WE RESIST

WE RESIST

Defending the Common Good
in Hostile Times

Edited by Cynthia Levine-Rasky and Lisa Kowalchuk

McGill-Queen's University Press

Montreal & Kingston · London · Chicago

ISBN 978-0-2280-0141-6 (cloth)
ISBN 978-0-2280-0142-3 (paper)
ISBN 978-0-2280-0280-2 (ePDF)
ISBN 978-0-2280-0281-9 (ePUB)

Legal deposit second quarter 2020
Bibliothèque nationale du Québec

Printed in Canada on acid-free paper that is 100% ancient forest free
(100% post-consumer recycled), processed chlorine free

We acknowledge the support of the Canada Council for the Arts.

Nous remercions le Conseil des arts du Canada de son soutien.

Library and Archives Canada Cataloguing in Publication

Title: We resist : defending the common good in hostile times / edited by
  Cynthia Levine-Rasky and Lisa Kowalchuk.
Names: Levine-Rasky, Cynthia, editor. | Kowalchuk, Lisa (Lisa Marie),
  editor.
Description: Includes bibliographical references and index.
Identifiers: Canadiana (print) 20200176285 | Canadiana (ebook)
  20200176331 | ISBN 9780228001423 (softcover) | ISBN 9780228001416
  (hardcover) | ISBN 9780228002802 (ePDF) | ISBN 9780228002819 (ePUB)
Subjects: LCSH: Common good. | LCSH: Social problems. | LCSH: Social
  action.
Classification: LCC JC330.15 .W4 2020 | DDC 320.01/1—dc23

CONTENTS

ACKNOWLEDGMENTS

This book came to be through the efforts of forty-two authors; it is them we wish to thank first. Some are academics representing the disciplines of communication, education, gender and sexuality, geography, health, industrial relations, media, philosophy, sociology, and a few others. They are practitioners, activists, and writers in law, the environment, human rights, Indigenous rights, education, disability rights, anti-racism, the media, and many other areas. This division of occupations and fields is arbitrary, since many contributors straddle them, as do the editors. Given the timeliness of the book, authors were pushed to produce within uncomfortably short deadlines. All of them stepped up to the challenge and wrote provocative and important essays on where we are today, how we got here, and what we can do to defend the preciousness of a common good subjected to multiple threats in our hostile times.

Elia Rasky and Adam Rasky provided thorough research assistance, creating individual files for over two hundred potential contributors who appeared on an original list early in 2017. Jen Danch, Dustin Galer, Adam Rasky, Herman Rosenfeld, Quentin Rowe-Codner, Stephen Sheps, and Jasmin Zine suggested a few of the authors. Our colleague nonpareil, Neil McLaughlin, provided his candid thoughts and welcome input through the inevitable ups and downs of the book-production process. Richard Day and David Murakami Wood offered valuable comments about its development and orientation. For the unconditional investment in our general well-being by our friends and families, we are extremely grateful.

At McGill-Queen's University Press, Kathleen Kearns's immediate "yes" to our proposal led to an excellent dialogue with editor Jacqueline Mason, who made the production process painless. We are grateful to our reviewers and to you, our readers. Together we amass the collective capacity to resist social and political forces that often feel overwhelming. Their consequences are not inevitable. We hope that readers find their people and seek their cause – and find authentic forms of resistance that bridge differences in politics and identities. We make the common good, indeed we are the common good, in all its complexity and uncertainty. We stand together to defend it.

WE RESIST

INTRODUCTION

Lisa Kowalchuk and Cynthia Levine-Rasky

The past fifty years have had their share of catastrophes, both natural and human-made. Some, like the assassination of revered leaders, war, or climate-related disasters, have had such profound and far-reaching effects that many people can say where they were when the news broke. The US presidential election of 8 November 2016, may qualify as one of those events. The largely unpredicted win of Donald J. Trump gave rise to a plethora of books and articles attempting to explain what happened and to analyze its likely impacts. The "monster's ball" (Blow 2016) of characters who came to make up his cabinet, his advisors, and the heads of highly sensitive governmental portfolios has confirmed the worst fears of people who were aghast at the success of Trump's audacious run.

As Canadian researchers, we are concerned with what the Trump victory implies for trends and events in Canada, specifically the problems that Trump's rise to power has exacerbated and made more visible. We recognize that the positioning of Trump at the centre of the picture implies that the outcomes of his presidency begin and end with his activities. This would be an error. Policies and legislation affecting citizenship, security, health care, education, employment, the economy, the environment, indeed everything that affects quality of life, were established long before Trump's arrival. Their consequences are endured by us all and are deepened by the particular violence exercised by the growing number of authoritarian leaders worldwide. Passionately motivated by these concerns, we invited forty-two Canadian scholars, community workers, and activists to describe their perspectives on the problems and the work they do to overcome them. Before we summarize a few of their themes, the next few sections explain the terms in our title.

What We Mean by the Common Good

Our conception of the common good is built on what Amitai Etzioni (2004) called "human flourishing," a state in which human beings thrive and enjoy physical, intellectual, and emotional well-being. This involves the complete range of human rights – civil, political, and social – and human capabilities that encompass the ability to think, learn, laugh, play, love, and grieve (Nussbaum 2002). The common good also involves the health of ecosystems and the natural environment, and the global climate conditions necessary for their sustainability. Though social justice in the form of socio-economic equality may be considered implicit in universal human rights and capabilities, it is worth underscoring it as a central element of the common good.

In this ideal sense, the common good has rarely been fully attained, at least since the dawn of stratification in human society. We part company with those analysts of the current-day threats to democracy and the rule of law (e.g., Frum 2018) who imply that there was a place and a period in the recent past (generally the United States in the latter third of the twentieth century) when things were about as good as we could expect them to be. We believe that what has become increasingly imperilled are gains and strides, however halting and incomplete, that have been made toward some aspects of the common good. Despite its aspirational quality, and the fragile progress toward its attainment, the common good is neither hypothetical nor utopian.

Among alternative conceptualizations of the common good is one that emphasizes shared norms and values. This approach is exemplified in Robert Reich's 2018 analysis of transformations in US politics, culture, and economy that gradually paved the way for Trump. In his book, simply entitled *The Common Good*, Reich defines the term as "shared values about what we owe one another as citizens who are bound together in the same society – the norms we voluntarily abide by and the ideals we seek to achieve" (2018, 18). Since laws are a sub-type of norms, this logically extends to people's "voluntary willingness to abide by laws … [e]ven if we dislike like them" (2018, 35). Unlike Reich, we do not regard a move toward greater convergence of values and norms as an assurance of the common good without specifying the content of those values and norms. For us, what matters are the conditions in which people find themselves. This means, for example, that the attainment of greater equality in rights and resources has often come not from compliance with the law but from challenging it. Nowhere is this more clear than in the struggle of Indigenous people for self-determination, despite the state's ongoing denials of its fiduciary responsibilities, indeed, of its laws and norms.

As a means of designating in one simple phrase what warrants defending in today's threatening political climate, however, "the common good" is a fraught term. The very word, "common," may strike many as presumptuous, since it could imply that some set of policies, laws, and rules are universally suitable to both the least well off and the most advantaged. We are mindful of the inequalities in substantive conditions stemming from a history of mass-scale collective domination and subjugation. The equal-worth premise implicit in the common good is violated by the confiscation and privatization of common resources, and by the subjugation of the powerless by the powerful for the latter's gain. As Vanessa Watts observes in her contribution to this volume, the common good has often been bandied about by Canadian political elites as a rationale for sacrificing the well-being of Indigenous peoples to economic "development." For Indigenous peoples, the land is not a resource to exploit, but integral to their identities (Lawrence and Dua 2011). Capital investment in extraction industries violates treaties and neglects obligatory consultations and the sharing of decision-making powers with affected Indigenous communities.

As we understand it, inequalities in access to society's rewards and resources, and in the endurance of its consequences, are antithetical to the common good. Yet inequalities are entrenched in, even a structural feature of, society. This is in sharp contrast to Indigenous epistemology that is predicated on a radical equality. No groups, persons, species, or lands are superior to another (Monture-Angus 1995, 233). This knowledge challenges settler groups, since it evokes deep questions about the assertion of power and entitlements to evoke the common good. Institutionalized inequalities affect vulnerable communities. Their elimination is conducive to the common good, and there are important instrumentalist arguments for assuring that elimination. Wilkinson and Pickett (2009) make a persuasive case that inequality has ill effects on society as a whole, including the most advantaged sectors, in the form of morbidity, premature mortality, crime, and other dimensions of well-being. Furthermore, inequality often goes hand in hand with political subjugation through violent force: the more unequal the system, the greater the level of coercion necessary to keep it in place.

This brings us to the question of the "temporal horizon" implied in our notion of the common good (Offe 2012). Do we have in mind only the well-being of people who exist today, or also those who will come after us? We conceive of a common good that recognizes "life course interdependence" (Estes 2017) between cohorts of people currently alive and between present and future generations bound up together in a "serial reciprocity for conduct and obligation" with past generations (Offe 2012, 678). This explication of the common good has parallels with the Seven Generations Principle found in Indigenous thought, in which a "kinship web" binds people to honour not only those who have died, but to care for the earth in the interest of those yet born (Sinclair 2004, 49).

What We Mean by Hostile Times

What are the forces that increasingly threaten progress toward the very idea of a common good? The 2016 US presidential election made visible a shift in political climate in the US and many other countries. No serious commentator thinks that the shift is embodied solely in Trump, or that the problems that brought him to office will dissipate when he leaves. It is widely understood that the most serious problems have been building for some time. For Lawrence Bobo (2017, 97), Trump "merely exploited the vulnerabilities of the moment, and upped the ante." Those who were unsurprised by the election outcome had been working for years on Indigenous rights, antiracism, labour issues, welfare-state programs, democratic freedoms, and immigration, despite setbacks in these and other sectors. Nonetheless, we acknowledge that something changed – and decisively so – in the aftermath of Trump's campaign and victory, if only by degree.

Several serious, interrelated problems have gathered force since 2016. One major dimension is a new permission for political elites and ordinary people to scapegoat marginalized and vulnerable minorities for the socio-economic dislocations occurring all over the world. A counterpart to this has been the rise of xenophobic, nationalist sentiment within civil society, and among power holders and viable contenders for political office. For some writers, this problem is ascendant. In the Republican's diehard support for Trump, the Tea Party, and the dismantlement of the Affordable Care Act, Lawrence Bobo, for example, sees "laissez-faire racism" in which all policy moves "must be read in substantial measure through a racial lens" (2017, 97). To this, Eduardo Bonilla-Silva (2018) adds Trump's preoccupation with The Wall, urban crime, the Muslim ban, and ISIS. Attributing support for these policies to the racism of poor, rural Whites is problematic, because it avoids not only the racism of other groups, but it also avoids the recognition of the "collective practices, mechanisms, institutions, and behaviours that reproduce racial domination" (Bonilla-Silva 2019, 17). A direct link can nonetheless be made between public acts of racism and the Trump election. This is suggested by a dramatic increase in hate incidents in the US and Canada over the weeks that followed, directed especially against Blacks, immigrants, Muslims, Jews, LGBTQ persons, and women (Southern Poverty Law Center 2016; Leber 2017). (On this issue, see Jamil, Elghawaby, Egan, and Robidoux, and Farber and Rudner in this volume.)

While it is a highly salient dimension of Trump's populism, the growing tolerance for racism is not entirely attributable to the 2016 election outcome. What we are observing is "only the most extreme expression of a brand of racial politics practiced by the Republican Party since the 1980s" (McAdam 2018, 1). First, Richard Nixon spurred what has become "extreme partisan politics" (McAdam 2018), as he and his successors appealed to their "base." Today, the impact of gerrymandering and voter-suppression practices favour Republicans and their host of "illiberal institutions." With this we come full circle: the consequences of these events are borne disproportionately by vulnerable communities, even extending to Indigenous peoples in Canada (Palmater 2018).

Trump may be the most recognizable face of this phenomenon, but the political ascendance of far-right nationalism is also seen in Britain (United Kingdom Independence Party), Denmark (Danish People's Party), France (Front National), Greece (Golden Dawn), Hungary (Jobbik), and Italy (The League and the Five Star Movement), as well as in the authoritarian leadership in India, Turkey, Brazil, and elsewhere. Meanwhile, an assortment of groups with various degrees of organizational capacity rely on the Internet to spread xenophobic views and mobilize public expressions of hate. Canada is not immune to this development (see Perry in this volume). Organizations are diffuse in their tactics and focus, but a shared hatred toward racial and ethnic minorities, refugees and new immigrants, women, and elites serve to bind them together. Infighting and lack of cohesion in these groups do not minimize the danger they pose: some of the worst xeno-phobic violence is committed by "lone wolves" who are directly inspired by discourse readily available on the Internet (Futrell and Simi 2017; Perry and Scrivens 2015). Bolstering popular receptivity to the ideas of these groups is the widespread devaluing of evidence-based knowledge and the unprecedented rise of junk research and fake news (see Reid in this volume), also transmitted by the Internet. This disturbing trend feeds a wilful ignorance about a range of other urgent problems, especially climate change (see Stewart in this volume).

A second major threat to the common good is the erosion of democratic institutions, such as a free press and judiciary, trade unions, and public ed-ucation. For several of the better-known commentators on the Trump phe-nomenon (for example Levitsky and Zablitt 2018; Hedges 2018), this is the uppermost concern. While their focus is on the United States, the pattern extends to other regions, including the Global South. It is safe to say that most de-democratization in the world today is occurring under the auspices of the political right. There are exceptions, such as the nominally socialist anti-democratic regimes in Latin America that have recently tightened their grip on power – the increasingly presidentialist and repressive regimes of Daniel Ortega and his wife, Rosario Murillo, in Nicaragua and of Nicolas Maduro in Venezuela (in transition at the time of writing). But more typical of deepening authoritarianism in this region is the ultra-right Nationalist Party in Honduras, and the 2018 presidential win in Brazil of Jair Bolsonaro, an unabashed admirer of that country's 1964–85 military dictatorship. Bol-sonaro's rise to power increasingly appears to have relied on the corrupt suppression of his chief opponent, Luiz Inacio Lula da Silva (Greenwald et al., 2019).

Parallel with setbacks in democracy have been episodes of mass-scale human-rights abuses the flagrancy of which points to perpetrators' increasing confidence in their own impunity. One of the worst examples is the late-2017 ethnic cleansing–style attack by Myanmar security forces on the Rohingya people in Rakhine state. Over 6,700 were killed by direct violence and over 650,000 were forced to flee into Bangladesh (Médicins-sans-Frontiers 2017). Another is the ongoing Philippine campaign of summary executions of alleged drug dealers and addicts – 20,000 in total by early 2018 (Regencia 2018). President Rodrigo Duterte, who spearheaded this orgy of violence when he took office in 2016, enjoys warm relations with President Trump. The friendliness between the US president and a number of strong-armed and even murderous autocrats like Vladimir Putin, Benjamin Netanyahu, Kim Jong-un, and Mohammed bin Salman suggests that the present turn in US politics is reinforcing de-democratization and assaults on civil and political rights around the world.

In regard to human rights, there is a special category of violation that parallels a discursive war on truth. We refer to the targeting of journalists with abuses ranging from sinister verbal bullying to imprisonment to assassination. Murders of journalists had diminished from 2006, but their imprisonments rose to a three-decade high in 2016 and 2017 (Auer 2018). Meanwhile, activists for the environment and the rights of Indigenous peoples among others have been singled out for harassment, threats, and violence (see Wood, Roach, Behrens, Oger, and Palmater in this volume). Even in countries with a reputation for tolerating peaceful dissent, authorities increasingly criminalize organized resistance activities under the rubric of national security (Wood and Fortier 2016). This is more pronounced when the protestors are Indigenous and are mobilizing against industrial development that will affect their livelihoods and health (Crosby and Monaghan 2018; Livesey 2017; Goujard 2017).

A third major dimension of our hostile times manifests in the stance of the US and several other governments toward international co-operation (Henley 2018) around peace, nuclear disarmament, and global climate change. In dealing with climate change, undoubtedly the most serious issue for the global common good is the need for concerted action to avert climate catastrophe. We concur with Naomi Klein (2017): the urgency of this issue makes the timing of Trump's election particularly unfortunate given the damage that will result from his administration's flagrant undermining of the Paris Accord and, domestically, its embrace of denialists and its dismantling of national safeguards.

In Canada, it would be inaccurate to describe the federal government of Prime Minister Justin Trudeau as more negligent and dismissive of climate goals than that of his predecessor, Conservative Stephen Harper. Canada's progress on this issue is nevertheless imperilled by the hollowness of

Trudeau's sparkling promises that Canada was "back" (Canadian Press 2015) – that it would now stand firmly with the international community to work on slowing global warming. His discourse on climate, which some argue helped get him elected in 2014, earned him international accolades during his first year in office. But it is contradicted in practice by his government's rigid determination to proceed with major projects such as the Kinder Morgan Trans Mountain pipeline. In May 2018, the Trudeau government opted to invest $4.5 billion of public money to purchase (and essentially nationalize) this project when it was clear that Kinder Morgan was losing interest in it (Chase et al. 2018). Despite fierce public opposition to the project, the Canadian government would triple the amount of bitumen transported from the Alberta oil sands to the BC coast and on to Asian markets. This will produce new greenhouse-gas emissions equivalent to the CO_2 from 2.7 million new cars on the road annually (Greenpeace n.d.) making it all but impossible to fulfill Canada's Paris Accord commitment to reduce emissions by 30 per cent by 2030 (Jaccard 2018). More recently, Trudeau's government dispatched the Royal Canadian Mounted Police to remove Wet'suwet'en land defenders at the site of the Coastal Gaslink pipeline in the northwestern central interior of British Columbia. The Indigenous community's actions were suppressed despite Delgamuukw, a 1997 Supreme Court decision in favour of Indigenous land claims and affirming the government's fiduciary responsibility toward Indigenous groups (Sterritt 2019).

How We Got Here

Discussion of the causal factors in our hostile times often reticulate with their impacts. Several writers (for example, Bonilla-Silva 2019; Eichengreen 2018; McAdam 2018; Klein 2017) document the dysfunctions of the US political system that facilitated Trump's rise, and how these vulnerabilities are heightened and exploited by the Trump administration. For reasons of space, and because we want to avoid too close a focus on the US election, we leave aside the fascinating and important demographic analyses of Trump's electoral base, such as that of Sean McElwee and Jason McDaniel (2017). Instead we confine our brief remarks here to analysts who review the broader historical backdrop.

One way that post-2016 explanations of the present crisis can be sorted is the attention they pay to political economy. We mean here particularly the widespread turn toward neo-liberal austerity, deregulation, and market fundamentalism in the 1980s. In one set of writings, which Jedediah Purdy (2018) calls the "crisis-of-democracy" literature, the explanation for the present crisis centres around changes in political culture, all but omitting political economy factors. As "disciples of norms" (Purdy 2018), these analysts emphasize an abandonment of "stabilizing, trans-partisan" codes of conduct across the political spectrum. The basic contention is that, at some point after the 1970s, US politics became much more polarized (Roberts 2018; Levitsky and Ziblatt 2018). For example, Reich (2018), in his book *The Common Good*, is primarily concerned with norms and culture underlying elite behaviour. While he roughly dates the culture shift to the onset of neo-liberal policies, he does not mention neo-liberalism or capitalism as part of the problem. He identifies corporations as major culprits in a shift toward the "whatever-it-takes-to maximize profits" approach. But his analysis is marred by a misplaced nostalgia for a time when CEOs of large corporations were stewards of the American common good, concerned with prosperity for their employees, consumers, and communities. These corporate statesmen of yesteryear, he observes, became "corporate butchers in the 1980s and 1990s" (2018, 76).

What Reich misses is the incremental-but-steady attack on labour unions in the United States and other countries, the decades-long trajectory of deregulation and privatization, cuts to social programs, intensified mechanisms of disenfranchisement of African-Americans in the United States, and the mounting threat to global climate and the environment. Also missing is a vision of any role for civil society collective action in countering these forces. We agree with Purdy (2018): norms and democratic ideals that matter vitally to the common good are being upended. However, we view as incomplete any analysis that does not consider the material basis for this, particularly the concentration of wealth and power that accelerated entrenchment of corporate power over policy-making since the 1980s. We are also critical of any analysis of the issues that does not acknowledge the role of ideology.

In a contrasting set of analyses, authors foreground the role of "unaccountable financial and corporate elites … [in] driving inequality and undermining democracy" (Lerner and Weeks 2017). Some of this literature predates the 2016 US election and helps place it in the context of broader threats to the common good. These works establish the ways in which

"gut-cut-and-privatize politics" (Estes 2012) entailed attacks on social programs that protected vulnerable groups. As David McNally observes, a new
wave of heightened austerity in many countries followed the aftermath of
the recession of 2008, as "[t]he ruling groups ... seized on the opportunities
this crisis has created to further neoliberalize society" (2016, 87). The poor
and middling sectors were made to pay for their governments' "Great Bank
Bailout" with cuts to social spending and corporate taxation. Even governments with no debt problem, like Canada, pursued (or renewed) these
kinds of measures because of "competitive austerity" between countries.
The result has been increasing precarity, deteriorating conditions of work,
and a diminished ability of workers to push for higher wages and benefits
(McNally 2016).

The overarching policy orientation in which austerity measures are embedded erodes the common good in other ways, the most serious of which
is arguably the environment. Austerity in domestic policy has been accompanied by the ascendance of free trade agreements (FTAs) structured to dramatically weaken the regulatory capacity of states over corporations, and
oriented to the pursuit of unrestricted economic growth as an end in itself.
A central argument in Naomi Klein's (2014) *This Changes Everything: Capitalism vs. the Climate* is that "free market fundamentalism" has "helped
overheat the planet." One of the ways that FTAs in particular have done this
is by facilitating a massive increase in global CO_2 emissions by allowing
manufacturers to locate production wherever labour is cheapest and regulations on pollution are weakest (Klein 2014). Furthermore, FTAs' national
treatment provisions make it all but impossible for governments to subsi-
dize local production of green technology such as solar panels, since this is
considered protectionist. In general, challenging climate change requires a
range of actions that neo-liberalism opposes, including massive state spending in a greener "public sphere: new energy grids, public transit, and energy
efficiency" (Klein 2017, 81). It also requires more-progressive taxation to
generate the funds required for such investment (Klein 2017, 81) in addition
to the curtailing of offshore tax havens.

The relationship between neo-liberalism and the resurgence of far-right
xenophobia, another major element in the increasingly hostile times, is more
complex. Here, the explanation lies partly in changes in the media landscape

stemming from changes in the rules around news-media ownership and news production. In the United States, "Deregulation that began in the 1970s and accelerated under Reagan led to the concentration of media ownership, the centralization and reduction of newsgathering, and the integration of news and entertainment" (Polletta and Callahan 2017, 396). Media concentration is even more acute in Canada (Winseck 2015). Whether in the United States or Canada, these trends allow news content to be much more "provocative, indeed deliberately objectionable" (Polletta and Callahan 2017, 396). As the best-known offspring of these changes in the broadcast realm, Fox News has an outsized impact on viewers relative to its share of news viewership. Compounding the impact of Fox News is social media, ensuring pseudo-news narratives about immigrants, LGBTQ, African-Americans, and other minority groups spreads much more rapidly than in the past (Polletta and Callahan 2017). Communication technology causes the proliferation of far-right white supremacist groups (Blee cited in Moreau 2017), however loosely their movement is configured. With a focus on Canada, Barbara Perry and Ryan Scrivens (2015) observe that the websites of right-wing extremist groups offer people a sense of community in part by facilitating communication on many everyday, non-ideological interests. Internet linkages between groups in different countries has allowed a white supremacist far-right network and identity to form internationally.

What We Mean by Resistance

Attempting to characterize and explain the intertwined threats to the common good creates the foundation for the central objective of this book – to inspire thinking about ways that ordinary people can respond. One of our assumptions is that grassroots collective action has been effective in challenging detrimental change and shifting public discourse. In strategizing resistance, we take social movements seriously, given the significance of past struggles involving mass-based actions in public spaces, and, at times, civil disobedience. Some commentators suggest that, paradoxically, it was the success of historical labour and civil-rights movements that aroused a backlash of corporate-led economic globalization, and more recently a resurgence of far-right populism (Klein 2017; McAlevey 2016).

While this may be an overly optimistic take on what we are up against, there is an undeniable interplay between the advances of social movements and elite retaliation.

Social movements traditionally utilize non-formal or non-institutional avenues for pursuing change. Yet we also understand the importance of activism through institutional channels, especially in the electoral arena. Although some activists and analysts will put their faith in one or the other, these modes of action often dovetail. The fact that liberal democracy is in crisis now "opens doors to both left and right" (Purdy 2018) in the electoral realm. In the United States, the "Republican Lite" character of the Democratic Party has no doubt led many progressives to despair of electoral politics. But six months before the November 2018 Congressional mid-term elections, four new candidates, all young women of colour running on socialist platforms, made breakthroughs in Democratic primary races in both suburban and urban districts, defeating centrist incumbents from their party (Nichols 2018). All four were subsequently elected to Congress. This has injected renewed hope into social movements advancing women, antiracism, and socialism.

Of particular note is Black Lives Matter. Although the movement is often regarded as a collective revolt against police violence toward Blacks in the United States, Canada is also deeply implicated in the "demonization of Black bodies" in policing and border security and, as in the US, in extending its morbid profusion into the child-welfare system and public education (Maynard 2017). For Keeanga-Yamahtta Taylor (2016), making connections between police violence and other forms of oppression of Blacks is essential to building a robust resistance movement out of Black Lives Matter.

The mobilization of Indigenous peoples present another decisive moment for social movements. Fused to action, the goal of this mobilization is radical change (Alfred 2009b, 107). Much of the resurgence in Indigenous activism in both Canada and the United States has been kindled by new extractivist encroachment on traditional territory (Manuel 2015), but also by the tragedy of murdered and missing women and girls. Indigenous collective action on these issues flows across the national border (CBC Radio 2018). One culmination of this movement is Idle No More, "one of the most important moments in our collective history ... a watershed time, an emergence out of past efforts that reverberated into the future" (The Kino-nda-niimi Collective 2014, 21). Between the peak months of December 2012 and August 2013, solidarity gatherings occurred in countries as far flung as Japan and Norway, India and Mexico. Like Black Lives Matter, women's leadership was essential to Idle No More, a fact that bound its orientation to environmentalism as a specifically feminist project and intimately linked it to "helping our people decolonize our notions of government, land management, business and social relation[s] by going through a process of re-evaluating our connection to the sacred" (Thomas-Muller 2013). The movement was deeply anti-colonial and simultaneously anti-racist and anti-oppression. The power of Idle No More notwithstanding, Palmater (2015, 222) notes that any Indigenous resistance movement, regardless of its name, is secondary to Indigenous peoples' continuous assertion of their sovereignty. "Despite all the challenges, this movement will just continue to grow, expose the uncomfortable truths, and force the fundamental change that is needed to keep the status quo from continuing to kill our people."

Several recent intersectoral actions and platforms exist at both the national and state level, including the Vision for Black Lives articulated in 2016 by the Movement for Black Lives; the annual People's Summit spearheaded in 2016 by National Nurses United; the Moral Mondays movement that started in 2013 in North Carolina and that has spread to neighbouring states; and in Canada the Leap Manifesto issued in 2015 (Klein 2017), which has since generated the formation of Leap groups across the country. Several coalitions have emerged in the past few years that enact a recognition of how deeply intertwined Indigenous rights are with the protection of water, air, and land that we all depend on. A vivid recent example was the coalition that arose in 2016 to support the Standing Rock Sioux's struggle against the Dakota Access Pipeline, often referred to as the "No-DAPL" movement (Lim 2016). Other kinds of intercommunity alliances of the past decade or so include workers' centres that specialize in helping non-unionized workers, localized anti-foreclosure movements in the United States (Haiven 2014), and coalitions for migrant workers' rights. Going back to the 1990s, Klein observes that the international and multi-sectoral movement in opposition to neo-liberal globalization – decisive in thwarting the Free Trade Areas of the Americas – is one of the strongest examples of alliance-building. It was "an unignorable mass movement that changed the conversation in dozens of countries" (Klein 2017, 111).

Friendly critics of progressive social movements signal a number of hurdles to this kind of broad-based coordination. Some focus mainly on constraints that are external to the movements. Because organized labour is crucial to many if not most efforts at cross-sectoral alliance-building, blows to union density and influence hurt that capacity. Factors that have weakened labour unions in the United States are "the employer offensive, hostile courts, globalization, automation, and a changing employment structure" (McAlevey 2016, 18). Many of these circumstances pertain to Canadian unions as well, with unions considerably weaker in manufacturing, and with rising precarity in all sectors (Ross 2018). Other commentators emphasize challenges that are internal to the movements. These tend to identify a shift in their internal culture that may undermine unity across divides of income, education, race, gender, and other categories. This is emblemized in a practise of shaming would-be participants for failing to recognize how their speech or action reflects their own positionality (Amhad 2015; Maltz Bovy 2017). Terms like "solidarity," "alliances," and "the people," have fallen out of fashion. In their place are terms that reflect a concern with participants' privilege, and everyday, micro-level aggression. In addition to the wasteful infighting this creates, it may leave activists isolated from the "wider working-class public" (D'Arcy 2016, 153) that has yet to be organized.

In tandem with this impediment is the dependency on digital or networked communication platforms. With social media, activists can transform massive cross-sectoral participation from virtual space to a real presence in physical spaces. They have even shown massive disruptive capacity that compels elites to heed some movement demands. The problem is that such movements build with little prior creation of the capacities, skills, and movement infrastructure that can develop only through face-to-face actions. As a result, social media–reliant movements such as Occupy Wall Street and the Arab Spring erupt quickly and with impressive magnitude, but lack the ability to employ "tactical maneuvering" (Tufekci 2017). Black Lives Matter leader, Keeanga-Yamahtta Taylor, captures the problem well when she (2018, 175) asks, "How do you move from protest to movement?"

Intersectoral unity is arguably also a function of the ability of each movement group or organization to mobilize beyond the core group of relatively well-educated, articulate people. In this respect, another internal impediment is the way that activists and leaders attempt to connect with their adherents, members, and people whose support they wish to garner. For Jane MacAlevey (2016), the problem is seen most glaringly in US labour unions. but has also seeped into other kinds of movement organizations of the left. In McAlevey's view, at some point over the past forty years, both union leaders and movement activists gave up on "deep organizing" – trying to recruit or convert a mass of people who have a stake in the issues but have never been active before. In the case of movement organizations, even when they mobilize highly attended and visible events, the participants are "self-selecting," and it is the same group of committed volunteer activists that continually show up for activities, "without the full mass of their co-workers or community behind them" (McAlevey 2016, 10).

The Essays

No single movement, organization, or activist can be expected to tackle all the challenges outlined above. Rather, these concerns form the context in which Canadian-specific responses can be considered. The essays in this collection illuminate the problems we have described from the viewpoint of Canadian activists, community leaders, and academics who are deeply embedded within political and community struggles or engaged in research that defends the common good. In order to include as many perspectives as possible, we assembled a relatively large number of succinct pieces that are accessible to specialists and non-specialists alike. We invited each contributor to discuss their analyses of the social and political climate in the world today, especially as it affects their own sphere of inquiry, research, writing, teaching, or activism. They discuss a wide range of issues from their perspectives as Indigenous, Black, Muslim, Jewish, transgender, queer, and disabled persons. They take up matters of concern in the substantive areas of law, health, religion, education, health, media, sport, policing, and the state, hate groups, surveillance, poverty, labour, family, environment, electoral politics, and citizenship. Many of the authors propose concrete actions that readers may take at the collective or individual level to facilitate social change in Canada. Like their analyses of the problem, their solutions arise from diverse political positions, ranging from left-liberal to socialist to radical. Some seek to reform social policies through progressive incrementalism;

others pursue an anti-capitalist and revolutionary vision. While diverse in their politics, professional experience, and spheres of expertise, all contributors share a critical perspective on the hostile times in which we live, and a wish to promote the common good.

We grouped the essays into four themes: communities of resistance, institutions and the common good, social policies in hostile times, and social movements for change. These broad themes cut across the authors' occupations, ethnicity, race, gender, gender identities, religions, abilities, and areas of expertise. Just over half of the essays explicitly or implicitly foreground the rise of the far right in their characterization of core threats to the common good. These include the essays by Richard Day, Uzma Jamil, Neil McLaughlin, Alex Neve, Kim Sauder, and Vanessa Watts. A smaller number of essays focused more centrally on austerity and other neo-liberal economic policies as the core threat. Examples of this are the pieces by Pat Armstrong, Max Haiven, Janice Newson, and Alan Sears. One set of essays explicitly draws a link between those two broad phenomena of neo-liberalism and far right bigotry, pointing out ways that they are in fact intertwined. These include the essays by John Clarke, Stephen D'Arcy, Dan Irving, Tim McCaskell, and Pam Palmater.

On the topic of the way forward, with greater or lesser emphasis, the majority of contributors signal that the nature of the multi-frontal threat we are seeing calls for broad alliance-building. Some essays describe at length at least one specific collective action, organization, campaign, or initiative to confront forces hostile to the common good through such broad alliances. This is seen in the pieces by Aziz Choudry and Mostafa Henaway, Alia Hogben, Melissa Graham, El-Farouk Khaki, Lorne Waldman, and our own co-authored essay. Other suggestions involve non-violent collective action (Matthew Behrens, Caitlyn Kasper, and Kikéola Roach), individual action (Alex Neve, and Morgane Oger), participation in electoral procedures (Ed Corrigan), and appeals to specific occupational organizations to do better (Margaret Reid, Keith Stewart).

Those advocating for resistance to hostile measures against the common good disavow change that leads only to modifications of bad policies or routing of dangerous politicians. They realize in the present moment an opportunity to push for "non-reformist reforms" (Schwartz and Sunkara 2017), and they broadly agree that social movements now need a comprehensive understanding of the nature of the threats we are facing. This will involve making connections between different dimensions of the problem (Giroux 2017), and it will require multi-sectoral coalitions, since single-issue and single-sector movements are inadequate (Klein 2017). *We Resist* is imbued with the spirit of this undertaking.

REFERENCES

Ahmad, Assam. 2015. "A Note on Call-out Culture." *Briarpatch Magazine*, 2 March. https://www.filmsforaction.org/articles/a-note-on-callout-culture/.

Alfred, Taiaiake. 2009a. *Wasáse: Indigenous Pathways of Action and Freedom.* Toronto: University of Toronto Press.

Auer, Soraya. 2018. "World Press Freedom Day: Are Journalists Increasingly under Attack?" *BBC News*, 3 May. https://www.bbc.com/news/world-43961380.

Bobo, Lawrence D. 2017. "Racism in Trump's America: Reflections on Culture, Sociology, and the 2016 US Presidential Election." *British Journal of Sociology* 68 (S1): S85–S104.

Blow, Charles. 2016. "Donald Trump's Monster's Ball." *New York Times*, 1 December. https://www.nytimes.com/2016/12/01/opinion/donald-trumps-monsters-ball.html.

Bonilla-Silva, Eduardo. 2019. "'Racists,' 'Class Anxieties,' Hegemonic Racism, and Democracy in Trump's America." *Social Currents* 6 (1): 14–31.

Bonilla-Silva, Eduardo. 2018. "2018 Presidential Address. Feeling Race: Theorizing the Racial Economy of Emotions." *American Sociological Review*, 1–25. doi: 10.1177/0003122418816958.

Canadian Press. 2015. "We're Back, Justin Trudeau Says in Message to Canada's Allies Abroad." *National Post*, 20 October. http://nationalpost.com/news/politics/ were-back-justin-trudeau-says-in-message-to-canadas-allies-abroad.

CBC Radio. 2018. "US Activists Inspired by Canada's Inquiry into Missing and Murdered Indigenous Women." *CBC Radio*, 11 June. https://www.cbc.ca/radio/the current/the-current-for-june-11-2018-1.4700689/u-s-activists-inspired-by-canada-s-inquiry-into-missing-and-murdered-indigenous-women-1.4700779.

Chase, Stephen, Kelly Cryderman, and Jeff Lewis. 2018. "Trudeau Government to Buy Kinder Morgan's Trans Mountain for $4.5 Billion." *Globe and Mail*, 29 May. https://www.theglobeandmail.com/politics/article-trudeau-government-to-buy-kinder-morgans-trans-mountain-pipeline/.

Crosby, Andrew, and Jeffery Monaghan. 2018. *Policing Indigenous Movements: Dissent and the Security State*. Halifax and Winnipeg: Fernwood.

D'Arcy, Steve. 2016. "The Political Vocabulary of the Post-New Left: How Activists Articulate Their Politics and Why It Matters." In *A World to Win: Contemporary Social Movements and Counter-Hegemony*, edited by William Carroll and Kanchan Sarker, 141–56. Winnipeg: ARP Books.

Eichengreen, Barry. 2018. *The Populist Temptation: Economic Grievance and Political Reaction in the Modern Era*. New York: Oxford University Press.

Estes, Carroll L. 2017. "Older US Women's Economic Security, Health, and Empowerment: The Fight against Opponents of Social Security, Medicare, and Medicaid." In *Women's Empowerment and Global Health: A Twenty-First Century Agenda*, edited by Shari L Dworkin, Monica Gandhi, and Paige Passanno, 232–50. Oakland, CA: University of California Press.

Etzioni, Amitai. 2004. *The Common Good*. Malden, MA: Polity.

Frum, David. 2018. *Trumpocracy: The Corruption of the American Republic*. New York: Harper-Collins.

Futrell, Robert, and Pete Simi. 2017. "The [Un]Surprising Alt Right." *Contexts* 16 (2): 76.

Giroux, Henry A. "White Nationalism, Armed Culture, and State Violence in the Age of Donald Trump." *Philosophy and Social Criticism* 43 (9): 887–901.

Goujard, Clothilde. August 2017. "After Charlottesville, Canada's Spy Agency Expresses 'Concern' About the Far Right." *National Observer*, 22 August. https://www.nationalobserver.com/2017/08/22/news/after-charlottesville-canadas-spy-agency-expresses-concern-about-far-right.

Greenwald, Glen, Leandro Demori, and Betsy Reed. "How and Why the Intercept Is Reporting on a Vast Trove of Materials about Brazil's Operation Car Wash and Justice Minister Sergio Moro." *Intercept*, 9 June. https://theintercept.com/2019/06/09/brazil-archive-operation-car-wash/.

Greenpeace. (n.d.). Pipelines in Canada. http://www.greenpeace.org/canada/en/campaigns/Energy/tarsands/Kinder-Morgan-pipeline/.

Haiven, Max. 2014. *Crises of Imagination, Crises of Power: Capitalism, Creativity, and the Commons*. Halifax and Winnipeg: Fernwood.

Hedges, Chris. 2018. *America, The Farewell Tour*. New York: Knopf Canada.

Henley, Jon. 2018. "Rise of Far Right in Italy and Austria Gives Putin Some Friends in the West." *Guardian*, 7 June. https://www.theguardian.com/world/2018/jun/07/rise-of-far-right-in-italy-and-austria-gives-putin-some-friends-in-the-west?CMP=Share_iOSApp_Other.

Jaccard. 2018. "Trudeau's Orwellian Logic: We Reduce Emissions by Increasing Them." *Globe and Mail*, 20 February. https://www.theglobeandmail.com/opinion/trudeaus-orwellian-logic-reduce-emissions-by-increasing-them/article38021585/.

Klein, Naomi. 2014. *This Changes Everything: Capitalism vs. The Climate*. New York: Simon and Shuster.

– 2017. *No Is Not Enough: Resisting the New Shock Politics and Winning the World We Need*. Toronto: Knopf Canada.

Lawrence, Bonita, and Enakshi Dua. 2011. Decolonizing Anti-Racism. In *Cultivating Canada: Reconciliation through the Lens of Cultural Diversity*, edited by A. Mathur, J. Dewar, and M. DeGagné, 233–62. Ottawa: Aboriginal Healing Foundation.

Leber, Ben. 2017. Police-Reported Crime Statistics in Canada, 2016. Catalogue no. 85-002-X. Ottawa. https://www150.statcan.gc.ca/n1/en/pub/85-002-x/2017001/article/14832-eng.pdf?st=5n2oupwL.

Lerner, Steven, and Maurice Weeks. 2016. "Five Principles to Guide Our Work under Trump." *Nation*, 9 December. https://www.thenation.com/article/5-practical-principles-to-guide-our-work-under-trump/.

Levitsky, Steven, and Daniel Zablitt. 2018. *How Democracies Die*. New York: Crown.

Lim, Audrea. 2016. "Want to Know How to Build a Progressive Movement under Trump? Look to Standing Rock." *Nation*, December 20. https://www.thenation.com/article/want-to-know-how-to-build-a-progressive-movement-under-trump-look-to-standing-rock/.

Livesey, Bruce. 2017. "Canada's Spies Collude with the Energy Sector." *National Observer*, 18 May. https://www.nationalobserver.com/2017/05/18/news/canadas-spies-collude-energy-sector.

Maltz Bovy, Phoebe. 2017. "The Perils of Privilege." *New Republic*, 6 March. https://newrepublic.com/article/140985/perils-privilege-phoebe-maltz-bovy-book-excerpt.

Manuel, Arthur. 2015. *Unsettling Canada: A National Wake-up Call*. Toronto: Between the Lines.

McAdam, Doug. 2018. "Putting Donald Trump in Historical Perspective: Racial Politics and Social Movements from the 1960s to Today." In *The Resistance: The Dawn of the Anti-Trump Opposition Movement*, edited by D.S. Meyer and S. Tarrow, 27–53. University Press Scholarship Online. doi: 10.1093/oso/9780190088 6172.001.0001.

McAlevey, Jane. 2016. *No Shortcuts: Organizing for Power in the New Gilded Age*. Oxford University Press: New York.

Médecins San Frontières (MSF). 2017. "Myanmar/Bangladesh: MSF surveys estimate

that at least 6,700 Rohingya were killed during the attacks in Myanmar." 12
December. http://www.msf.org/en/article/myanmarbangladesh-msf-surveys-
estimate-least-6700-rohingya-were-killed-during-attacks.

McNally, David. 2016. "Neoliberalism and Its Discontents: Austerity and Resistance
in an Age of Crisis." In *World to Win: Contemporary Social Movements and
Counter-Hegemony*, edited by William K. Carroll and Kanchan Sarker, 75–92.
Winnipeg: ARP Books.

Monture-Angus, Patricia. 1995. *Thunder in My Soul: A Mohawk Woman Speaks*.
Halifax: Fernwood Publishing.

Moreau, Julie. 2017. "Race, Gender, and the Study of Far Right Social Movements:
An Interview with Kathleen Blee." *Mobilizing Ideas*, 19 April. https://mobilizing
ideas.wordpress.com/2017/04/19/race-gender-and-the-study-of-far-right-social-
movements-an-interview-with-kathleen-blee/#more-10595.

Nichols, John. 2018. "The 2018 Progressive Honor Roll." *The Nation*, 20 December.
https://www.thenation.com/article/2018-progressive-honor-roll/.

Nussbaum, Martha. 2002. "Women's Capabilities and Social Justice." In *Gender
Justice, Development, and Rights*, edited by Maxine Molyneux and Shahra Razavi,
45–77. New York: Oxford University Press.

Offe, Claus. 2002. "Whose Good Is the Common Good?" *Philosophy and Social
Criticism* 38 (7): 665–84.

Palmater, Pamela. 2015. *Indigenous Nationhood: Empowering Grassroots Citizens*.
Halifax, NS: Fernwood Publishing.

– 2018. "Trump's 'Crazy Town' Represents a Clear and Present Danger to Canada."
Blog post. 27 December. http://indigenousnationhood.blogspot.com/2018/12/
trumps-crazy-town-presents-clear-and.html.

Perry, Barbara, and Ryan Scrivens. 2015. Right-Wing Extremism in Canada: An
Environmental Scan. Public Safety Canada: September. https://www.public
safety.gc.ca/cnt/ntnl-scrt/cntr-trrrsm/r-nd-flght-182/knshk/ctlg/dtls-en.aspx?
i=116.

Polletta, Francesca, and Jessica Callahan. 2017. "Deep Stories, Nostalgia Narratives,
and Fake News: Storytelling in the Trump Era." *American Journal of Cultural
Sociology* 5 (3): 392–408.

Purdy, Jedediah. 2018. "Normcore." *Dissent* (summer). https://www.dissent
magazine.org/article/normcore-trump-resistance-books-crisis-of-democracy.

Regencia, Ted. 2018. "Senator: Rodrigo Duterte's Drug War Has Killed 20,000."

Al Jazeera, 21 February. https://www.aljazeera.com/news/2018/02/senator-rodrigo-duterte-drug-war-killed-20000-180221134139202.html.

Reich, Robert B. 2018. *The Common Good*. New York: Knopf.

Roberts, Kenneth M. 2018. Populism, Democracy, and Resistance. In *The Resistance; The Dawn of the Anti-Trump Opposition Movement*, edited by D.S. Meyer and S. Tarrow, 54–73. University Press Scholarship Online. doi: 10.1093/oso/9780190 886172.001.0001.

Ross, Stephanie. 2018. "The Challenges of Union Political Action in the Era of Neoliberalism." In *Divided Province: Ontario Politics in the Age of Neoliberalism*, edited by Greg Albo and Bryan M. Evans, 522–48. Montreal and Kingston: McGill Queen's University Press.

Sinclair, Raven. 2004. "Aboriginal Social Work Education in Canada: Decolonizing Pedagogy for the Seventh Generation." *First Peoples Child and Family Review* 1 (1): 49–61. https://www.google.com/search?client=safari&rls=en&q=vine+deloria+seven+generations&sa=X&ved=2ahUKEwiXkZii_rbgAhXHzIMKHZBEDKw4ChDVAigCegQIBhAD&biw=1680&bih=969#.

Southern Poverty Law Centre (SPLC). 2016. *Hatewatch*, 16 December. https://www.splcenter.org/hatewatch/2016/12/16/update-1094-bias-related-incidents-month-following-election.

Sterrit, Angela. 2019. "Wet'suwet'en Arrests Spark Debate about Indigenous Relations with RCMP." CBC.ca, 18 January. https://www.cbc.ca/news/canada/british-columbia/wet-suwet-en-conflict-spurs-debate-about-indigenous-relations-with-rcmp-1.4980695.

Taylor, Keeanga-Yamahtta. 2015. *From #BlackLivesMatter to Black Liberation*. Chicago: Haymarket Books.

The Kino-nda-niimi Collective. 2014. *The Winter We Danced: Voices from the Past, the Future, and the Idle No More Movement*. Winnipeg: ARP Books.

Thomas-Muller, Clayton. 2013. "The Rise of the Native Rights-Based Strategic Framework." *Canadian Dimension*, 23 May. https://canadiandimension.com/articles/view/the-rise-of-the-native-rights-based-strategic-framework.

Tufekci, Zeynep. 2017. *Twitter and Teargas: The Power and Fragility of Networked Protest*. New Haven and London: Yale University Press.

Wilkinson, Richard G., and Kate Pickett. 2009. *The Spirit Level: Why Greater Equality Makes Societies Stronger*. New York: Bloomsbury Publishing.

Winseck, 2016. Media and Internet Concentration in Canada Report, 1984–2015.

Canadian Media Concentration Research Project. Carleton University. http:// www.cmcrp.org/media-and-internet-concentration-in-canada-report-1984- 2015/.

Wood, Lesley, and Craig Fortier. 2016. "Consent, Coercion, and the Criminalization of Dissent." In *World to Win: Contemporary Social Movements and Counter- Hegemony*, edited by William K. Carroll and Kanchan Sarker, 128–40. Winnipeg: ARP Books.

PART ONE

COMMUNITIES OF RESISTANCE

1

TRADING OUR HISTORY
The Importance of Indigenous Resistance in Today's Hostile Times

Caitlyn E. Kasper

On the physical nature of the Two Row Wampum:

> The belt consists of two rows of purple wampum beads on a white background. Three rows of white beads symbolizing peace, friendship, and respect separate the two purple rows. The two purple rows symbolize two paths or two vessels travelling down the same river. One row symbolizes the Haudenosaunee people with their law and customs, while the other row symbolizes European laws and customs. As nations move together side-by-side on the River of Life, they are to avoid overlapping or interfering with one another. – John Borrows, Indigenous legal scholar (cited in Keefer [2014], 10).

We have been accused of no greater crime than to be born Indian. Our story from the first breath was not chosen, and the resistance that defines our life is relentless. To give in would mean we cease to exist as either an individual or as a community and to our people; this is one and the same.

It is the cold and uncompromising truth that Indigenous communities and people across Canada have been fighting in defence of our rights, for the return of our land, protection of our resources, and for self-determination since the first European settlers laid claim to Turtle Island and called it their own. The times of hostility for us did not begin with the rise of nationalism or the upset of broken international trade agreements, but with the earliest European settlers in the sixteenth century who destroyed our way of life and common good for their benefit. The methodic destruction of Indigenous people followed the steady march of colonialism, where the firm belief in Western superiority demanded that Indigenous culture and all institutions within Canada be created in the likeness of the rest of the Western world, without exception.

We resisted. And in our story, there is much to learn for non-Indigenous people who are likewise searching for their common good in this country and where government policies and destructive legislation seek the elimination of our nation's sustainable future. The teachings of the wampum are clear that the Indigenous and non-Indigenous people are brothers and that, in the movements that are happening right now, there is a place for lessons of Indigenous resistance to be shared for the benefit of all of us, as we each search for the common good of our own people.

Broken Treaties and the Indian Act

Our shared history begins around four hundred years ago, when the increasing European presence on Turtle Island required that treaty be made to ensure peaceful relationships between First Nations and foreign subjects, whose numbers were so few that safety concerns were very real as we lived side by side. In 1763, approximately sixty-two years after the first treaty was signed on Canadian soil, the British won the Seven Years War against the French and issued a Royal Proclamation. The proclamation confirmed the original occupancy of Indigenous people in North America and determined how further settlement and relationships between the British Crown and Indigenous people would occur. Land not ceded under treaty remained under Aboriginal title, and the British Crown was designated as the only legal entity permitted to buy land and sign treaty with Indigenous people.

This proclamation, ironically utilized by Indigenous people in the twenty-first-century fight for legal recognition of their rights, was initially created for the sole purpose of monopolizing Indigenous lands for the British Crown. It was designed unilaterally by the British monarchy without the consultation or the participation of First Nations people, and was a foundational document in the history of Canada. It was also a foreboding symbol of the insatiable need and desire for the land and resources of Indigenous people that would lead us into dark shadows of colonization, although no one in our communities knew or understood that yet.

The official creation of Canada through Confederation in 1867 established democracy for the settlers in this country and cemented the legacy of the British monarchy forever. Between 1871 and 1921, the last of the major eleven treaties covering payments of goods and cash, cession of First Nations land title and creation of reserves, provision of education and health care, as well as the protection of fishing, hunting and harvesting rights were signed between Indigenous people and Canada.

By 2018, the entire 9.985 million square kilometres that Indigenous people formerly called home was in the possession of Canada, and our presence within it was confined to reserves under Crown title, comprising 0.2 per cent of its land mass. Today, we comprise 4.9 per cent of the population, and Canadians question why our people are in poverty, without stopping to ask whether the dispossession of all Indigenous peoples' territory is at the heart of it.

We're not ethnic minorities. We are Indigenous peoples, we have the right to self-determination … we have our own lands, we have our own laws, we have our own languages, we have our own identifiable peoples and we have our own identifiable forms of government. That inherent right must be respected. – National Chief, Assembly of First Nations, Perry Bellegard, in Kieridden (2017).

Fewer than ten years after the formation of Canada, the Indian Act was created to consolidate all the various laws that had existed concerning Indigenous people prior to Confederation. These applied to registered Indians, their bands, and the system of Indian reserves. Despite numerous major amendments, the Indian Act is still in force today and continues to affect the majority of First Nations people in Canada. Its purpose was to prescribe how the government of Canada was to interact with and control the over six hundred First Nations bands and their members, and was wide-ranging enough to cover their governance, land use, health care, education, the operation of reserves and bands, and who is recognized – or not – as an "Indian."

The Indian Act has been amended over the years, but it still remains an oppressive, racist piece of legislation that continues to inflict irreparable damage upon our peoples. – Ontario Regional Chief Isadore Day (Chiefs of Ontario 2016).

Most importantly, it must be remembered that the Indian Act is not a treaty; it is Canada's answer to these agreements and was created without the involvement or input of Indigenous people.

Why We Resist

After the Royal Proclamation, the number of treaties signed between the British Crown and Indigenous people increased, and the reserve system began in earnest. The Indian Act functioned as the legal framework for the federal government's widespread colonial policy and, almost immediately after its passing, the traditional forms of First Nations governance were replaced with the elected chief and council system in place today.

Indian agents were appointed for each reserve, and dictated marriage, travel, and food rations (among other things) for First Nations people. For the federal government to keep track of us better, we were given European surnames. We could not leave the limits of the reserve without permission and were no longer allowed to hunt and travel in our traditional ways. The ability of our communities to sustain themselves disappeared, and thus the system of welfare dependence began.

In the 1920s, Indigenous people began organizing themselves to protest the federal government's failure to respect treaties. In response, the federal government amended the Indian Act so that Indigenous people could not hire lawyers. Outside of the church, we were no longer permitted to gather in public in groups of three or more and were prohibited from practising our traditional ways. The potlatch and other ceremonies integral to keeping our Indigenous communities and relationships strong were made illegal.

The Indian Act outlined many ways in which First Nations people could lose their Indian Status and, with it, all their rights as Indigenous people. This process, which began with the Gradual Civilization Act of 1857 even before the Indian Act was created, was called "enfranchisement," and no group suffered more than Indigenous women. Since they were the stalwarts of our communities, it was necessary for the federal government to devalue our women in order to break down our societies. The provisions of the Indian Act related to band membership dictated that our Indian Status and right to live within our communities would be taken away if we married non-Indigenous men or men from another reserve. The patriarchal discrimination against women characteristic of Western society became part of our story, creating dysfunction and power imbalances within our own families. By the time the Charter of Rights and Freedoms was enacted by Canada in 1982, and Indigenous women forced the federal government to change these provisions, the damage had already been done. A century of discriminatory policy had already caused tens of thousands of Indigenous women to become dislocated from their homes and from their families, both geographically and in their traditional self-identity.

The role of the Canadian government as complicit in the tragedy of missing and murdered Indigenous women is well known. Numerous studies and reports have indicated that the root causes of violence toward Indigenous women in Canada are poverty, homelessness, and historical factors such as racism, sexism, the legacy of colonialism, and the devastation of the residential school system. Across Canada, Indigenous women are six times more likely to be homicide victims than non-Indigenous women; the number of missing and murdered Indigenous women is unknown, but is estimated to be between twelve hundred to four thousand.

Finally, Canada came for our children. The Indian Act directed that Indigenous children be forcibly removed from our homes by the Royal Canadian Mounted Police to attend off-reserve residential schools run by the churches. Today, the inhumane conditions of these institutions are well known. Children came home years later without their language and culture and with the scars of physical, mental, and sexual abuse. Indigenous children were taught to hate themselves and who they were as Indigenous people. Many children did not come back at all.

The federal government's Royal Commission on Aboriginal Peoples noted that "Repeated assaults on the culture and collective identity of Aboriginal people have weakened the foundations of Aboriginal society and contributed to the alienation that drives some to self-destruction and antisocial behavior. Social problems among Aboriginal people are, in large measure, a legacy of history" (Piétacho and Basile 1996).

In 2018, the picture is grim from the outside looking in. Despite the phasing out of residential schools during the 1960s, Indigenous children continued to be taken from their traditional families by child-service programs and adopted into non-Indigenous households. An overwhelming number of these adoptions broke down, and/or the children were abused. Today, Indigenous women are most likely to experience poverty. As the primary caregivers, single women with children experience the most extreme levels of this. A shocking four out of ten Indigenous children live in poverty.

The movement toward placing children in foster and group homes has for the most part replaced the policy of adopting out, but the number of Indigenous children in care has only grown. Approximately 48 per cent

of the thirty thousand children and youth in care across Canada are Indigenous (Yükselir and Annett 2016).

The federal government has overwhelmingly failed in its responsibility
to provide basic infrastructure within our communities and adequate funding for our social services. Ninety-one First Nations have no access to clean
drinking water (Amnesty International n.d.), while health and education
services are funded at a lower level than identical services offered off-reserve
and paid for by the provinces.

In 2018, the rhetoric of the Liberal government under Prime Minister
Justin Trudeau, elected in 2015, continues to stress that "There is no relationship more important to me – and to Canada – than the one with First
Nations, the Métis Nation, and Inuit" (Trudeau 2015). Yet there continues
to be an overwhelming implementation gap between Canada's human-
rights obligations within domestic laws, policies, and programs toward Indigenous people. We cannot wait. And for all the reasons above and more,
we resist.

Movements for the Common Good

But words are also easy, cheap ... too often we see the tendency –
especially in politics – to use important words that have real meaning
and importance, carelessly ... We see 'recognition' applied to ideas that
actually maintain 'denial.' We see 'self-government' used to refer to ideas
or processes that actually maintain control over others. – Jody Wilson-
Raybould, Member of Parliament (2018).

The United Nations has condemned colonization in every form. Dispossession of someone's land and the dependency that colonizers attempt to
create can only result in a community willing to fight to be free and independent again. There cannot be peace when there is colonization.

Indigenous movements have been steadfast in their resistance, both
taking up arms and using non-violent methods. While they have faced a
number of setbacks, many victories have also come through these struggles. The Northwest Rebellion in 1885, led by Louis Riel, was also supported
by various chiefs in Saskatchewan and Alberta who recognized that the
disappearance of bison and relocation to reserves meant starvation for their

people. Although the rebellion was short lived, each side took many lives, and the Indigenous men who were hanged are said to have cried out their defiance of the Canadian government with their last breaths.

As the policies of the Indian Act displaced and fragmented communities during the late-nineteenth and twentieth centuries, a quieter and more-secretive resistance of hiding children from Indian agents occurred, along-side the secret teaching of ceremonies and language. During this period, the settler colonial violence shifted from outright physical force via battle to a suppression characterized by negotiation and law.

In the last thirty years, Indigenous movements have grown in number, with more communities standing together against the federal and provincial governments. These protests, sit-ins, and blockades have received increasing exposure in the media, with the government relying heavily on police or armed forces to "handle" the situation. This has led to serious consequences, including physical violence, criminal charges, and even death.

The Oka crisis in 1990 in Kanestake, Quebec, saw the Mohawk nation attempt to prevent their sacred territory from becoming a golf course through a seventy-eight-day armed standoff between the Canadian armed forces and the Mohawk citizens. Many Indigenous communities across Canada showed their support through their own actions of solidarity.

Five years later, another request by the Kettle and Stony Point First Nation for the return of land led to a standoff in Ipperwash Provincial Park. During a heated moment of this crisis, an Indigenous man by the name of Dudley George was shot and killed by a member of the Ontario Provincial Police. An inquiry into his death concluded that this deadly violence on the part of the officer was a direct result of the fractured relationship between Indigenous people and Canada.

In 2012, a handful of strong Indigenous women dedicated to fighting Prime Minister Stephen Harper started the Idle No More movement. Thousands of Indigenous people and their allies organized sit-ins and marches across the country to protest the legislation proposed by the Conservative government, especially the omnibus Bill C-45, or the "Jobs and Growth Act," which portended far-reaching, destructive effects on Indigenous livelihood, health, and the environment.

At the same time, Indigenous advocates were calling on the government to launch an inquiry into missing and murdered Indigenous women and girls. The Conservative government refused, but the federal election in 2015, which saw the Liberal party under Justin Trudeau take power, offered some initial hope. Finally, the Canadian government officially launched an inquiry into murdered and missing Indigenous women. Its sluggish progress after being launched in January 2017 left the communities, families, and friends of the victims dismayed. They believe that the process is just another example of Prime Minister Trudeau's treatment of Indigenous issues – all rhetoric, with little to no action, all tied up in the bureaucracy. The inquiry finally issued its report in June 2019.

The growing disdain for the Liberal government's commitment to reconciliation has only increased with the number of pipeline projects approved by Trudeau's office. Supporting a future for fossil fuel and taking a huge environmental risk does nothing to enhance the image of a government that has repeatedly dedicated itself to introducing progressive and cleaner energy sources. And while Indigenous and environmental allies work tirelessly on the ground to halt work on these projects before irreparable harm is done, the issue of who should be consulted continues in light of the confusion that the Indian Act has created with elected versus traditional hereditary chiefs. The silence from the Prime Minister's Office speaks volumes, given its historic role in the manufactured disarray.

And so it becomes clear that, while Prime Minister Justin Trudeau may be better than most at renaming government departments, buildings, and parks and in unequivocal outbursts of expressive emotion decrying the harms that have been done to Indigenous people, we continue to be the most disenfranchised group in the country.

There is no doubt today that the federal party in power has had little effect in changing the destiny of our people. That destiny does not lie in the federal creation of an Indigenous-rights framework; nor does it lie in the constitution of a country that drew its power from the processes of colonialization. Rather, the answer lies in reliance on the treaties made between equal but separate nations and a continual push for self-determination through self-governance. It definitely does not come through the Indian Act.

Once the Indian Act is done away with, only then will First Nations have control of our own destiny to become self-sufficient and self-governing.
– Grand Chief Derek Nepinak (Fontaine 2016).

Conclusion

That Indigenous people in Canada can never truly regain their status as healthy, autonomous, and self-governing nations through the Canadian political and legal process is not a novel concept. The history of the federal government's attempts to control us through legislation such as the Indian Act has only led to the destruction of our culture, governance structures, and traditional identities. It falls on us, then, as Indigenous people, to search and fight for the common good of our own people. It must be shared and beneficial for all members of our community and sought through the collective work and participation of everyone.

The era of disillusionment for Indigenous people is over, and we have recognized the Canadian government for what it has been, what it is, and what it cannot be. It cannot be the servant of two masters; the interests of the non-Indigenous public are not necessarily the same as the common good of Indigenous communities who identify as land defenders and water protectors. As Cree lawmaker Romeo Saganash pointedly asked in the House of Commons shortly after the Federal Court of Appeal ruling that the Liberal government had failed to adequately consult with the First Nations affected by the Trans Mountain pipeline project in August 2018: "Why doesn't the prime minister just say the truth and tell Indigenous people that he doesn't give a fuck about their rights?" (Cecco 2016).

The leader of Canada is not the leader of our people. As Indigenous people, we have our own responsibilities to protect the land, the water, and the environment around us as part of our Original Instructions as provided by the Creator. These instructions explained our responsibilities to each other and to the natural world and how we were to govern ourselves.

At times, these responsibilities that we were given clash with the interests of the wider world of finance and resource extraction, where the greed of nationalist policies and the emphasis on securing trade and fiscal balances for the next election are more important than protecting the earth for seven generations to come. This is a dark place for politics and a place where the exploitation of people and divisiveness between "us" and "them" allows for continued mistreatment and blame to be placed on everyone else.

When this happens, the history and experience that Indigenous people have in asserting their treaty rights or challenging the government to create policy that protects the land and the water – with attention focused on the future – is invaluable. Increasingly, non-Indigenous people and groups are recognizing the importance of living in harmony with the natural world and are becoming allies of the grassroots movements that are central to Indigenous activism. Co-operation also fosters a closer relationship between Indigenous and non-Indigenous people as the historical context of colonialism and infringement on treaty rights and land claims becomes increasingly apparent.

This new understanding on the part of non-Indigenous allies is in itself an integral part of reconciliation, and breaks down the barriers encouraged by a far-right ideology that turns a blind eye to injustice while continuing to perpetuate it. The use of media to further partner with like-minded people and organizations is an important first step, while continued education of colleagues, friends, and family by Indigenous and non-Indigenous alike comes next. There has never been a more relevant time for widespread civil resistance to the national agendas and global regimes that are determined to expropriate non-renewable resources while distracting the public with protectionist propaganda.

We, Indigenous and non-Indigenous alike, were born during these sacred times to be relentless warriors for the defence of our resources and to protect the world we live in for future generations. And though we search as separate nations for the good of our own communities, we have in this moment come to a place of learning where the history of the Indigenous resistance and the traditional teachings of respect and harmony can be passed along for the good of the water; for the good of the earth; and for the good of each other.

REFERENCES

Amnesty International. n.d. "Canada: The Right to Water in First Nations Communities." Amnesty International Canada. https://www.amnesty.ca/our-work/issues/indigenous-peoples/indigenous-peoples-in-canada/the-right-to-water.
Cecco, Leyland. 2016. "Canadian MP says Trudeau 'Doesn't Give a Fuck' about Indigenous Rights. *Guardian*, 26 September. https://www.theguardian.com/world/2018/sep/26/trudeau-romeo-saganash-indigenous-rights-parliament.

Chiefs of Ontario. 2016. "Ontario Regional Chief Isadore Day Statement on 140th
    Anniversary of Indian Act: Oppressive, Racist Legislation that Condemns First
    Nations to 21st Century Poverty Must be Replaced with a True Nation-to-Nation
    Relationship." http://www.chiefs-of-ontario.org/news_item/ontario-regional-
    chief-isadore-day-statement-on-140th-anniversary-of-indian-act-oppressive-
    racist-legislation-that-condemns-first-nations-to-21st-century-poverty-must-
    be-replaced-with-a-true-nation/.
Fontaine, Tim. 2016. "Indian Act Turns 140, but Few Are Celebrating." CBC News,
    12 April. https://www.cbc.ca/news/indigenous/indian-act-turns-140-but-few-
    celebrating-1.3532810.
Keefer, Tom. 2014. "A Short Introduction to the Two-Row Wampum." Briarpatch,
    10 March. https://briarpatchmagazine.com/articles/view/a-short-introduction-
    to-the-two-row-wampum.
Khieridden, Tasha. 2017. "What a Nation-to-Nation Relationship with Indigenous
    Canadians Should Look Like." iPolitics, 17 July. https://ipolitics.ca/2017/07/17/
    what-a-nation-to-nation-relationship-with-indigenous-canadians-should-
    look-like/.
Piétacho, Chief Jean-Charles, and Sylvie Basile. 1996. "Gathering Strength." People
    to People, Nation to Nation: Highlights from the Report of the Royal Commission
    on Aboriginal Peoples. Canada. Royal Commission on Aboriginal Peoples.
    https://www.aadnc-aandc.gc.ca/eng/1100100014597/1100100014637.
Trudeau, Prime Minister Justin. 2015. Speech to Assembly of First Nations Special
    Chiefs Assembly, 8 December. https://pm.gc.ca/eng/news/2015/12/08/prime-
    minister-justin-trudeau-delivers-speech-assembly-first-nations-special-chiefs.
Wilson-Raybould, Jody. 2018. "Recognition, Reconciliation, and Indigenous
    People's Disproportionate Interactions with the Criminal Justice System."
    Department of Justice, 13 September. https://www.justice.gc.ca/eng/news-nouv/
    speech.html.
Yükselir, Murat, and Evan Annett. 2016. "Where the Kids Are: How Indigenous
    Children Are Over-Represented in Foster Care." Globe and Mail, 13 April. https://
    www.theglobeandmail.com/news/national/indigenous-kids-made-up-almost-
    half-of-canadian-foster-children-in-2011statscan/article29616843/.

2

HAVE YOU EVER SEEN A REAL, LIVE RACIST?

Post-racialism and the Crisis of Recognition in the Rise of the Far Right

Philip S.S. Howard

31/10/2010, Campbellford, ON: Two Halloween party-goers – one in Ku Klux Klan costume, the other in blackface with a noose around his neck – won first prize for most original costume. During the ensuing controversy, one of the party-goers' sons declared, "My dad's not racist, his best friend is Black."
(Dempsey and Allen 2010)

30/9/2017, St-Bernard-de-Lacolle, QC: Québec anti-immigration groups gathered to intimidate Haitian migrants at the Québec-US border. Antifascists gathered in counter-protest chanted, "Tout le monde déteste les racistes" ("Everyone detests racists"), and were momentarily flummoxed when the anti-immigrant groups began chanting along.
(Antifasciste Info Montreal 2017)

29/1/2017, Québec, QC: A white nationalist terrorist murdered six people and injured several other worshippers at a mosque. His longtime friend, despite disagreeing with his views, declared, "I wrote him off as a xenophobe. I didn't even think of him as totally racist, but he was enthralled by a borderline racist nationalist movement."
(Perreaux and Andrew-Gee 2017)

The incidents above reveal the Canadian crisis of recognition with respect to racism in the contemporary moment. The inability to apply the term *racist* to acts that celebrate or perpetuate racist violence and intimidation is at issue. I argue that this crisis of recognition has been integral to the ostensible rise in the far right in North America.

Canadian scholars Perry and Scrivens (2015) define the far right as: "characterized by a racially, ethnically, and sexually defined nationalism. This nationalism is often framed in terms of white power, and is grounded in xenophobic and exclusionary understandings." While Perry and Scrivens also identify racial violence as a factor, in recent, everyday usage, the term "far right" need not imply this factor. In general usage, then, "far right" refers to unapologetic expressions of racial nationalism.

Mindful of this definition, there can be little question that there has been a rise in the far right. The emergence of such populist parties as Germany's Alternative für Deutschland and the Dutch Partij voor de Vrijheid, the increased influence of the Freedom Party of Austria, the Golden Dawn in Greece, and the National Front in France, and the election of such parties to government in Germany, Hungary, and Poland make this rise evident.[1] It is also worth mentioning Donald Trump's Republicans in the United States, for while they may differ somewhat from the aforementioned groups, the differences appear to be those of degree rather than substance. Racial nationalism is at the root, as evidenced by the number of white supremacist groups galvanized by Trump's rhetoric.

In Canada, we see similar trends. Federal politicians have employed racist dog-whistle concepts like "barbaric cultural practices" and "tests of Canadian values." In 2017 the province of Quebec passed Bill 62, the "Act to Foster Adherence to State Neutrality," prohibiting those providing or using public services from wearing face coverings – a thinly-disguised effort to eject Muslim women who wear the niqab or burqa from public life. A Quebec court suspended this aspect of the law in 2018 (Shingler 2018b), and with the ruling Liberal party's electoral loss that year, it was essentially shelved. But the rhetoric of Bill 62 is consistent with that of the eighty to a hundred far-right groups across Canada (Perry and Scrivens 2015) that have conducted demonstrations and patrols to oppose and directly intimidate racialized people, especially recent migrants, asylum seekers, and Muslims. In June 2019, the Coalition Avenir Québec, elected to a majority government on 1 October 2018, passed the more far-reaching "Act Respecting the Laicity of the State," popularly known as Bill 21, which bans all religious symbols, including the hijab, being worn by public servants. It also invokes the "notwithstanding clause" in the Canadian Charter of Rights and Freedoms to pre-empt constitutional human-rights challenges, and alters Quebec's own Charter of Rights to loosen protection of religious expression (Perreaux 2019).

However, it is crucial to set this rise of the far right in context. First, racialized relations are the foundation of modernity that has produced Western nation-states. Indeed, settler-colonial nation-states like Canada are established, and only able to persist, through originary and ongoing racist-colonial violence that dispossesses and "disappears" Indigenous peoples, dehumanizes Black people, and exploits all racialized people within the broader context of neo-liberal capitalism. Violence against Indigenous, Black, and Muslim lives, and against the lives of a host of other intersecting ethnic, sexual, gendered, classed, and dis/abled identities is longstanding, routine, and constitutive.

In the wake of the Second World War, global independence movements, and civil-rights/anti-apartheid struggles, Western nations shifted attitudes about overt racism, claiming commitments to racial and social justice (but notably *not* toward decolonization). However, these commitments were largely the nominal results of interest convergences (Bell 1980). Further, if we take a long historical view, these commitments are recent and conspicuously the exception rather than the norm. Instead of ushering in substantive anti-racist change, this superficial consensus against racism provoked discourses of denial that laid the foundations for the crisis of recognition I am interested in here.

I am insisting, then, that racist violence and values are not aberrations in countries like Canada. To suggest otherwise, or to think about the rise of the far right apart from this framing, is to deny the embedded racism to which Indigenous, Black, and other racialized people in Canada are routinely subjected. Thus, the rise in the far right cannot be understood as a reversal of moral commitments to racial justice. Rather, it is a re/turn by some to an overt, unapologetic assertion of racialized and colonial relations that are always already in play. It is expression and threat of violence that simply defies the cultivated norms that normally obscure everyday racialized state violence and civil society's racial antipathy.

What is perhaps new about the current rise in the far right are the ways in which it makes racist claims in the name of reasonableness and democracy. This is a symptom of the post-racialism that characterizes a post-9/11, post-Obama world. Post-racialism refers to the ideological climate within which racism continues to structure the state and civil society, while the conditions for recognizing and redressing it are dissolving (Goldberg 2012, 125). Post-racialist logic asserts that, as societies and individuals, we have transcended whatever racism may have been in our past, thus there is no (further) need for legal or structural racial remedies or for individuals to refrain from "telling it like it is" – even if that involves expressing unpleasant racist "truths." The logic continues: the persistence of "diehard" anti-racists (and multiculturalists) places White people in harm's way and at risk of racial injustice.

The events of 9/11 precipitated an intensified rationale for accusing racialized people of being security threats and drains on social resources. Simultaneously, Barack Obama's presidency provided post-racialist "evidence" that racial injustice is no longer an issue in the United States, while exacerbating long-standing Canadian post-racialist myths that the nation was not birthed through colonial violence, and has transcended racism. Indeed, Canadian post-racialism significantly predates the US version, dating at least as far back as Canada's 1988 Multiculturalism Policy, but also implicating Canada's selective accounts about the Underground Railroad, its role as international peacekeeper, and its self-image as tolerant alternative to the United States.

Canadian post-racialism is particularly pronounced in Quebec, given the dual positioning of its dominant population as linguistic minority in Canada but White-settler majority in Quebec. In fact, Quebec nationalism has historically co-opted Black struggle in ways that obscure Quebec's anti-Blackness (Austin 2013). This dynamic was poignantly illustrated in a blackface incident during the Quebec student protests in 2012. Here, an effigy of then–Quebec Liberal premier, Jean Charest, emblazoned with the original anglicized version of his name, sits on a cart and towers over protesters in blackface pushing the cart. By using blackface to signify the Black body and its ostensible servility, this display intimated that Charest's proposal to raise university tuition represented oppression of Quebec's francophones by anglophones. In the tradition of Pierre Vallières' *Nègres blancs d'Amérique* discourse from his 1971 book, this incident conflated race, class, and language to represent the student movement (Hampton 2012), and re-inscribed anti-Blackness. It thus exemplified the crisis of recognition enabled by linguistic struggle in Quebec that refuses intersectionality.

Post-racialism is therefore fertile context within which to manipulate what counts as racism, producing the crisis of recognition. But to be clear, this crisis of recognition is not an actual inability to identify racism, but rather a will to restrict *what counts* as racism. The contemporary far right routinely engages in this post-racialist manipulation to express its racist nationalism with impunity, while denying racism.

Racist humour has long functioned to communicate racism in a post–civil rights climate that nominally disapproves of racist expression (Pérez 2013; Howard 2014), and in some contexts, the far right has become savvy at using it to broadcast its views (Wilson 2017). The humour context allows a crisis of recognition by creating ambiguity about whether the humorist is "seriously" racist. My research into contemporary blackface in Canada (Howard 2018) has examined the role of racist humour in conveying Canadian racial national mythologies. However, where it comes to far-right expression in Canada, and particularly in Quebec, the far right appears not to need the cover of humour.

I argue that this has to do with how deeply post-racialism and its attendant crisis of recognition of racism are embedded in Quebec and the rest of Canada. In Quebec, we saw abundant evidence of this in relation to the white supremacist terror attack of 29 January 2017, when six Muslim men were killed at the Centre Culturel Islamique de Québec. While high-profile Quebecers denounced the attack and had a short-lived conversation admitting that their Islamophobic discourse influenced the conditions that produced the attack, this was quickly succeeded by denials. Even now, the Quebec City police department's website has a single reference to hate, and the city's mayor has rejected the need for a hate-crimes unit (Solyom 2017). This although far-right groups had been organizing regular patrols in Quebec City to "make [Muslims] aware of Quebec values" before the attack (Montpetit 2017a). This although race-related hate crimes in Quebec City more than doubled from 2015 to 2016 (Solyom 2017). This although anti-immigrant, Islamophobic marches have occurred in the city since the massacre (Montpetit 2017b). At the first anniversary of the massacre, Quebec opposition parties insisted the term "Islamophobia" should not be used in reference to the incident. They thereby individualized the attack and disconnected it from the broader Islamophobic climate (Shingler 2018a). Similarly, to gain political favour, the provincial Liberals, the ruling party at the time, cancelled an inquiry into systemic racism, replacing it with "a commission on valuing diversity and fighting against discrimination" (Shingler 2017). At the federal level, the crisis of recognition was evident when, in the name of free speech, opposition politicians vehemently resisted a parliamentary motion to recognize and commit to challenging Islamophobia (CBC News 2017b).

Finally, while Islamophobia clearly also affects Muslims who are Black (two of the Quebec massacre victims were African), demonstrating that Islamophobia and anti-Blackness are not mutually exclusive (see Jiwani, in this collection), we also see the anti-Blackness of the crisis of recognition in many other ways as well. For example, Quebec's far right strongly protested the arrival of Haitian asylum-seekers crossing the border from the United States at St-Bernard-de-Lacolle in 2017, all the while denying racist motivations. Further, the profiling and harassment of Black people is widely practised and defended in Canada as necessary and non-racist, as it is for Indigenous people. Law enforcers who brutalize and kill Black and Indigenous people, particularly those with mental-health challenges, too often go free – as in the cases of Andrew Loku, Clayton Willey, Alain Magloire, and Brydon Whitstone. Overall, then, the crisis of recognition in Canada holds firm, even in the face of killings that involve race-related disregard.

Canadian researchers of the far right have indicated that the broader racist climate in Canada fosters far-right groups and legitimizes their racist expression (Perry and Scrivens 2015, 62). Under these conditions, there is no need to use humour to cover far-right expression. The entrenched crisis of recognition emboldens the far right to express its racial nationalist principles while denying racism. Indeed, the boundary is unclear, if there is one, between far-right ideas and those racist ideas in evidence more broadly. The crisis of recognition in Canada and its effect on the rise of the far-right is aptly summed up in the observations of a former Quebec neo-Nazi:

It's ... more open now ... when I was a kid, and even when I was a young adult, you didn't get to say these things without being blasted ... you can't radicalize without a context. It doesn't happen out of the blue. It's common now to hear Islamophobic things everywhere in the media, on social media, at work, at school. You hear these things, and it becomes normalized. It has normalized racism. (CBC News 2017a).

There are neither simple solutions to this crisis of recognition nor neat strategies for addressing the rise of the far right. Nevertheless, the considerations above suggest some important directions for activists, academics, and popular educators. First, the way forward cannot be conceived in terms of any kind of return to some better, less-racist time. Rather, the contemporary post-racialist moment has been produced by the insistence on a stubborn racial liberalism that denies our racist settler-colonial histories, and fails to take a hard look at ongoing racial-colonial violence. The crisis of recognition instantiates precisely the contradictions of our current ways of living together that claim egalitarianism while being constituted in/through racist-colonial relations. Thus, far-right ideas cannot be countered with mythical allusions to an ostensibly tolerant Quebec and Canada whose values the far right is betraying. Instead, when responding to far-right expression, it is imperative that those who truly desire change – whether they occupy visible public office or participate in everyday conversations – resist smug declarations that "this is not who we are." Similarly, we must avoid resorting to simplistic explanations, such as "implicit bias," that blame racism on the individual's unconscious, and obscure how people consciously engage in racist violence that has been socially normalized and rationalized.

Second, and related, we must reconsider the somewhat arbitrary distinction between the far right and broader settler-colonial relations. As worrisome as the impunity of the far right is, it easily becomes a scapegoat, allowing equally problematic racist discourse and violence enacted in/through the state and civil society to go unexamined. Resistance to the far right cannot be separated from a sustained critique of the entire settler-colonial arrangement that produces the socially unjust, racially violent conditions we experience. Critical educators – whether popular or academic – must continually engage the intersectional, anti-colonial, race-class analysis that makes these connections evident. We must circulate clear, accessible definitions of racism. For example, xenophobia, racialized anti-immigrant sentiment, talk of the threat posed by racialized people – all of these depend upon racializing logics and count as racist. It is important that racist ideas be named as such, *using the label racist*, in addition to more specific labels such as anti-Black, Islamophobic, colonial, etc., where applicable. As such, educators might devise, teach, and rehearse successful strategies for having these critical conversations that push back against the crisis of recognition in varied social contexts, from the casual to the professional.

Third, we must educate to create greater literacy around global neo-liberalism and the erosion of the welfare state, which create the desperate conditions that many Whites blame on migrants and racialized people, who, themselves, are more deeply challenged and made migrants by these conditions.

Finally, the way forward is one of imagination – one in which we imagine ways of living together and relating that few, if any, of us have yet experienced. Like Roach in this volume, I note that this creative vision requires imagining a world that does not depend upon carceral relations, the violence of national boundaries, and the relations of neo-liberal capitalism, or upon the racist logics that are crucial to how they play out. This is why the way forward is not easily reduced to a few actions. It does not require tweaks to a largely good system, but the dismantling of all that many of us have ever known.

NOTE

1 I would like to thank Rosalind Hampton for the many good conversations we have had about the far right, which have greatly contributed to my knowledge of its current manifestations.

REFERENCES

Antifasciste Info Montreal. 2017. "Storm Alliance at the Border: 'We're Not Racists, but …': Documenting the Far Right." 10 October. https://montreal-antifasciste. info/en/2017/10/10/storm-alliance-at-the-border-were-not-racists-but/.
Austin, D. 2013. *Fear of a Black Nation: Race, Sex, and Security in Sixties Montreal.* Toronto: Between the Lines.
Bell, D.A. 1980. "*Brown v. Board of Education* and the Interest-Convergence Dilemma." *Harvard Law Review* 93 (3): 518–33.
CBC News. 2017a. "Former Quebec Neo-Nazi Speaks Out about How He Learned to Hate Minorities." *CBC News* [online], 27 August. http://www.cbc.ca/radio/the

sundayedition/august-27-2017-the-sunday-edition-1.4260430/former-quebec-
neo-nazi-speaks-out-about-how-he-learned-to-hate-minorities-1.4260438.

– 2017b. "MP Who Launched Anti-Islamophobia Motion Received Hate Mail,
Death Threats." *CBC News* [online], 18 September. https://globalnews.ca/news/
3753972/anti-islamophobia-bill-hate-mail-mp/.

Dempsey, A., and K. Allen, 2010. "Campbellford Reels after Halloween Costume
Furore." *Star* [online], 4 November. https://www.thestar.com/news/ontario/2010
/11/04/campbellford_reels_after_halloween_costume_furore.html.

Goldberg D.T. 2012. "When Race Disappears." *Comparative American Studies:
An International Journal* 10 (2–3): 116–27.

Hampton, R. 2012. "Race, Racism, and the Quebec Student Movement." *New
Socialist*, 8 July. http://newsocialist.org/race-racism-and-the-quebec-student-
movement/.

Howard, P.S.S. 2014. "Drawing Dissent: Postracialist Pedagogy, Racist Literacy,
and Racial Plagiarism in Anti-Obama Political Cartoons." *Review of Education,
Pedagogy, and Cultural Studies* 36 (5): 386–402.

– 2018. "A Laugh for the National Project: Contemporary Canadian Blackface
Humour and Its Constitution through Canadian Anti-Blackness." *Ethnicities* 18
(6): 843–68. (Published online: 8 July 2018).

Montpetit, J. 2017a. "Inside Quebec's Far Right: Soldiers of Odin Leadership Shake-
Up Signals Return to Extremist Roots." *CBC News*, 8 January. http://www.cbc.ca/
news/canada/montreal/quebec-far-right-soldiers-of-odin-1.3896175.

– 2017b. "Did Quebec City Police Help Legitimize Province's Far Right?" *CBC News*,
2 December. http://www.cbc.ca/news/canada/montreal/quebec-city-police-help-
legitimize-far-right-analysis-1.4420370.

Pérez, R. 2013. "Learning to Make Racism Funny in the 'Color-Blind' Era: Stand-Up
Comedy Students, Performance Strategies, and the (Re)Production of Racist
Jokes in Public." *Discourse & Society* 24 (4): 478–503.

Perreaux, L. 2019. "Quebec Passes Bill Banning Public Servants from Wearing
Religious Symbols". *Globe and Mail*, 16 June. https://www.theglobeandmail.com/
canada/article-quebec-legislature-expected-to-pass-bill-21-late-sunday/.

Perreaux, L., and Andrew-Gee E. 2017. "Quebec City Mosque Attack Suspect
Known as Online Troll Inspired by French Far-Right." *Globe and Mail*, 30 January.
https://www.theglobeandmail.com/news/national/quebec-city-mosque-attack-
suspect-known-for-right-wing-online-posts/article33833044/.

Perry, B., and R. Scrivens, 2015. "Right-Wing Extremism in Canada: An Environ-

mental Scan." *Public Safety Canada*. https://www.publicsafety.gc.ca/cnt/ntnl-scrt/
cntr-trrrsm/r-nd-flght-182/knshk/ctlg/dtls-en.aspx?i=116.

Shingler, B. 2017. "Reduced Mandate of Quebec's Racism Inquiry 'Very Political'
and 'Unacceptable,' Community Groups Say." cbc *News*, 27 October. http://
www.cbc.ca/news/canada/montreal/quebec-mosque-shooting-islamophobia-
1.4478861.

– 2018a. "Quebec Opposition Parties Against Marking Mosque Shooting with Day
Against Islamophobia." cbc *News*, 9 January. http://www.cbc.ca/news/canada/
montreal/quebec-mosque-shooting-islamophobia-1.4478861.

– 2018b. "Judge Suspends Quebec Face Covering Ban, Saying It Appears to Violate
Charter." cbc *News*, 28 June. https://www.cbc.ca/news/canada/montreal/quebec-
bill-62-face-covering-july1-1.4724863.

Solyom, C. 2017. "What to Do About Hate Crimes in Quebec City?" *Montreal
Gazette*, 1 September. http://montrealgazette.com/news/local-news/what-to-
do-about-hate-crimes-in-quebec-city.

Wilson, J. 2017. "Hiding in Plain Sight: How the 'Altright' is Weaponizing Irony
to Spread Fascism." *Guardian*. https://www.theguardian.com/technology/2017/
may/23/alt-right-online-humor-as-a-weapon-facism.

WHO'S AFRAID OF MUSLIMS?

Uzma Jamil

We live in political times, as Brexit and the election of Trump have given political legitimacy to the far right in Europe, the United States, and Canada.
Far-right demonstrations have numbered in the thousands, making explicit
their supporters' xenophobic and Islamophobic views, nationally and internationally. It seems as if these political events are unprecedented, but in
truth, they are not. They are not outside history; they are part of it.

Despite different national contexts, far-right groups have political and
ideological elements in common: the belief that White majorities are the
true "owners" of the nation and that racialized minorities, immigrants, Indigenous peoples, and Blacks are outsiders to this "white nation" (Hage
1998). Hage uses this phrase to describe the racialized hierarchies that operate in Australia, but this racialized view of the nation has also been present
in North America for centuries, even if it has taken different forms and been
named differently.

Canada came into being as a colonial settler society, settled by British
and French explorers. Their respective claims to "founding a nation" were
based on a racialized hierarchy that excluded the Indigenous peoples from
what became known eventually as Canada. In the late 1800s and early 1900s,
Canada implemented "White Canada" policies that were designed to ex-
clude Asians, Blacks, and other non-Europeans from entering and settling
in the country. For example, the Chinese head tax, in place between 1885
and 1923, was meant to discourage immigration by charging a steadily increasing fee for each Chinese person entering Canada. The Continuous
Journey clause, enacted in 1908, was designed to prevent the entry of Asian
immigrants by prohibiting those who did not travel directly (continuously)
from their country to Canada. It was challenged by the Indian passengers
of the ship *Komagata Maru* in Vancouver Harbour, in 1914.

Today, the political discourse on the arrival and settlement of racialized immigrants and refugees continues to echo from these themes and policies, maintaining a racialized hierarchy between immigrants and "founding peoples" that questions the belongingness of the former. In the past nineteen years, even though the "war on terror" has made Muslims extremely visible, and normalized the perception of them as potential racialized "threats," it is part of a broader and much longer historical and colonial preoccupation with Muslims as racialized Others in relation to the West.

It is out of this history that the contemporary rise of the far right and the increased visibility of Islamophobia in Canada are linked together. Both were already present, but have become controversial topics for debate in recent years. Though they are separate events, a look back shows a political trajectory.

In December 2016, MP Iqra Khalid introduced a non-binding motion, M103, condemning Islamophobia, which was debated in parliament in February 2017. Her motion brought the term "Islamophobia" and its contested meanings into public view, and initiated vigorous controversy, ironically giving space to Islamophobic sentiments themselves. Even though Islamophobia existed before this moment, now there was a name to it. It became a way to talk about the presence of Muslims collectively, as both a racialized and religious minority group in the country, rather than as Arabs, South Asians, Blacks, and Muslims. The disagreements about M103, the term "Islamophobia," and who or what it includes and excludes all illustrate the visibility of Muslims as a political identity (Jamil 2018). This is important, because the categories in which we speak about an issue are relevant to how we think about it and how we address it.

Another event took place in January 2017, before M103 came up for parliamentary debate. On January 29, Alexandre Bissonnette walked into a mosque in Quebec City and killed six Muslim worshippers and injured nineteen others. In 2018, when he pleaded guilty to his crime, court documents made public Bissonnette's support for the xenophobic and Islamophobic sentiments of the far right in France and Trump's immigration policies, especially the "Muslim travel ban," which had come into effect a few days earlier. He expressed fear that White majorities, people like him and his family, were at risk of being killed by racialized Muslim immigrants, demonstrating a link between the views of far-right White nationalists and this act of violence. The mosque shooting was the first incident of explicit violence against Muslims in their place of worship in Canada. In the aftermath, politicians and the public expressed short-lived sympathy and support for Muslims, without acknowledging how the constant demonization of Muslims in political discourses might have led to this horrific event (Jamil 2019).

This demonization has existed for a long time and has become normalized over time, most recently in provincial (Quebec and Ontario) and federal election campaigns. It has created a fertile ground for La Meute, a far-right group in Quebec with about forty-five thousand members. Though it started as a secret Facebook group, it held several demonstrations in Quebec City and Montreal in 2017, with increasing numbers of protestors. The group calls for the protection and preservation of white francophone majority culture and identity in Quebec against what it sees as the threat posed by increasing numbers of racialized immigrants, particularly Muslims. Members of the group have publicly criticized radical Islam, illegal migration, and the increasing numbers of immigrants in Montreal (Montpetit 2017).

The Quebec mosque shooting and La Meute are connected; they are part of the same spectrum (Mastracci 2017). La Meute represents both the global crisis of whiteness, as well as national fears of the loss of a distinct Quebec francophone identity in an anglophone country. The crisis of whiteness is based on a fear of loss of power by White majorities, a fear of the loss of white privilege in a world where the historically dominant position of the western nation is no longer a given (Jamil 2018). This crisis of whiteness is linked to Islamophobia, because the perceived loss of the "white nation" is seen as an outcome of the "Muslim threat" represented in the presence of Muslims as racialized and religious minorities in the West. While M103 was a political move to give space to the discussion of Islamophobia, the mosque shooting was an extreme example of it. It was the ultimate response to the perception of threat – to erase Muslims altogether from the nation.

Islamophobia without Muslims

Islamophobia does not require actual Muslims in order to exist, but it does require the idea of a Muslim as a racialized threat to whiteness. The far right requires this Muslim figure in order to assert their nativism, xenophobia, and Islamophobia. This is why the actual size of the Muslim population doesn't matter. Even if there are very few Muslims in proportion to the total population in Quebec (about two hundred thousand Muslims, many of whom live in or near Montreal, out of eight million Quebecers) or in Canada (just over one million Muslims among thirty-five million people in Canada), it does not prevent Islamophobia.

Islamophobia is an expression of a racialized way of thinking that draws a line between the West and the non-West. It is an expression of coloniality, which reflects the racialized logic that endures without the formal institutions of colonialism, maintaining the distinction between the former colonizer and the formerly colonized (Sayyid 2014, 37–8). Muslims are postcolonial subjects who continue to be seen as cultural outsiders and threats, as the "uncivilized" to those believed to be part of the "civilized" West.

What Do We Do Now?

If Islamophobia does not depend upon the actual number of Muslims, the question of how to address it remains unanswered. The explicit desire of the far right to "return" to an imagined national homogeneity and racialized purity through a stop on Muslim immigration will not solve the problem either.

Addressing the rise of the far right and Islamophobia means that we must first acknowledge that they are connected; they are based on white anxieties about power and privilege. The common factor is whiteness and the racial inequalities and hierarchies that emerge from it. This is not an isolated contemporary problem. It comes out of histories of colonialism, genocide, and slavery in this country, all of which have led us to this racialized present, as Howard also notes in his essay. Thus, there is no better past, there is no "again" (of the "Make America Great Again" type), because it never existed in the first place.

Refocusing the analytical lens for understanding the present means embracing the idea of resistance as a collective endeavour and is not just about one issue or one racialized minority group, as Roach, Farber, and Rudner also point out in their essays. This is parallel to the way that far-right groups have also come together to protest against what they see as related threats, that is refugees, Muslims, and immigration and government policies on these issues. For example, in August 2017, the pro-refugee and immigrant activist group Solidarity across Borders mobilized a counter-protest at the Quebec-US border near Lacolle against far-right groups who were protesting the arrival of refugees from the United States. Two months later, a group called Ottawa against Fascism brought together protestors around a loosely unified anti-racist, anti-fascist, and anti-colonial agenda. The members organized a counter-protest against far-right groups in that city who wanted to express their disagreement with federal government policies on immigration.

In addition to protests and demonstrations, there are also opportunities to build coalitions across groups and parties on relevant issues. For example, the 2018 call for the federal government to designate 29 January, the day of the Quebec mosque shooting, as an annual National Day of Remembrance and Action on Islamophobia had potential to mobilize support from the government, community groups, and citizens across Canada. Although instigated by the National Council for Canadian Muslims in 2018, the idea received scattered support – from the Green Party, from Toronto city councillor Neethan Shan, from some grassroots interfaith groups, and from Muslim community groups. Unfortunately, it received a non-committal response from the Liberal government and vocal resistance from Quebec political parties. January 29 can be a political symbol of inclusion, even as it demonstrates resistance to the far-right and white-nationalist agenda. It has the potential to be politically meaningful, in addition to marking the anniversary of a tragic event (Jamil 2019).

Lastly, scholars and activists need to be vigilant in calling out and criticizing the normalization of the views of the far right in contemporary politics. These are not "just" another point of view in the marketplace of ideas of a liberal democracy. Far-right groups have created false equivalencies that all views are equal, and that they are simply "correcting the imbalance" by insisting on the power of White majorities. In fact, their perspective deliberately obscures the structural and historical inequalities in society that mean that non-White minorities are not and have never been treated equally to White majorities. In fact, far-right political views have violent consequences for non-White minorities, as the mosque shooting demonstrated so clearly.

In conclusion, Canadians like to think of themselves as nice, polite people, who apologize readily for the smallest of things. But although comforting, this idea is part of a national myth. This country has deep-seated, racialized divisions between the Indigenous and those of white colonial-settler heritage, between "immigrants" and "founding peoples," between White majorities and non-White minorities. The far right and Islamophobia emerge out of these divisions. We need to acknowledge this history, because, as other authors in this collection also point out, we are all in it together.

REFERENCES

Hage, Ghassan. 1998. *White Nation: Fantasies of White Supremacy in a Multicultural Society.* Sydney, Australia: Pluto Press.

Jamil, Uzma. 2018. "Islamophobia, One Year Later." *ReOrient*, 22 January. https://www.criticalmuslimstudies.co.uk/islamophobia_one_year_later/.

– 2019. "Remembering Is a Political Act." *ReOrient*, 22 January. https://www.criticalmuslimstudies.co.uk/remembering-is-a-political-act/.

Mastracci, Davide. 2017. "Why Canada Missed Its Best Chance to Deradicalize the Alt Right." *The Walrus*, 7 September. https://thewalrus.ca/why-canada-missed-its-best-chance-to-deradicalize-the-alt-right/.

Montpetit, Jonathan. 2017. "How Quebec's Largest Far Right Group Tries to Win Friends, Influence People." CBC *News*, 21 August. http://www.cbc.ca/news/canada/montreal/quebec-la-meute-far-right-1.4255193.

Sayyid, Salman. 2014. *Recalling the Caliphate.* London: Hurst Publishers.

Statistics Canada. 2011. *National Household Survey Data Tables.* Statistics Canada Catologue no. 99-010-X2011032. Ottawa. Released 8 May 2013.

4

WHY WE MUST SHARE OUR STORIES

Amira Elghawaby

I had long ago understood the power of storytelling. As a journalist, working at the CBC shortly after 9/11, I did all I could to interject experiences and
stories from Canadian Muslim communities reeling from the double impact of that awful day. Not only did we have to deal with the pain and horror
of the event itself, but we also had to deal with the backlash following the
news that so-called Muslims had committed the senseless act. Sitting
around a large boardroom table with reporters, hosts, and associate and
senior producers, I remember not fully understanding a colleague's analysis
of the Middle East and feeling that, as the only Muslim in the room, I was
expected to.

The burden felt heavy. All I could do was share stories. The first interview
I booked in the days that followed was with a former professor of mine,
Karim H. Karim, who had just that year published an in-depth analysis
of the Western media's often disjointed and orientalist view of Muslims
and Islam. Foreshadowing the coverage that was to come, Professor Karim
talked to our "Ottawa Morning" listeners about the stereotypical and uni-
dimensional view of Muslims that is often presented, particularly following
terrorist acts or social and political upheaval somewhere in the world in
which Muslims are implicated.

As a new graduate from journalism school at Carleton University, I felt
I had a whole lot of growing up to do in a very short span of time. Until
then, my main focus as a student journalist had been on the increasing corporatization of our university campuses and of turbulent organizing during
the Harris years and the so-called "Common Sense Revolution." Suddenly,
I found myself part of the "Western media" as its gaze fell squarely and sus-
piciously on a community I had only a year before decided to fully make
my own. It was a year prior to 9/11 that I had decided to don the *hijab*. I

went from White-passing to visible minority, or racialized, or what-have-you, in one afternoon – and it had taken me that year to fully come to terms with what the political and social ramifications my personal decision meant for who I was, and who I was perceived to be. It wasn't an easy transition even back then, though my friends, professors, and peers seemed to accept me, even respect me, for the choice I had made to skip clubbing and spend more time focusing on nurturing a spiritual dimension I had neglected for most of my adult life.

The grudging respect, or mild curiosity, I had seen in some people's eyes all but disappeared after 9/11. But the negative change I felt was nothing close to the discrimination and eventual suspension of civil liberties that too many Western Muslims would come to experience. Of particular note is Maher Arar. I remember his story in particular because it was while I was preparing for one of our radio programs that I was first introduced to Monia Mazigh, his wife. She had just learned that he was missing and had come to the CBC to meet with a reporter. I remember her entering our space, then on the top floor of the Château Laurier in Ottawa's downtown, and determinedly sharing her story. Her husband, a Canadian-Syrian, had been renditioned to Syria based on suspicions that he was involved in terrorist activities. He would later be fully exonerated. Canadians would later learn that his detention in a grave-like cell for over a year was due to faulty information shared by Canada's Royal Canadian Mounted Police with American officials. It was a story she would share over and over again, on the radio, on television, with politicians, at rallies; her young children, Barâa and Houd, as well as her beloved mother, were always close by. I remember watching her in awe, knowing that finding such resilience when it felt as though the entire world was falling apart represented a fearless stoicism that few people would ever have to demonstrate, even if they could.

All of this felt deeply personal – as though it were happening to members of my family. At the time I was also writing and editing a community newspaper called *Muslim Link*, which now exists online only (and which has become one of the country's main portals for Canadian Muslim stories). Back then, we struggled to bring community stories to our pages, finding it challenging to report on ourselves, with our own lens, with our own nuances, at a time when the narratives of who we were and what we believed seemed limited to what others reported. Monia and Maher's story would become part of Canadian lore; their struggle for justice became symbolic of all that went wrong in the post-9/11 world. It was a time of heightened anxiety, during which politicians rushed to appease a frightened public by stereotyping, scapegoating, and eventually suspending the human rights of people whose religion matched those of the terrorists. I never imagined that, ten years later, I would join one of the key Canadian Muslim advocacy organizations that had fought so tirelessly for Maher – and for the human rights of countless Canadian Muslims who were also deeply affected by the Islamophobia that crashed over North America.

By the time I joined the National Council of Canadian Muslims (NCCM), a new normal had set in. This twilight zone was one in which terrorist acts were being committed all too regularly by so-called Muslims around the world, a world in which the stereotyping of Muslims in return was as common. In 2012, a Quebec political party, the Parti Québécois was campaigning on a platform that would prevent religious clothing from being worn by public servants – and eventually by anyone in the public sector. A year later, Quebecers representing a vast number of religious communities, and their allies, marched frequently to protest the discriminatory campaign. At the federal level, the government conflated terrorists with Muslims at every turn, and the Conservative prime minister coined the term "Islamicism," describing it as the most serious security threat to Canada. The RCMP had warned officials that it was unfair to be "casting all Muslims as terrorists or potential terrorists." But, as we would learn at the NCCM, some politicians couldn't resist scoring political points off the backs of vulnerable communities. Scaring people about the "other" is a sure-fire way of winning support among certain segments of the population. It's a tactic that continues today (and which has been entrenched in American foreign policy with the so-called Muslim ban and the obsession with building a wall at the border with Mexico).

At the same time as all of this was happening in 2012 and 2013, Daesh (also known as ISIS) was growing in strength and once again raising fears of violent extremism taking root in our communities. An attack by a drug addict and habitual offender on Parliament Hill in Ottawa, my own hometown, would lead to the murder of Corporal Nathan Cirillo and the onset of new security measures that would again take us down a path of human-rights violations. I won't soon forget that horrible day. The news sent shockwaves across Canada and shook Ottawa's Muslim communities to their core. We quickly organized a press conference, bringing together community representatives from across the diverse spectrum of the Muslim population. I remember standing there, in front of the Human Rights monument, thinking of Corporal Cirillo, a father, and his young son, and almost breaking down then and there in front of the cameras. The burden felt heavier than it had ever been – and yet, the story we had to tell was one of a community that shared the sadness with fellow Canadians. Many members of our communities resented the constant need to demonstrate our humanity, time and time again, and yet, what else could we do? No other communities were expected to apologize for the crimes of individuals. Perceived silence would be used to assume our complicity and tacit approval of terrorist acts. Mourning privately wasn't good enough.

A few days later, I happened to interview Glenn Greenwald for rabble.-ca, an alternative media site. Greenwald, a lawyer and author, had been one of the key individuals reporting on the information leaked by former CIA analyst Edward Snowden. He predicted that the Harper government would rush to push through national-security legislation that would severely hinder civil liberties – and that Canadians would accept it. He was right about the government actions, at least to a certain extent, but Canadians would resist.

It had become rare for me to be the one interviewing someone else. Since taking on the role of director of communications at the NCCM, I was frequently in front of microphones, no longer behind them. I was often called upon to speak out about the rising numbers of hate crimes targeting Muslims in Canada and against our previous government's smear of our mosques when they were falsely linked with radicalizing people and the curtailment of the religious freedoms of Muslim women to wear whatever they wanted. It felt good to have a voice at a time when it seemed that our communities were being spoken for by too many who knew far too little about us. According to authors like Nathan Lean and think tanks like the Center for American Progress, there is a multi-million-dollar American-based Islamophobia industry pumping out misinformation. How could we keep up? We were the victims of fake news, like other communities before us. It used to be called propaganda. The tools have grown more sophisticated, and the impact as deadly.

On 29 January 2017, a young man, consumed with hatred, walked into a Quebec City mosque and started shooting indiscriminately. He killed six men. Six pillars of strength for their wives, for seventeen children who are now fatherless. He left several more severely injured, including one man who will never walk again. The young man who did that to them, to all those families, had been consuming hatred online, growing to hate Muslims so deeply that he would commit the deadliest massacre at a place of worship to ever occur in our country.

As I stood shoulder to shoulder with hundreds of Ottawa folks who had braved a cold January night following the attack to stand in vigil around the centennial flame on Parliament Hill, next to cabinet ministers and various MPs, I found reason to hope, despite the sadness. Similar vigils were happening across the country, with thousands of Canadians showing solidarity with the Muslim community. I ventured to think that maybe the tide had finally turned, and Islamophobia would lessen, that our communities were finally seen as fully human, fully vulnerable, fully real.

But in the weeks ahead, thanks to a contentious debate about Islamophobia, the anti-Muslim rallies grew in number and in strength in various cities across Canada. There were counter-rallies, too, but the hate would not, and has not, abated. Neither has the scapegoating, nor the political pandering, nor the intimidation. What lingers strongest is the fear that my children will never feel safe practising their religion in this country, that they won't even want to in a country where an overwhelming number of Canadians see Islam as damaging to Canada. This despite all the efforts we've been making to prove that this is wrong; to showcase our faith's true teachings of generosity, caring, empathy, love. To showcase our humanity.

I recently had to take a bit of a break from all this. I didn't realize it, but the burden was taking its toll on me, and on my family. It's difficult to keep running and running, only to realize that very little distance has been covered. Yet to those who have shown what allyship truly looks like, thank you. By showing up at counter-rallies, by sending kind messages, by donating to causes that defend the rights of other people, by speaking out, you give me, and many others, the hope we need to get through another day. And to those of you who continue to raise your heads proudly as Canadian Muslims, thank you as well. By holding true to our values and principles, by being proud of our heritage and of our beliefs, we show the way forward for our children, making it easier for them to one day contribute as positively as we keep trying to.

There's a lot more we need to build. I don't think civil society is as organized as it needs to be to take on the challenges of our time. It's far too easy for governments to withhold funding, to make illegal what is legal – like protesting, or striking, or wearing certain clothing. Yet, we must gather, we must think, we must plan, and we must collaborate.

We must hold our institutions and our elected officials to account. We must speak out, and we must rally. We must resist the stereotyping, the fake news, the oppositional narratives that some politicians and movements use to their own advantage. We must find ways to build and rebuild a culture of civic engagement that is rooted in our communities, in our very own neighbourhoods, with the myriad of people we share space with on public transit, in public institutions, on the streets, in our parks. As we struggle as individuals to make it in the world, we need to provide ways to collectively make it. It's about resisting our hyper-individualized culture that elevates personal satisfaction far above the public good. It's also about holding our own community institutions to account, to demand that they be run democratically, transparently, and in a way that is inclusive of our diversities. To do all this, we must keep sharing our stories – in order to tell better ones tomorrow.

5

ANTISEMITISM
Everything Old Is New Again

Bernie M. Farber and Len Rudner

The authors of this essay combine more than sixty years of experience in advocating for the rights and protection of the Jewish community – and other communities – in Canada. Just as importantly, they combine almost 130 years of lived experience as Jews born and raised in Canada in the post-Holocaust era, in times when hostility against Jews ebbed and flowed with the activities of white supremacist groups.

Although the fresh horror of the Holocaust silenced antisemitism for a time, the pause was shockingly brief. In the mid-1960s, John William Beattie and David Stanley became leaders of what they named the Canadian Nazi Party. Their numbers were infinitesimal, but the impact on the Jewish community was devastating. A short, publicized appearance by Beattie, Stanley, and fewer than a dozen followers wearing Nazi uniforms in Toronto's Allen Gardens erupted in a counter-demonstration led by Jewish Holocaust survivors, trade unionists, and hundreds of others. The Nazis had to be led away by police. That movement withered and died.

There were minor eruptions of antisemitism in the years that followed, but it really wasn't until the appearance of antisemitic schoolteacher James Keegstra and Holocaust denier Ernst Zundel in the mid-1980s that we saw a significant increase again in Canada. Zundel and Keegstra helped spawn a new look for neo-Nazism and antisemitism in a group that called itself the Heritage Front, possibly the most successful fascist group since the 1930s. It took the combined efforts of the Canadian Security Intelligence Service, police, and anti-racism activists to finally shut them down.

While the collapse of the Heritage Front signalled for many the end of this threat, the optimism was misplaced. Like-minded individuals continued to meet in small groups or to form communities through the growing online capabilities of the Internet. Antisemitism, ever ready to give form to a list of old and new grievances, awaited only the right opportunity. Like the creature in Yeats's poem "The Second Coming," "what rough beast, its hour come round at last, slouches towards Bethlehem to be born." Today, encouraged by the shameful behaviour of an American president who in tweets and public comment has given racists and antisemites new energy, we once again see the rise of those with hate in their hearts.

Historian Robert Wistrich observed that antisemitism is the longest hatred. Theodor Adorno, when asked for a definition of antisemitism, offered that it was "a rumour about the Jews." The rumours to which Adorno referred are the conspiratorial whispers that have echoed through the corridors of history from its first recording, and are now magnified through the megaphone/loudspeaker of the Internet. These electronic tools have made *The Protocols of the Elders of Zion* a fashionable read for antisemites. A forgery that purported to contain the plans of a Jewish conspiracy for the domination and enslavement of the world, the *Protocols* was first published in 1903 and remains available in numerous languages. The document was useful fuel for antisemites, and for the Nazis in particular. An important ideological pillar for the notion of the Jew as an eternal and diabolical enemy, the *Protocols* was rightly described by author Norman Cohn as a "warrant for genocide." Stephen Eric Bronner (2000) observed that the *Protocols* was a foolish and dangerous answer to a very important question: why does the world work the way it does? More poetically, why do bad things happen to good people? More personally, why do bad things happen to me?

Tragedy, whether natural or man-made, is not unique to our time. The identification of scapegoats satisfies a human need for both revenge and justice. Illness ravages communities, economies collapse, and wars end in defeat. We render the inexplicable explicable and the intolerable bearable by blaming others, not infrequently shedding our own culpability in the process. In a sense, antisemitism persists because it satisfies two deep human needs: to "understand" the world and to avoid taking responsibility for our own behaviour.

Antisemitism in the early decades of the twenty-first century is, at its root, no different from what preceded it. The racial-biological form of Jew hatred which came into being in the late nineteenth century – and was raised to lethal perfection by the Nazis – is still with us today. To the writers, it matters less what name we apply to the messengers than that we understand what the message means. Nazis. Neo-Nazis. "Alt-Right." Fascist. The words generate more heat than light as we waste energy demanding that our opponents (and sometimes even our allies) "define their terms." All the while, the usual suspects, their ranks bolstered by new generations of the disaffected and disenfranchised (that they believe themselves to be such is as important as any reality we care to argue about), fill the public square as they did in Charlottesville, Virginia, in the summer of 2017 with cries of *you will not replace us* and *blood and soil!*

While it's tempting to give in to the notion that these tiki-torch-bearing marchers are no more than a confederacy of dunces who also perplexingly chant that "Harry Potter is not real," it is a mistake to do so. There is no such thing as "Nazi-lite." As the Southern Poverty Law Center (SPLC) makes clear, the slogans shouted out in Charlottesville and other places tie the "alt-right" movement to some of the most dangerous extremist notions. *You will not replace us* expresses the deep fear of white-nationalist elements that their culture and their whiteness is under attack by the forces of multiculturalism and non-Whites. The fear finds clear expression in dire warnings of the coming (or now-arrived) "White Genocide." The target of white rage was made clearer as the chant became "Jews will not replace us." More disturbing, but also more illuminating, is use of the phrase *Blood and Soil*. According to SPLC (2017), "this is the English rendition of Nazi Germany's most fervent chant, 'Blut und Boden!'" Originally devised as a slogan of nineteenth-century German nationalists and popularized by Nazi ideologue Richard Walter Darre, the phrase is intended to invoke patriotic identification with native national identity, built on a foundation of virulent antisemitism and racism. As Hitler sought to expand territories occupied by Germans, the slogan later became a key component of his "Lebensraum" program, a major factor in the Holocaust. "Blood and Soil" has been adopted as a rallying cry by White supremacists, particularly their openly neo-Nazi element, to emphasize its own nativist and eliminationist agenda.

What shocks in all of this is not the novelty of the message, for as we have noted there is little here that is new. What *is* shocking, however, is the effrontery of the marchers and the ease with which they have introduced the language of genocide into public discourse. We suspect that many in our community, and other communities as well, had hoped that the reality of the Holocaust had permanently inoculated democratic societies against such manifestations. But the image of Jews barricaded into a synagogue while racists marched was too stark to be ignored. This was but a foretaste of what was to come fourteen months later, as eleven Jews were murdered at prayer in a Pittsburgh synagogue.

So, what needs to be done? And who needs to do it?

The writers are advocates of free speech, but are not absolutists in this regard. We believe that current laws in Canada against hate propaganda (which make offences of advocacy of genocide, incitement of hatred, and wilful promotion of hatred) are sufficient to meet extreme forms of hatred, but that they are insufficiently used. We believe that police services require dedicated hate-crime units or ready access to procedural expertise. We also believe that provincial attorneys-general need to be mindful of the impact of hate crimes and be more willing to authorize the laying of charges.

We also believe that the government of Canada should reinstate Section 13 of the Canadian Human Rights Act, thus reversing the 2012 decision of the House of Commons. This section, which provided the Canadian Human Rights Commission with the authority to receive complaints regarding hate on the Internet, was an important bulwark against hate speech that did not rise to the level of a criminal offence. Although the Supreme Court of Canada found that Section 13 was constitutional, we believe that, should Section 13 be restored, it would be improved by removing the financial penalty associated with a finding of wrongdoing. This will make it clearer that resolution of complaints within a human-rights framework is intended to safeguard society from the harmful effects of hate speech rather than to punish individuals.

While education does not provide a perfect cure to racism in general or antisemitism in particular, it has an important role to play. Ministries of education should ensure that there is a robust anti-racism component embedded in both the elementary- and secondary-school curricula. Where external resources are available, such as local Holocaust Education Centres or educational programs such as *Facing History and Ourselves*, *Choose Your Voice*, and *The Tour for Humanity*, they should be deployed wherever possible.

Challenging antisemitism – and other forms of hatred – is not a task that can be delegated to government and then ignored. Antisemitism can manifest itself in a variety of ways. One of our colleagues once spoke of the "atmospherics" of antisemitism. By that he meant that antisemitism not only showed itself through actionable behaviours but also through comments and behaviours that do not meet the test for prosecution but should meet the test for public condemnation.

One such example occurred in late 2017 in Toronto, where white nationalist organizations were able to rent rooms in public libraries in order to hold events that were racist in nature. The organizers hoped to gain legitimacy through the use of respected public space, and the ease with which those bookings were made suggests that anti-hate and anti-discrimination policies need to be reviewed. In this case, grassroots activists were able to bring sufficient pressure to bear, and authorities cancelled the room bookings. Citizens rather than systems were responsible for this outcome.

Like all hatred, antisemitism is persistent and opportunistic. It cannot be ignored. It requires confrontation. Individually we must all be ready to "open a mouth" when antisemitism appears, whatever its manifestation. One way is to utilize media, both social and conventional, to show support for local Jewish communities that have been targeted by antisemitic outbursts. A simple letter to the editor of a local newspaper, or a statement on a Facebook/Twitter site, can go a very long way.

Consider those cases where inappropriate workplace behaviour masquerades as humour or calls upon the victim to be "less sensitive." Such behaviour needs to be challenged. We recall hearing of a case where, on public transit, a passenger's Islamophobic tirade against a woman was short-circuited when another rider sat down next to the woman and engaged her in polite conversation, making it physically clear that this woman was not alone. It is inadequate to be a bystander. Alliances are especially important. Jewish groups should enter into partnership with other communities to present a united front against antisemitism and all forms of hatred. An attack on one must be understood as an attack on us all.

Hate speech has a corrosive effect on the cords that bind us together in a civil society. When a group of citizens is singled out as the object of hateful or discriminatory practices, then the entire society becomes brutalized as a result. The emergence of right-wing extremism and its new purchase in the public square is more than a matter of brazen audacity. The ghosts of a not-dead past still beckon us to join them in their dark projects. We ignore their dangerous whispers at our peril.

REFERENCES

Bronner, Stephen Eric. 2000. *A Rumor About the Jews: Reflections on Antisemitism and the "Protocols of the Elders of Zion."* New York: St. Martin's Press.
The Southern Poverty Law Centre. 2017. "When White Nationalists Chant Their Weird Slogans, What Do They Mean?" 10 October. https://www.splcenter.org/hatewatch/2017/10/10/when-white-nationalists-chant-their-weird-slogans-what-do-they-mean.

6

ESCAPING NEUROTIC JUSTICE
Learning from a Trans* Male Survivor of Workplace Violence

Dan Irving

Introduction

Gender transition is a public affair that forces others to confront the inevitability of change. Trans* people are monstrous (Stryker 2006) – their bodies tell stories of metamorphosis, unintelligible states of in-betweenness, the chimera of sex and gender in ways that disrupt all gendered bodies. The experiences of trans* people exceed the personal and reveal significant intersections in power relations governing society. The ways that cis-gender people react and respond to visible sex and gender difference points to their own efforts to grapple with significant shifts in cultural, political, and socio-economic terrains.

In this chapter, I contextualize such trans-monstrous revelations amid the current socio-political climate in Canada, where neo-conservativism is palpable. I analyze an excerpt taken from an interview I conducted with Kevin (a pseudonym), a White trans* man who participated in my qualitative study addressing trans* un(der)employment. Kevin tells of being sexually assaulted within his unionized workplace. While I cannot make any definitive claims about this incident, since I have not interviewed Kevin's attackers, I read it in conjunction with broader socio-economic and political dynamics. I do not interpret Kevin's assault as an isolated act of transphobic violence. Rather, Kevin's story opens spaces to reflect upon the interconnectedness of masculinity, economic security, and whiteness in austere times. I suggest that the ways a select group of Kevin's co-workers projected their anxiety and rage onto his transitioning body rather than toward systemic power relations challenges organizational efforts to fight for the common good in the form of a more equitable and substantively democratic society.

War in the Workplace: Kevin's Story

I was at lunch break [...] sitting on a bench and a guy walked up and said "Can I talk to you for a minute?" and I knew he belonged to a group of guys that had an issue with me. And they used to call themselves the SS group, the Secret Society [...] Where he waved me to go [...] there were eight guys and they locked me in the room. One guy stood and guarded the door while they proceeded to tell me [...] I had no business lying to them. I tricked them, what kind of fucking human being am I? They were going to teach me what it was like or show me that I wasn't a man. They were going to teach me what it was like to be a woman because I should be a woman. And they started getting physically aggressive [...] I am like going under desks as they are pinning desks up against me against the wall. I had a guy grab me ... I really thought that was it. And, as the sparks start to unfold, a guy broke the goddamn door open [...] and I bolted out of the room.

Monstrous Performances of Masculinities in Crises

The attack on Kevin can be analyzed in relation to dominant social expectations of what it means to be a proper White, working-class, man in these austere times. In Canada, the era of postwar compromise between capital and the labour movement (i.e., both agreed to a livable family wage, benefits, and job security) and the state (i.e., through social-welfare policies to shield citizens during times of temporary hardship) gave way to neo-liberalism in the early 1980s. The tenuousness of the economic stability and upward mobility for unionized workers that was definitive of the postwar boom became evident through anti-unionist back-to-work legislation, outsourcing, and plant relocations and closures (Workman 2009; Fanelli 2013).

The postwar boom, in the Canadian context, cannot be understood apart from whiteness tied to nationalism, heteronormativity, and ruling ideals that define masculinity and who counts as a proper man. White working and middle-class men benefited most from the postwar compromise and – mediated by invisible discourses of whiteness and heteronormativity – *came to expect* a stable job with good pay and benefits. They came to naturalize the privilege afforded through a nation grounded in settler-colonialism, white supremacy, and heteropatriarchy that denigrated the feminine. This land, economic security, safe neighbourhoods, and promising futures were naturalized as their birthright. The roots of "aggrieved entitlement" (Kimmel 2013, 12), or the rage that many White men feel when they cannot secure all they believe they naturally deserve, stem from the ways that white and male privilege is embedded within these golden years of capitalism when the (North) American Dream seemed more within reach.

Three decades of neo-liberalism have produced a noxious affective atmosphere. Discourses espousing competition, instability, austerity, and crises usher in a reactive mindset befitting these dangerous times. The disparity between whiteness and "sturdy individualism" (Evans and Sewell 2013, 37) as governing ideals and the lived experiences of White, working-class men produce feelings such as fear, depression, and rage that charge the social environment with toxic energy. The material conditions for economic security, comfort, and satisfaction have become unsustainable for many men; nevertheless, hard work, autonomy, fortitude and resilience remain integral to – and a moral imperative of – performing normative white masculinity in the wake of capital's assaults.

Kevin's attackers behave like "neurotic citizens" (Isin 2004) demanding "neurotic justice" (Isin 2004, 233). In other words, they are so consumed by their anxious feelings that they attempt to manage by increasingly expecting "the impossible [from the capitalist class and neo-liberal state both ensconced in austerity measures] … the right to security, safety, body, health, wealth, and happiness as well as tranquility, serenity and calm" (Isin 2004, 232). Furthermore, White, working-class men are "external[izing] stress … and … feeling like an angry victim" (Holloway 2016) as they confront the material limits of their privilege, while retaining the entitlement such privilege affords. Plant closures, layoffs, the roll-back of benefits, and other attempts to drive wages downward threaten workers' economic security and well-being. Many White, working-class men are not mobilizing against governing systems of power framing these perilous times. Rather, some men attempt to assuage their real and perceived vulnerability by misdirecting their rage toward – and committing violent acts against – immigrants, racialized populations, women, and trans* people. Their victim mentality and their misogynist, racist, xenophobic, queer, and transphobic rallying cries for protection amid these dangerous times is grounded in nostalgic fantasies for a time when these White, working-class men felt more in control. Such material positionality, entitlement, and feelings such as rage and fear both undergird expressions of toxic masculinity and galvanize and propel neo-conservative movements forward (Kelly 2017, 73).

Trans-Monstrous Bodies as Harbingers of Crisis

I place Kevin's narrative of his attack at the workplace within the broader socio-economic context detailed above. These working-class tradesmen work within a unionized environment, and their jobs are secure – for now. Nonetheless, they live amid a climate of crises, where there are no guarantees.

During the initial phases of his taking testosterone, Kevin's *visible gender difference* further shakes what some White, working-class men may already understand as trembling ground. His body personifies transition, flux, states of in-betweenness, the unknown, as well as the porousness of the borders of white masculinity. Members of the Secret Society are enraged and demand answers. They use sexual assault – a gendered weapon of war (Kirby 2013) – to battle against the perceived enemy among them.

Two phrases in particular reveal the ways that these men "manage [their] anxieties and insecurities" (Isin 2004, 232) by holding Kevin personally responsible for the fear and rage they feel, and demand forcibly that this monstrous body account for itself. First, they inform Kevin that: "[he] had no business lying to them." Michael Kimmel argues that White men have actually been "duped" by governing structures and discourses of meritocracy (2013, 12). The scene of Kevin's attack demonstrates the perversion of reality to match the feelings of insecurity and frustration and the sense of being deceived that many White working men experience. These unionized warehouse workers position themselves as victim to Kevin, who is believed to be an "evil deceiver" (Bettcher 2007, 47–8).

Despite the increasing gulf between dominant and ideal forms of masculinity and the felt experiences of White, working-class men that demonstrate the constructed nature of such governing categories, Kevin via his visible gender in-betweenness becomes the lie. Once behind closed doors, these eight Secret Society members, whom Kevin described elsewhere as "burly men," attempt to assuage their fears and act out their rage through "[a] performative utterance [that] can only succeed if it repeats a coded or

iterable utterance: it works precisely by citing norms ... that already exist"
(Ahmed 2014, 93). Not only do they refuse to recognize him and attempt to
resecuritize masculinity by telling him he "wasn't a man," they reduce his
embodied trans-male subjectivity to a lie. These men refused to be "tricked"
by Kevin and fortify the perimeters around proper masculinity by violently
denying his entry into the realm of manhood.

Second, his assailants demand Kevin account for his humanity when they
cry out: "What kind of fuckin' human being *are you?*" Demonstrative of
neo-liberal discourse of individual accountability, marginalized subjects are
called upon increasingly to demonstrate their humanity, particularly in the
midst of crises and austerity. Kevin's attackers forcibly demanded that this
monstrous body account for itself.

The Secret Society's performative refusal to accept Kevin as a man, and
their questioning of his humanity as his transition, positioning him as vis-
ibly between genders, can also be comprehended as an act of annihilation.
These working-class men – whose race, gender, and class privilege remain
intact in the midst of their feeling under siege – work to securitize the
boundaries of whiteness and masculinity by rendering Kevin's existence
near impossible and declaring that he "should be a woman." They revert to
restoring their own position of masculine privilege by degrading someone
they perceived as feminine. As indicative of the rising neo-conservative
backlash in Canada, these men shut down any space afforded by socio-
economic crises to question ruling power relations, engage in alternative
meaning making, and seize the opportunity to struggle in solidarity with
trans*, racialized, queer, and women-identified workers for more socially
just and equitable ways of living.

Conclusion

Kevin's violent ordeal at work must not be dismissed as an isolated act
by a fringe group. I have drawn from Stryker's work on the potentiality
of trans-monstrosity to buttress our thinking through the growing tide of
neo-conservatism, toxic masculinity, and white supremacy in Canada. I
suggest that Kevin's visible gender in-betweenness when he began to take
testosterone rendered him a ghastly reminder of the mutable nature of

both masculinity and economic security in these austere times. The fear, anxiety, and rage of these White men is real, albeit misguided, toward a body that personifies change to the unrestricted access to the privileges that white hegemonic masculinity afforded. Within a neo-liberal Canadian society, where recognition and gains are perceived as a "zero-sum game" (Kimmel 2013, 16), Kevin's very existence in the workplace agitates their feelings of losing ground.

Over the past few decades, organized labour and other leftist movements have been weakened significantly and have failed to produce viable alternatives to these precarious times (Camfield 2011; Sears 2014). This means cries of deception and trickery have been directed toward monstrous Others, while the ravages of capitalism, white supremacy, and hetero-patriarchy on society have not been called to account. Trans* individuals, queers, immigrants, and people of colour have been constructed as enemies, denied their humanity, and targeted for elimination (Haritaworn, Kuntsman, and Pocosso 2014).

Emotional justice must be a central pillar of social justice to resist the groundswell of neo-conservatism. The right panders to the aggrieved entitlement of White, cisgender working and middle-class men who are funnelling their depression, anxiety, fears, and failures into rage targeted toward feminized and racialized Others. The left needs to create spaces where White men can come to grips with their emotions and develop the psycho-social tools needed to problematize such feeling states as the affective dimensions of governing relations that oppress us all. While concrete solutions depend on specific locations and particular workplace cultures, some general suggestions include peer-led educational interventions. Inspired by the White Ribbon Campaign to address violence against women (https://www.whiteribbon.ca/), training peer facilitators to run anti-oppression workshops for White, cisgender men is one way to address aggrieved entitlement. These workshops – run outside of the workplace and offering attendees full pay for their time – can enable men to be heard as they voice negative feelings and violent emotion. They can also challenge participants to reframe their perceptions concerning the source of the alleged threats to their well-being. Such workshops, together with union-sponsored film festivals and comedy and artistic events rooted in social justice to which members are admitted free may provide the educational and social grounds toward allyship. Perhaps then their guttural screams can shift from "What kind of fucking human are you?" to demanding that systems of power account for a question that plagues us all: "What kind of fucking life is this?"

NOTE

The asterisk following trans is used by transgender studies scholars and activists to acknowledge the plurality of existing trans identities, as well as to gesture to the acceptance of future gender non-normative identities.

REFERENCES

Ahmed, Sara. 2004. *The Cultural Politics of Emotion*. New York: Routledge.

Bettcher, Talia. 2007. "Evil Deceivers and Make-Believers: On Transphobic Violence and the Politics of Illusion." *Hypatia* 22 (3): 43–65.

Camfield, David. 2011. *Canadian Labour in Crisis: Reinventing the Workers' Movement*. Halifax: Fernwood Press.

Evans, Peter B., and William H. Sewell, Jr. 2013. "Neoliberalism: Policy Regime, International Regime, and Social Effects." In *Social Resilience in the New Era*, edited by Peter A. Hall and Michele Lamont, 35–68. Cambridge: Cambridge University Press.

Fanelli, Carlo. 2013. "Fragile Future: The Attack Against Public Services and Public Sector Unions in an Era of Austerity." Unpublished dissertation for Carleton University.

Haritaworn, Jin, Ali Kuntsman, and Silvia Posocco, eds. 2014. *Queer Necropolitics*. New York: Routlege.

Holloway, Kali. 2016. "Toxic Masculinity Is Killing Men: The Roots of Male Trauma." https://www.alternet.org/gender/masculinity-killing-men-roots-men-and-trauma.

Isin, Egin. 2004. The Neurotic Citizen. *Citizenship Studies* 8 (3): 217–35.

Kelly, Ann. 2017. "The Alt-Right Reactionary Rehabilitation for White Masculinity." *Soundings* 66: 68–78.

Kimmel, Michael. 2013. *Angry White Men: American Masculinity at the End of an Era*. New York: Nation Books.

Kirby, Paul. 2013. "How Is Rape a Weapon of War? Feminist International Relations, Modes of Critical Explanation, and the Study of Wartime Sexual Violence." *European Journal of International Relations* 19 (4): 797–821.

Sears, Alan. 2014. *The Next New Left: A History of the Future*. Halifax: Fernwood.

Stryker, Susan. 2006. My Words to Victor Frankenstein above the Village of Chamonix. In *Transgender Studies Reader*, edited by Stephen Whittle and Susan Stryker, 244–56. New York: Routledge: 244-256.

Workman, Thom. 2009. *If You're in My Way, I'm Walking: The Assault on Working People since 1970*. Halifax: Fernwood.

7

RIGHT, RISE, REDUX

Tim McCaskell

People talk about "the rise of the right" as if it were something new. But to gay dinosaurs like me, it all seems eerily familiar.

I came out in Toronto in the mid-1970s. Thanks to the Keynesian welfare state, the city was far more socially equal than today, with more than two-thirds of the population living in middle-income areas. Nevertheless, lesbians and gay men faced open and legally sanctioned discrimination, exclusion, and violence. We were only a few years past "decriminalization," and largely still considered a criminal class. Social equality co-existed with legal inequality. The city's young gay movement set itself the task of challenging that, and its first major victory was the 1973 inclusion of sexual orientation in Toronto's anti-discrimination policy. Several US groups won similar battles.

Rise of the Right, Take One

But by the late 1970s, the wind began to shift. In June 1977, Anita Bryant won a referendum repealing the gay-rights ordinance in Dade County, Florida. Copycat referenda were organized in other US municipalities. Things soon spilled across the border. Early in 1978, Bryant was invited by Renaissance International, a far-right Christian organization, to visit Toronto and extend her crusade into Canada. Only a month before, the police had raided *The Body Politic*, Canada's leading gay-liberation journal, laying obscenity charges. Both gay material and artistic work dealing with sexuality faced increasing censorship.

In April 1980, CBS broadcast a new documentary, "Gay Power, Gay Politics," to millions of people across the continent. It portrayed gay communities as a political threat, and a danger to children and society. The program was widely cited in the 1980 Toronto municipal elections, when, after a campaign marked by homophobic rhetoric and active participation by the Toronto police against "pro-gay" candidates, both George Hislop, the city's first openly gay aldermanic candidate, and progressive mayor, John Sewell, went down to defeat. The same month, Ronald Reagan won the US presidential election with the support of the new religious right, headed by The Moral Majority. In February 1981, the Toronto police smashed into the city's gay baths, arresting nearly three hundred gay men – at the time, the second-largest mass arrest in Canadian history.

The hard shift to the right was far from spontaneous. The economy was in crisis. Elite think tanks decided that it was necessary to displace those who had managed the Keynesian system of wealth redistribution, and to engineer a turn to neo-liberal "free market" economics to drive down the cost of labour. Their strategy was to mobilize and amplify the voices of ultra-conservative religious and racist networks around the dual mantra of smaller government and traditional values. Focusing on issues that stirred up xenophobia, misogyny, and homophobia masked tax cuts for the rich and benefits cuts for the rest. Although this movement began in the United States, its cultural echoes emboldened right-wing forces across Canada.

In that struggle about how capitalism would be managed, lesbians and gay men became the symbol of everything the resurgent right felt was wrong. Their rhetoric incited and enabled the daily violence of cops, queer bashers, and neo-fascist groups. When AIDS came along, governments were silent.

Responses

There were different responses to this crisis. Protests against Bryant's Toronto visit ultimately led to the formation of Gay Liberation Against the Right Everywhere (GLARE) and Lesbians Against the Right (LAR). Although few really understood the neo-liberal sea change that was inciting the new right-wing politics, GLARE and LAR's socialist-inflected analysis identified the common danger to lesbians and gays, women, racialized minorities, and workers. They proposed horizontal alliances with such constituencies against the right as a first step in a struggle for deeper social change. But neither GLARE nor LAR managed to mobilize large numbers in their generalized struggle against the right, and neither lasted more than a few years. Their major legacy was the establishment of the annual Lesbian and Gay

Pride Day celebrations, an event which soon drifted away from explicit politics to take on a more carnivalesque character.

After the bath raids, the Right to Privacy Committee (RTPC) took a different tack. It focused on a more concrete enemy – the police – organizing massive street actions, financing and coordinating the defence of those charged, making common cause with Black and immigrant groups also facing police violence, demanding community control of the cops, and establishing a volunteer street patrol to protect people from homophobic attacks. The strategy helped the RTPC to establish itself as an important voice in the broader struggle for police reform, cement an alliance with the gay petite bourgeoisie of bar and bath owners, and mobilize the sexual networks of gay men anchored in such establishments.

The RTPC was successful in its more-limited aims. The vast majority of those charged were acquitted, and although there was no change in the Criminal Code, police raids on baths were halted. Lesbian and gay communities gained increased recognition and acceptance through the visibility of our resistance. In the fight against increasing censorship, LGBT groups united with artists, writers, and filmmakers, deploying freedom-of-expression arguments. We were finally successful in winning acquittal in the obscenity charges against *The Body Politic*, and ultimately helped dismantle the Ontario Censor Board. So, while the more-limited goals of building alliances to defend the community against violence and censorship did win victories, the strategy of building a broad horizontal front against the right was less than successful. It is always easier to mobilize around concrete issues than amorphous political philosophies.

"Liberal" Neo-liberalism

Then the climate changed again. With the collapse of "socialism" in 1990, neo-liberalism was ascendant. With the work of dismantling the welfare state largely accomplished, and the rapid redistribution of wealth to the very rich proceeding apace (the point of the exercise all along), elites no longer needed the social conservative baggage. Prejudice became embarrassing. A more liberal logic of "equality" became hegemonic. In Canada, the Charter of Rights was used as a lever to pry open a window for LGBT communities. Rights advocates turned to the courts and focused their efforts on legal challenges to discrimination. This period saw rapid advances in legal equality – spousal benefits, discrimination protections, gay marriage, recognition for trans people. Rights to free speech were strengthened.

But these demands for *legal equality* were embraced at the same time as neo-liberal economic policies worsened *substantive social inequality*. Some groups, notably Toronto's growing Black communities, found themselves pushed to the bottom of the barrel as racism combined with the dismantling of redistributive policies. Well-paying jobs were replaced by precarious ones. Unions were on the defensive and in decline. Wages (except those of corporate executives) stagnated. The "middle class" shrank. For LGBT people, class differences within the community deepened, leading to more internal political conflict.

Instability

The neo-liberal system has been far from stable. It has lurched from crisis to crisis. It has never really recovered from the 2008 crash. Social disparity unimaginable in the 1970s is now taken for granted. As more people find themselves out in the cold, frustration and resentment build. A stressed and angry population becomes more vulnerable to the bluster of demagogues – racist, sexist, homophobic, Islamophobic. Economic crisis and increasing disparity lead to political crisis.

Trump promises to make America great again, but before we get too smug, Canadians should remember that, well before Trump, we had Harper, and Toronto had Rob Ford. Like Trump, these right-wing politicians bullied and silenced their critics, and enabled more-radical groups to intimidate and marginalize minorities. A system that is unable to meet people's needs shifts to more authoritarian means of control.

The strength of the right reflects a more general deterioration of democracy. That deterioration has many proximate causes, but its root is that political democracy no longer reflects the material reality created by neo-liberalism. Democracy rests on the fiction of equality – that in the public sphere, all persons are equal – one person, one vote. It tends to work best when that fiction is more in correspondence with reality – when, in terms of wealth and influence, most people are at a similar level. But the more real power, wealth, and influence are unequally distributed, concentrated in

fewer and fewer hands, the more democracy becomes an exercise in legitimation for an unjust system, as different elite factions use their considerable
institutional powers of persuasion and competing forms of demagoguery to
mobilize a vulnerable public in their interests.

Democracy is not just under attack from right-wing extremists. It is being
hourly eroded by neo-liberal elites whose sunny-ways messages distract
from the realities of intensifying disparity resulting from their economic
policies. Who is responsible for hate? The smiling liberals who till the fields,
or the snarling fascists who reap the crop?

Resistance

There was major resistance to neo-liberal globalization in Seattle in 1999.
In April 2001, when the Summit of the Americas sought a new continent-
wide free-trade deal in Quebec City, there were similar demonstrations and
a brutal police response. That year at Toronto Pride, veterans of the Quebec
battles organized a Glamorous Outcasts contingent that marched behind a
banner, "Fight Oppression – Fight Capitalism – Make Love," and targeted
increased corporate influence on the festival. There are similarities here to
GLARE and LAR's organizing in the 1980s. But like GLARE and LAR, Glamorous Outcasts was short-lived.

In 2010, under pressure from the Israel lobby and several levels of government, Pride Toronto attempted to ban the Palestinian solidarity group
Queers Against Israeli Apartheid (QUAIA). The move to silence voices condemning Israel's colonial apartheid policies was part of a wider effort led
by the Harper government to shield its main Middle Eastern ally from criticism. Only after a public campaign around the issue of freedom of expression led by an ad-hoc group, The Pride Coalition for Free Speech, was Pride
forced to drop its ban. It was a successful strategy, and QUAIA continued to
march in Pride until the group dissolved in early 2015. A parallel could be
drawn here with the more-limited goals and liberal framing of the RTPC.

In 2016, Black Lives Matter Toronto blocked the Pride parade with a list
of demands to challenge the organization's racism, including a call for the
end of participation by uniformed police officers in the parade. That action
sparked a backlash and a major crisis in Pride Toronto, but in the end, after
several large public meetings, Pride members overwhelmingly voted to ac-

cept all of BLM's demands. Again, like the RTPC, BLMTO's concrete demands were winnable.

But in the Long Run, What's a Queer to Do?

While the rise of the right in the 1980s was sparked by the crisis in the Keynesian system and was orchestrated to facilitate the shift from the welfare state to neo-liberalism, its rise today is about more than a change in economic paradigms. It is the product of deeper and linked crises exacerbated by the neo-liberal system – the globalization of production, growing class and regional inequality, ecological crisis, and the decline in American hegemony. Unlike the more finite crisis of the 1980s, these seem unlikely to be resolved any time soon. Especially in the United States, elites are divided, and demagoguery and scapegoating are out of control. Finally, the capacity of the state to surveil, spy, and violate fundamental rights is far greater now than thirty years ago.

Queers face this generalized crisis with a community far more divided by class and race disparities. While some, marginalized because of race or poverty, push back to reclaim community spaces, the professional/managerial class that now generally speaks on our behalf through established NGOs, cleaves to liberal power. "Sure, Trudeau's economic policies are no less neo-liberal than Harper's, but there is no alternative, and at least he marches in Pride." Other voices even embrace ultra-right politics and Islamophobia on our behalf, to protect "us" from the racialized other.

Successful past models of resistance – the deployment of liberal freedom-of-expression arguments to shield radical protest or the demand for reform on specific issues, such as policing – are basically conservative, since they are oriented toward preserving or perfecting the liberal order in the face of the authoritarian, right-wing challenge that neo-liberalism has spawned. In the United States, where anti-democratic and racist forces now control both the legislative and executive arms of the state and threaten to turn on LGBT communities, alliances with less-racist and homophobic sectors of the elite are proposed. In Canada, however, we are already governed by such a liberal elite, who, despite buoyant rhetoric, continues to deepen the neo-liberal transformation. Given the breadth of the global economic, social, political, and environmental crisis they are producing, it is hard to see how an alliance with liberal elites does anything more than postpone the day of reckoning. Worse, it abandons bold visions of a different future to the atavistic fantasies of the right.

I think we need to recognize that there is no returning to the golden age of Keynesianism. A more-long-term strategy of horizontal alliances is appropriate. Many queers are already active in alter-globalization – socialist or anarchist, anti-racist, anti-poverty, anti-austerity, union, or ecological movements – as progressive *individuals*. If organized, we could constitute a bridge toward a popular anti–neo-liberal movement that could challenge the fundamental processes that undermine democracy.

8

VICTIMS AND VILLAINS
Disabled People as Rhetorical Pawns in Political Discourse

Kim Sauder

People don't know how to reckon with history. Doing so would require them to fully understand the actions of their ancestors and, as a result, they run the risk of, if not repeating history, at least falling prey to the same false self-conceptions that allowed for the rise of harmful social movements. This is relevant to the current political climate, which seems like a clash of political extremes but is at least in part an unwillingness to grapple with the reality that we are as capable of cultural violence as any other generation in history.

The rise of the far right is of particular concern to disabled people, because of the way we have been culturally framed as "less than," but are also somehow a group that society is convinced they care about greatly. Consider the American election, during which Donald Trump mocked the journalist Serge Kovaleski. This moment entered the cultural consciousness as the moment that Trump should have lost all hope of winning. The act of mocking Kovaleski was somehow seen as being in a completely different class of inappropriate behaviour than proposing a ban on Muslims entering the country and referring to Mexicans as criminals and rapists. This certainty that the mockery of Kovaleski was somehow fundamentally worse than the racism and religious intolerance on which Trump had largely built his campaign was widely held, despite the fact that Kovaleski was frequently dehumanized in discourse around the incident. He was rarely named, people tending to refer to him only as the disabled reporter (CNN 2015).

Stripping Kovaleski of his name is relevant in understanding how disabled people are framed as victims. Culturally, people seem to find it easier to empathize with a vague image of disablement, which can be framed around helplessness. Understanding who Kovaleski is and the context of why Trump mocked him specifically on the grounds of his disability undermines narratives of helplessness.

Trump's mockery of Kovaleski was actually a very effective tactic in deflecting attention away from the fact that Kovaleski had challenged Trump's interpretation of an article he had written after September 11. Trump had used a misreading of the article to justify Islamophobia. Kovaleski had attempted to set the record straight, which is what inspired Trump to publicly mock him. As a result, the discourse around the event became about the mockery and not about why it happened, effectively directing attention away from the Islamophobia that had initially inspired it. Ignoring that context presents Kovaleski as a passive, nameless victim of Trump's bigotry, as opposed to someone who was actively attempting to challenge him. This fact was lost in the moral panic as people rushed to condemn the unspeakable awfulness of mocking a disabled person.

Disabled people are, however, more difficult to champion when we are not vague, nameless individual victims. As a group we are a problem. It is far easier to denounce a single act of injustice against a victim whose victimhood was largely culturally created to serve a political purpose. As a marginalized group that experiences systemic prejudice and discrimination, we're not so palatable. While people might condemn systemic acts of discrimination, they are far less likely to undertake meaningful action to end them.

Society has for far too long held conflicting views of disabled people. We can be pitiful victims, but that seems to apply only when we do not challenge cultural understandings of what disability is and what disability justice looks like. Justice for disabled people is easy when it involves the condemnation of fleeting mockery of a nameless, faceless concept of disability. As a group, our needs are more nuanced.

Disabled people disproportionately live in poverty and are disproportionately represented among the unemployed and underemployed (CCD n.d.). This means that, as a group, we are more likely to seek help from various forms of social assistance. In larger discussions around assistance for disabled people that consider issues of increased likelihood of poverty and increased medical needs, suddenly we're far more likely to be framed in negative ways. Qualifying for disability-specific social assistance requires meeting a particular definition of disability that may be out of step with the reality and not adequately meet the needs of the disabled population. In times of national financial strain (which seems to be all the time), governments may narrow the qualifying definition in order to limit the number of people who have access to disability-specific programs as a cost-saving measure. This is often justified by the suggestion that the system is full of cheats.

This allows for society to hold conflicting opinions. They believe that disabled people have a right to additional assistance to offset the poverty they experience as a result of their disabilities, while simultaneously demonizing disabled people for attempting to take advantage of those services by applying narrow definitions of disability which do not reflect the reality of the need. This tends to lead to disabled people being framed not as a disadvantaged group but as a genuine social problem of their own making. Some social-assistance programs are run on the assumption that people will try to cheat, and are therefore designed to stop people qualifying in the first place (Malacrida 2010).

Disabled people are often victims of austerity measures. We're seen as expensive, which can lead to the idea that we're expendable. While government policies are unlikely to overtly suggest this, it is a potential consequence. Consider the austerity measures of the United Kingdom, a country that routinely cut disability benefits and narrowed qualifications. More disabled children are placed in segregated schools, and rates of poverty for disabled citizens are rising. The impact of these measures is so egregious that the United Nations stated that they amounted to systemic violations of the rights of disabled people, and argued that the British government had failed to consider the impact of austerity measures on the well-being of disabled people (Butler 2017). This conclusion is also supported by a recent study that links the same austerity measures to as many as 120,000 deaths (Watkins et al. 2017). The British government has rejected the UN's assessment of their assistance programs. These human-rights violations are shielded from being perceived as such, because, despite austerity measures, the official written intention of those social-benefits programs is to provide assistance for disabled people. The consequences are unintended and are publicly visible only after scrutiny from outside parties.

Shedding light on injustices against disabled people has been historically difficult. In fact, some of the most worst government actions against disabled people came to the public's attention only because of their negative impact on non-disabled people. Consider the Canadian and American eugenics programs, which saw disabled people (or those perceived to be disabled) forcibly institutionalized and sterilized. These programs were based on the false belief that poverty and other social ills were consequences of genetic disability that could be fixed by controlling who had children (MacLaren 1990). As a consequence of eugenics programs in Canada and the United States, thousands of people – mostly women (particularly women of colour) – were forcibly sterilized. This is now perceived to be a grave injustice. It also did not solve North America's issues with poverty or remove disabled people from the population.

While legislated eugenics is accepted as a dark point in history, it exists in the modern consciousness as such not because of a recognition that forcibly sterilizing disabled people is wrong, but because it was sometimes done to people who turned out not to be disabled. The horrors of Canadian eugenics are known and condemned because of Leilani Muir (2014). In 1995, she successfully sued the Alberta government over her 1959 sterilization. She won not on the grounds that sterilization was wrong in and of itself, but rather because it was later determined that she was not in fact disabled, and was therefore wrongfully sterilized. There is a similar case in the United States surrounding Carrie Buck, who was sterilized after losing a Supreme Court case in 1927, during which she was labelled an imbecile. This diagnosis is now generally considered to have been in error (Lombardo 2010).

It is important to remember that eugenics was considered to be a social good – supported by people like Tommy Douglas and members of the Famous Five like Nellie McClung and Helen MacMurchy, who are celebrated for their progressive ideas – not just because of the belief that it would rid society of the poor and indigent but because, through its application, disabled people would be cared for through institutionalization and segregation from the rest of society (Douglas 1933).

Disabled people are a convenient scapegoat. While they can be used as a palatable victim to rally behind in opposition to Donald Trump's bigotry, paradoxically, they can also be used to delegitimize him. As we look at the presidency of Donald Trump and the political movement that gave him that position of power, detractors often focus specifically on the president and ignore the context that put him in office. A lot of the language in the opposition to Donald Trump is a language of disability. His incompetence and bad behaviour are routinely described as arising from mental illness or intellectual disability. People took great pleasure in hearing that Rex Tillerson, the former Secretary of State, might have referred to the president as a "fucking moron." Moron is a term that is connected to eugenics and used as a classification for people perceived to have intellectual disability. There is also a movement among some mental-health professionals, and widely adopted by the public, to #DiagnoseTrump with some kind of mental illness, often Narcissistic Personality Disorder (NPD). So popular is this idea that many people have largely rejected the previously held ethical guidelines that say mental-health professionals should not diagnose people, particularly public figures whom they have not treated. The goal behind labelling Donald Trump as mentally ill is to see him deemed incompetent and removed from office. So prevalent is this idea that the doctor responsible for writing the criteria for NPD came out to denounce such armchair diagnosis (Frances 2017).

This assumption that mental illness or disability is invariably paired with incompetence is not only false but is also harmful to the disability community at large. It is also ironically the same argument that Trump implied in his much-maligned mockery of Kovaleski.

Mental illness and disability are red herrings. They provide a way to ignore the cultural realities that led to millions of people electing Donald Trump as president. These motivations are entirely separate from whether Trump is himself disabled. He did not come to power on his own. His actions often solicit support. Trump and his actions do not exist in a vacuum. He is a symptom of widespread social unrest that extends beyond the borders of the United States of America.

People don't want to believe that social upheaval, particularly turmoil that hinges on widespread bigotry, can be consequences of the culture in which they live, so they apply the same scapegoat criticism to Trump as he did to Serge Kovaleski. They rely on a vague conception of what they presume mental illness to be, one that is as divorced from reality as the idea that Serge Kovaleski is a helpless, disabled man whose mocking by Donald Trump was worse than planning to ban Muslims from the United States and building a wall on the US- Mexico border. Both of these were proposed by Trump before he ever mocked Kovaleski.

Disabled people have been and still are a convenient scapegoat for societies that do not want to deal with the complexities of the social ills they are experiencing, and this misdirection only increases inequality. This operates regardless of the political leanings of the people doing the scapegoating. The consequences also invariably end up hurting more than just disabled people. It is imperative to avoid becoming easily distracted by casual ableism when it is used to sidetrack people from other bigotries which come with the intention for real policy follow-through. We have seen this happen with the Muslim ban and the southern border wall. People must also come to recognize that casual ableism, regardless of the target, can be used to erode the rights of disabled people. This stands whether or not it is being used to conveniently deflect attention away from the suffering of others. Only then will we be able to move on to concrete solutions to build a resistance that is accessible to and inclusive of all people.

REFERENCES

Alvi, Kiran. 2017. "US: Most Mass Shootings Not Committed by Mentally Ill." *USA News / Al Jazeera*. Retrieved 23 November 2017. http://www.aljazeera.com/news/2017/11/mass-shootings-committed-mentally-ill-171111162521074.html.

Blake, John. 2017. "Becoming White Supremacists by Default." CNN. Retrieved 9 November 2017. http://www.cnn.com/2017/08/18/us/ordinary-white-supremacists/index.html

Butler, Patrick. 2017. "UN Panel Criticises UK Failure to Uphold Disabled People's Rights." *Guardian*. Retrieved 19 November 2017. https://www.theguardian.com/society/2017/aug/31/un-panel-criticises-uk-failure-to-uphold-disabled-peoples-rights.

CCD. n.d. "As a Matter of Fact: Poverty and Disability in Canada." *Council of Canadians with Disabilities*. Retrieved 23 November 2017. http://www.ccdonline.ca/en/socialpolicy/poverty-citizenship/demographic-profile/poverty-disability-canada).

CNN. 2015. "Donald Trump Mocks Reporter with Disability – Video." https://www.theguardian.com/us-news/video/2015/nov/26/donald-trump-appears-to-mock-disabled-reporter-video.

Douglas, Thomas C. 1933. "The Problems of the Subnormal Family." Unpublished Master's thesis.

Frances, Allen. 2017. "I'm an Expert on Diagnosing Mental Illness. Trump Doesn't Meet the Criteria." *Stat News*. Retrieved 23 November 2017. https://www.statnews.com/2017/09/06/donald-trump-mental-illness-diagnosis/.

Lombardo, Paul A. 2010. *Three Generations, No Imbeciles: Eugenics, the Supreme Court, and Buck v. Bell.* Baltimore: The Johns Hopkins University Press.

MacLaren, Angus. 1990. *Our Own Master Race: Eugenics in Canada, 1885–1945.* Toronto: McClelland & Stewart.

Malacrida, Claudia. 2010. "Income Support Policy in Canada and the UK: Different, but Much the Same." *Disability & Society* 25 (6):673–86.

Muir, Leilani. 2014. *A Whisper Past: Childless after Eugenic Sterilization in Alberta: A Memoir.* Victoria, BC: Friesen Press.

Watkins, Johnathan, Wahyu Wulaningsih, Charlie Da Zhou, Dominic C. Marshall, Guia D.C. Sylianteng, Phyllis G. Dela Rose, Viveka A. Miguel, Rosalind Raine, Lawrence P. King, and Mahiben Maruthappu. 2017. "Effects of Health and Social Care Spending Constraints on Mortality in England: A Time Trend Analysis." *BMJ Open* 7 (11). Retrieved http://bmjopen.bmj.com/content/7/11/e017722.

"OUR HOME AND NATIVIST LAND"?

Vanessa Watts

The increase in far-right attitudes and social movements within Canada is not independent from the social gains of racialized communities, Indigenous peoples, and LGBTQ people. As socio-political space and power are cleaved from whiteness by and for these varied communities, the intensification of the far-right correspondingly proceeds. One of the tenets of the far-right movement that is particularly salient (and troubling) for Indigenous peoples is the argument that the far-right is "indigenous," in the sense that their own particular national identity is natural. As to the far right's ideological values, Saull et al. (2014, 5) notes a "concern with the preservation of what it regards as the essential and Indigenous social, ethnic, moral and cultural bases of society in the face of change." This sort of Indigenization by nativist groups is increasing and taking on unique formations. One of the leaders of La Meute, a far-right group in Quebec, claimed that, while he holds no Indigenous ancestry, he is "aboriginal" as a second-generation citizen of Quebec (Cook 2018). This self-framing accentuates an artificial self-righteousness based on a claim that eclipses Indigeneity with a particular sort of Eurocentric settler nostalgia. It exemplifies a redux of *terra nullius* – a denial of nationhoods prior to the arrival of Europeans. Further it signifies an entrenchment of colonialism: the shaping of Canada as a so-called righteous and moral pursuit. This is all the more perplexing because this sort of nostalgia can only be imagined through the dispossession of Indigenous peoples.

For actual Indigenous communities and nations in Canada, the ongoing denial of our socio-political systems by the state (and propped up by individual Canadians) continues to serve statist social, economic, and political interests. Far right or not, the current state of the nation must be recognized as existing and functioning upon this disavowal of authentic Indigenous people. The claims of the far right thrive on historic erasure.

In this sense, their rise is made possible by a century and a half of colonization. Now, in an era of reconciliation, promises to Indigenous peoples and communities by governments (whether artificial or not) may be perceived as a threat to far-right goals of the restoration of their "indigeneity." This premise rests on that question of artificiality. What is reconciliation discourse in Canada, anyway?

In February 2017, I attended the public-policy forum Expanding the Circle: What Reconciliation and Inclusive Economic Growth Can Mean for First Nations and Canada. It was hosted by the National Aboriginal Economic Development Board (NAEDB), the National Aboriginal Capital Corporations Association (NACCA), and Indigenous and Northern Affairs Canada (INAC). The theme of the conference was economic reconciliation and how to get there. I had never heard this term before. Reconciliation, yes, but not "economic reconciliation." Since the introduction of the Indian Act of 1876, First Nations have faced legislated economic precarity. Forced bans on the sale of goods off-reserve, forced enfranchisement of status Indians who attended post-secondary institutions, forced relocations of entire communities, and the policing of Indigenous peoples who attempted to leave and re-enter reserves via the Pass System are but a few examples of social and economic segregation. These long-standing efforts toward suppression of Indigenous life must be considered in the practice of reconciliation. Given this context, I wondered then and now if economic reconciliation is about restitution, or whether it is about reconciling ourselves to a legacy of state land theft?

At the conference, I heard that a pathway toward economic reconciliation could be found in reframing the traditional origin stories of Indigenous peoples in order to justify an indigenist rationale for resource extraction. This was, specifically, that the principle of "sharing," common to many Indigenous origin/creation stories, could justify our participation in the resource extraction of our lands. Sharing with mining companies is (suddenly, now) made consistent with Indigenous traditions. The framing of our creation stories as pretext for the extraction of minerals from traditional lands and resources and as a logical contemporary extension of an Indigenous value system was stunning yet unsurprising. Is this how reconciliation will be achieved? Under the expectation that we reconcile ourselves to state interests by compromising our own traditions? These are not the creation stories, nor the values, that I know as an Anishinaabe and Kanienkehaka person. The message was clear: to no longer be barred from a common interest, we are advised to extend ourselves into it.

Perhaps we should interrogate the common good. Indigenous interests and rights have continuously been violated for the "common good" of Canada through some of the most draconian government laws and policies created by any state anywhere. This was crystallized in 1973 when Quebec courts ruled that, even if the Cree and Innu disappeared because of the flooding of their territory for hydroelectric development, that outcome would be justified because the majority of Québécois would benefit from selling electricity at below market price to Americans. Indeed, even on lands the Supreme Courts recognize still belongs to Indigenous people, governments can permit extractive and violent development that will harm us, all in the name of the public good. This was the Supreme Court of Canada's "infringement" test in the 2013 Tsilqot'in decision, made overwhelmingly clear for the judiciary, but also for the executive branch of government. One year earlier, Prime Minister Stephen Harper presented Bill C-45, The Jobs and Growth Act, that sought to erode treaty rights. That legislation would inspire the counter-movement Idle No More. United Nations Special Rapporteur on the Rights of Indigenous Peoples, James Anaya, reported that Canada "faces a crisis when it comes to the situation of indigenous peoples of the country," citing the well-being gap between Indigenous peoples and Canadians (Anaya 2013). This state of affairs continues with the government of Prime Minister Justin Trudeau, who champions pipelines across lands in British Columbia that Indigenous peoples have not agreed to share. So, a presumption of a "common good" is not commonly held.

For the Haudenosaunee, the first time the common good was recognized as a prospect with Europeans was during the era of the Kaswentha treaty (or the Two Row Wampum), originally negotiated in 1613 with the Dutch. This agreement resolved that Haudenosaunee and the Dutch (later the British Crown) would share the land and resources in common, provided that the actions of one did not impede the other. One hundred and fifty years later, this agreement, and most that followed in Canada between Indigenous peoples and the state, have been violated or ignored in one way or another. These violations of treaties did allow for a common good to be established within

Canada – but one that excludes Indigenous title, laws, and rights. Considered in this light, the common good is based on theft and dishonesty.

In contrast, Indigenous values consistently demand a radical alternative. Anishinaabe scholar and artist Leanne Simpson (2013) reflects on an Anishinaabe version of economic reconciliation (if it can be called such). In an interview with Naomi Klein she stated:

> If I look at how my ancestors even 200 years ago, they didn't spend a lot of time banking capital, they didn't rely on material wealth for their well-being and economic stability. They put energy into meaningful and authentic relationships. So their food security and economic security was based on how good and how resilient their relationships were – their relationships with clans that lived nearby, with communities that lived nearby, so that in hard times they would rely on people, not the money they saved in the bank.

The mode of economy for Anishinaabeg that Simpson describes is indicative of what might resonate as the "common good," but is more properly understood as *mino bimaadiziwin* (Klein 2013), a phrase borrowed from Anishinaabe activist Winona LaDuke. Simpson elaborates that *mino bimaadiziwin* can be understood as "continuous rebirth." For Anishinaabeg, economic life was intimately tied to relationships, and these relationships were vital to rebirthing. Similarly, for the Haudenosaunee, "the Good Mind" or "the Great Peace" can be described as individuals engaging in economic, social, political, and spiritual life in ways that fostered peace, power, and righteousness. This underscores the principles and tenets of the Great Law (the Haudenosaunee approximation of a constitution), in which Haudenosaunee nations came together as a formalized confederacy in the twelfth century to create an everlasting peace between the nations – one that lasted five hundred years. Peace between nations, within communities, and in the minds of individual citizens was generative of a common good. For the Haudenosaunee, Anishinaabe, and other Indigenous nations, living a good or peaceful life is not an abstract concept. It is the basis in which systems of governance can continue or be continuously rebirthed for future generations. Our understanding of the common good is not irreconcilable with other peoples or nations, although it continues to be perceived as threatening to state interests.

These, and the hundreds of other forms of Indigenous socio-political systems being re-articulated and asserted, undoubtedly pose a threat to the far-right's nativist interests. Canada's 150th birthday on 1 July 2017 is an example. In response to a group of Mi'kmaq peoples who had gathered at the Cornwallis statue in Halifax to mourn his violent legacy, the "Proud Boys" organized a counter-protest, confronting the Indigenous group and displaying their pride at Cornwallis's bounty on Indigenous scalps. Of course, the statue stood as a commemoration of Edward Cornwallis, the founder of Halifax, who during his time as governor in the 1750s offered a cash bounty for the imprisonment or scalping of any Mi'kmaq who resisted the establishment of Halifax (Williams and Patil 2018). Instead of celebrating, Mi'kmaq peoples engaged in ceremony to acknowledge this past. Their ceremony was halted by the Proud Boys (who were also members of the Canadian Armed Forces), who alleged that the Indigenous peoples were being disrespectful of Cornwallis – and by extension, of their heritage.

We can link this example to the broader project of Canada. It is emblematic of the same ethic of the nineteenth century when the Indian Act was amended in 1885 to ban Indigenous ceremony because it was perceived as a threat (Leslie and Maguire 1978). Assimilationist policies of the time were designed to remove the Indianness from the Indians and design new patriots. The act of ceremony was seen as an insult to a particular national identity then, and by the Proud Boys now. This comparison is all the more acute, considering these were military servicemen (McMillan and Patil 2017).

In the province next door, posters directing students to far-right online sites were found plastered on a Maliseet welcome sign at the University of New Brunswick (Gill 2017). In October of 2017, on the other side of the country, members of the Department of Native Studies at the University of Alberta arrived at their offices to find an "It's Ok to Be White" poster taped to the front door on the morning of Halloween (Khandaker 2017). Just the day before, someone had placed a carved pumpkin in front of the building and adorned it with multicoloured feathers as an effigy. The intention of the pumpkin is clear: Indigenous students were made to feel unsafe. And yet, the poster that appeared the next day ("It's Ok to Be White") also communicates an ostensible desire to feel safe, though for a different group of people. Incidents such as these are characteristic of a perceived threat against national identity, and the usurping of dispossession politics to drive nativist fears (Boyd 2017).

As Indigenous peoples rebirth, reconstitute, and renew our philosophies, values, and relations with our territories, this seems to be viewed as an affront to the philosophies, values, and relations to our territories that far-right activists exalt. As we fight for justice, those whose power has been largely unfettered for generations see injustice (King 2017). For some, our successes in holding fast to Indigenous ways of understanding the "good" or the "peace" present a threat to one of the goals of the far right: to articulate a defence of "nativist" interests. The nostalgic longing of the far right is attempting to establish itself as fundamental to the common good in which a common national identity is under siege by communities of colour, LGBTQ communities, immigrant populations, feminist groups, and Indigenous peoples. The laws and principles that continue to be rebirthed from the multiplicity of Indigenous territorial identities are modes of understanding and practice that we can look to in re-establishing the "good."

Indigenist claims are being re-asserted in movements like the Ogimaa Mikina Project (established in 2013) that, through art, seeks to reclaim and rename captured settler colonial spaces in Toronto. You will find it on the street signs, bridges, and sides of buildings that are being de-named and re-named in Anishinaabemowin (the language of the Anishinaabe). You will find it among the Inuit of Labrador, who are fighting against a hydroelectric dam project at Muskrat Falls that would see environmental devastation to their territories, land they share with non-Indigenous neighbours. Beatrice Hunter, an Inuk grandmother who refused to abide by an injunction that required her to stay one kilometre away from the construction site of the dam, was incarcerated for ten days in a federal men's prison for attempting to protect her territory and people (Breen 2017). The Nibi Emosaawdamajig (Those Who Walk for the Water) are another example. Inspired by Anishinaabe elder Josephine Mandamin and the Great Lakes Water Walk that began in 2003 on Lake Superior, Nibi Emosaawdamajig walk around the waters in the Kawartha region during the summer months as both an act of ceremony for, and resistance to, environmental contamination of the waters (Johnson 2017). Resistance movements like these, and countless others, may be seen as an affront to preservation tactics embedded in nativist, far-right ideology, because they present another world. Or, rather, the original one. The flimsy nativist-cloaked-as-Indigenous claims are without merit and can only exist within the limits of the state. Indigenous resistance and protection of our Native lands is ideologically and materially opposed to the preservation of narrow nativist conceptions of the common good. As we reclaim space for our families, in the cities, in the bush, in universities, on the ground, or through the courts, a right to maintain *our* common good will continue to be asserted.

REFERENCES

Anaya, J. 2013. "Statement upon Conclusion of the Visit to Canada." http://unsr. jamesanaya.org/statements/statement-upon-conclusion-of-the-visit-to-canada.
Boyd, A. 2017. "'This Is Racist': University of Alberta Investigates Jack-o'-Lantern Found on Campus." *Metro News* Edmonton, 30 October. http://www.metronews. ca/news/edmonton/2017/10/30/a-stupid-little-pumpkin-university-of-alberta-investigating-racist-jack-o-lantern-found-on-campus.html.
Breen, K. 2017. "Beatrice Hunter Released from Jail, Allowed to Protest Outside Muskrat Falls Gate." CBC *News*, 9 June. http://www.cbc.ca/news/canada/ newfoundland-labrador/beatrice-hunter-jail-court-murphy-1.4153349.
Cook, B. 2018. "Quebec Far-Right Leader Claims He's Aboriginal." *i heart radio*, 3 January. http://www.iheartradio.ca/cjad/news/quebec-far-right-leader-claims-he-s-aboriginal-1.3533935.
Gill, J. 2017. "Alt-Right Propaganda Posted on Maliseet Welcoming Sign." CBC *News*, 30 September. http://www.cbc.ca/news/canada/new-brunswick/alt-right-poster-st-thomas-university-maliseet-sign-1.4315282.
Johnson, R. 2017. "'It's Really Very Crucial Right Now': Great Lakes Water Walk Focuses on Protecting 'Lifeblood.'" CBC *News*, 23 September. http://www.cbc.ca/ news/indigenous/great-lake-water-walk-meant-to-spread-awareness-open-to-all-1.4303050.
Khandaker, T. 2017. "White Nationalist Posters Are Popping Up on Canadian University Campuses." *Vice News*, 3 November. https://news.vice.com/en_ca/ article/pazqb9/white-nationalist-posters-are-popping-up-on-canadian-university-campuses.
King, H. 2017. Personal Communication. 7 November.

Klein, N. 2013. "Dancing the World into Being: A Conversation with Idle No More's Leanne Simpson." *Yes! Magazine*, 5 March. http://www.yesmagazine.org/peace-justice/dancing-the-world-into-being-a-conversation-with-idle-no-more-leanne-simpson.

Leslie, J., and R. Maguire. 1978. *The Historical Development of the Indian Act*. 2nd ed. Ottawa: Treaties and Research Centre, Research Branch, Department of Indian and Northern Affairs.

McMillan, E., and A. Patil. 2017. "Forces Members Who Disrupted Indigenous Rally Face Severe Consequences." cbc *News*, 4 July. http://www.cbc.ca/news/canada/nova-scotia/proud-boys-canadian-military-indigenous-protest-disrupted-1.4189615.

Ogimaa Mikana. 2018. http://ogimaamikana.tumblr.com.

Patil, A. 2017. "Who Are the Proud Boys Who Disrupted an Indigenous Event on Canada Day?" cbc *News*, 4 July. http://www.cbc.ca/radio/asithappens/as-it-happens-tuesday-edition-1.4189447/who-are-the-proud-boys-who-disrupted-an-indigenous-event-on-canada-day-1.4189450.

Saull, R., A. Anievas, N. Davidson, and A. Fabry. 2014. *The Longue Durée of the Far-Right: An International Historical Sociology*. New York: Routledge Press.

Williams, C., and A. Patil. 2018. "Controversial Cornwallis Statue Removed from Halifax Park." cbc *News*, 31 January. http://www.cbc.ca/news/canada/nova-scotia/cornwallis-statue-removal-1.4511858.

PART TWO

INSTITUTIONS AND THE COMMON GOOD

10

WE'VE BEEN RESISTING SINCE WE ARRIVED

Kikélola Roach

I am a recovering lawyer. After sixteen years of being on the front lines trying to "get justice" for my often poor, Brown, and Black clients, brutalized at the hands of police, I've stepped away – to catch my breath, to grieve and mourn the loss of lives made vulnerable by the cruel persistence of racial violence.

"What's next?" I've often asked myself. I wanted to be a lawyer to fight for justice, but ironically the law protected the very injustice that led me to law school. I've been dealing with this conundrum ever since. How could I enter the legal arena and extract any justice from it? How can I continue to labour in a system I don't believe in – one designed to turn me into what one colleague called "a noble loser." Extracting five- and six-figure settlements for clients after protracted proceedings could not be my measure of success. Audre Lorde said it best when she said that the master's tools will never dismantle the master's house.

We as Black people have continually engaged a legal system that was never designed to even recognize our humanity, but we've engaged, trying our best to extract a measure of justice. Understanding the sacrifice and bravery of my ancestors is what sustains me. Searching for the Black Canadian history never taught to me in school, I came to know of three different Black women in Canada, each of whom found herself confronting the legal system: Viola Desmond, Estena Mundle, and Nancy Morton. None saw justice in their lifetime, but each of their cases was righteous and each shapes the story of who we are as Canadians and people of African descent.

Viola Desmond

Hearing in 2016 that the federal Liberal government had chosen Viola Desmond to grace a new Canadian ten-dollar bill, I wondered about the choice. What is the meaning the government wishes us to learn from her story?

Years before Rosa Parks sat on a bus, Viola's courageous stand against segregation in Canada would spark a flame for justice. It was 1946 when Viola went to the Roseland Theatre in New Glasgow, Nova Scotia, to watch a movie while waiting for her car to be repaired. Even though she had requested, and was willing to pay for, a forty-cent seat on the main floor of the theatre, she was sold a thirty-cent balcony seat ticket. The ticket taker told her that "you people" cannot purchase a downstairs ticket. Instead of going to the balcony seats designated for Black folks, she sat in the Whites-only section and refused to budge. Soon she was confronted by a police officer, who grabbed her by her shoulders, and a manager, who grabbed her by her legs, injuring her knee and hip. They carried her out into the street and threw her into a waiting car. They took her down to the police station, where she was jailed for twelve hours in a cell, and then she was tried without a lawyer, convicted, and fined twenty-six dollars. Her spontaneous-but-deliberate decision to defy the segregationist practices of this theatre is one that I was excited and proud to learn about.

Curiously, at her now-historic trial on 9 November 1946, no one mentioned the fact that Viola Desmond was denied a main-floor theatre ticket because she was Black. Today, government officials give her the title "Entrepreneur and Social Justice Defender." Terms like "resistance" and challenging "white supremacy" are avoided, even though these are defining features of the struggles of Black people in this land.

In December 2016, announcing the new banknote, the federal Minister of Status of Women said: "The choice of Viola Desmond reminds us that Canada is a diverse country where everyone deserves equality and respect" (Bank of Canada 2016). Stating that we are a diverse country is simply stating a fact. Stating that everyone *deserves* equality and respect is a truism that does not speak to our actual lived conditions, nor does it hint at a concrete program for the achievement of that ideal. Neither does it even speak to the intense and *ongoing* struggle that African-Canadians have had to wage to have our humanity and our inherent dignity recognized. In the evolving techniques of maintaining white supremacy, we must guard against the superficial ways in which Blackness can be strategically deployed. As Sara Ahmed (2012, 185) writes: "Bodies of color provide organizations with tools, ways of turning action points into outcomes. We become the tools in their kit." Instead of justice for Indigenous people, we get an Indigenous minister of justice. Instead of just immigration laws for refugees, we get a minister of immigration who was a refugee. Instead of the safety and well-being of Black people becoming a chief concern of police, we get a Black chief of police. And so, to the government, Viola is a symbol of "diversity" to be displayed and traded – one that is not however accompanied by an equal sharing of power or a resolute commitment and action to end systemic racism.

While Viola herself may have become a historic figure, several aspects of her experience have a very contemporary feel. Negative encounters with the legal system and the police remain a defining feature of Black Canadian life. Recently the issue of carding (the unconstitutional practice by police of randomly stopping Black people and collecting their data, despite the fact that no crime is being committed), has received more notice, but the brutal nature of the police use of force on our people is generally not well understood by mainstream society.

I've had people as old as seventy and as young as twelve years of age come to my office having been wrongfully detained, maliciously prosecuted, abused, humiliated, beaten by the police. I've represented people who have been clobbered over the head, who've had their arms broken, their eyes rammed with the butt of a gun, their foot stomped on and damaged, people who have been strip-searched and left naked by the police. I've represented families whose loved ones were denied emergency medical care while in custody, with fatal consequences, or killed by being shot in the back or strangled to death with a baton by the police. This is the ugly face of policing that wished to be masked behind the rainbow flag at Toronto Pride. A force that has meted out injury and death, all without apology, all without remorse, all without making amends, should not be allowed to colonize our celebration born of resistance to police brutality. This is the hypocritical police presence that, thankfully, Black Lives Matter – Toronto (BLM–TO) successfully demanded be removed from the Toronto Pride.

But what are we to make of a system that shelters police from virtually all wrongdoing? In the 1980s, a group of Caribbean-Canadian activists in Toronto formed the Black Action Defense Committee (BADC) to pursue an end to police violence. I was proud to be a member and part of the legal team for the group. We sought systemic changes through the inquest system. We demanded that an independent body investigate police wrongdoing and charge the police criminally. We sued the police over and over and over again. We rallied and we chanted. We submitted proposals for legislative change. We lobbied politicians. We made deputations. We argued that the police force must diversify its personnel to be more reflective of the community. We called for the police to be disarmed. We called for crisis intervention teams to respond to civilians who were experiencing mental-health crises. We demanded that the whole system be examined from top to bottom. And examined it has been, in numerous reports and inquiries. And after years of leading mass protests in the streets and speaking out in the media and other forums, BADC was instrumental in forcing the creation of the Special Investigations Unit (SIU), thus making Ontario the only jurisdiction in North America to have an independent civilian-led body to investigate excessive use of force by police.

However, the SIU has let us down; we discovered it is not so independent after all. Police killings have continued, and the daily violations of our constitutional rights persist. What has come of all those recommendations, most of which the system has ignored? What can we learn from those reports? Can we continue working with tools that are not designed to deliver a transformative justice? True freedom and equality are antithetical to a racist, sexist, capitalist, and colonial state. Liberation would require revolutionary change.

Estena Mundle

In the same 2016 Bank of Canada press release announcing the new ten-dollar bill, the finance minister said the following of Viola Desmond: "She represents courage, strength and determination – qualities we should all aspire to every day" – sentiments that sweep us all into a basket of sameness. But consider for a moment the kind of courage, strength, and determination that a woman like Estena Mundle had to call upon when she learned that a police officer had shot her twenty-two-year-old son Tommy Anthony Barnett to death nineteen seconds after arriving on the scene. The year was 1996, and the Special Investigations Unit cleared the officer involved, despite dubious circumstances. When lawyers walked out during the inquest into Tommy's death to protest unfair procedures, Estena decided to question the officer herself. As a lawyer, I know how taxing it can be to cross-examine a police officer. I can't imagine how I would feel cross-examining an officer who had killed my child as Estena Mundle did. Here again was an "ordinary" woman finding her voice in hostile and intimidating circumstances, resisting injustice and seeking accountability. We have had to be brave to be heard.

In 2016, when BLM–TO stopped the Toronto Pride parade, in dramatic fashion, unleashed clouds of colour and staged a sit-in in the middle of an usually high-traffic intersection surrounded by thousands of onlookers, it produced much-needed discussion and a vigorous debate on structural racism that was unprecedented. This is an example of how you have to shake up your tactics when the folks you're negotiating with are not listening. BLM–TO reminded people that the police continue to harass the poor, the racialized, queer people of colour, people with disabilities. They were saying, "Don't ever forget your queer histories." It was queer folks fighting police violence that launched Pride in the first place.

When news broke that there would be no charges laid against the Toronto officer who killed Andrew Loku on 5 July 2015, BLM–TO kicked into action by marching down and setting up tents in front of police headquarters on College Street. They would spend the next two weeks camped out day and night in a determined bid for answers, justice, accountability, and trans-parency from the police and politicians. The police chief never emerged to talk to the protestors. But something more important happened: the pro-testers created community. BLM–TO's Tent City became a place not just of protest but one where people consoled each other, fed each other, created artwork, made memorials to the dead, and held press conferences. They created a space where people could express solidarity, which is what all good movements show us: that we're not alone; that we share a common struggle.

So, in these and other ways, BLM–TO has: (1) recentred progressive politics and progressive demands; (2) changed people's consciousness by shedding light on marginalized issues; and (3) helped build solidarity and alliances. With determination, a clear voice, and a passion to see justice done, it got results. Community support, followed by media attention, forced the legislature to act, with vows to review police oversight bodies and address anti-Black racism with the establishment of an Anti-Racism Direc-torate. These measures don't go far enough, but signal that these issues cannot be ignored.

Nancy Morton

On the same occasion that the new ten-dollar bill was announced, the finance minister said: "Viola Desmond's own story reminds all of us that big change can start with moments of dignity and bravery." Big change also starts with resisting oppression, challenging the status quo, and imagining a better future. Nancy Morton chose to do all these things. After a failed attempt to escape bondage, Nancy Morton became one of the first persons to legally challenge slavery in Canada. With two lawyers arguing on her behalf, she brought her case to a Fredericton, New Brunswick, court in 1800, arguing she should be freed from her owner Caleb Jones. A year-long trial ensued, culminating in a divided decision that forced her return to enslavement. Though her case was unsuccessful, it was instrumental in turning public opinion against slavery. Thirty-four years later, slavery would be abolished in Canada.

Conclusion

We must guard against the erasure of our history of resistance and struggle for justice. We must become the new abolitionists, who make the case for abolishing the need for police, for lawyers, for courts and jails and prisons and punishment. What would our society look like if we didn't need any of those things? Of all the jobs that will soon become obsolete, surely the one that I did for sixteen years should be among them. How can we strengthen each other? How can we spirit our family members away from the forces that would harm them? How can we use what we've got to get what we want?

How deep was Nancy Morton's faith that a New Brunswick court in 1800 would vindicate her and set her free? Did Viola Desmond have a hope that the legal system would treat her fairly? How much trust do we now hold that the SIU will truly be reformed and that the system will deliver us justice? Do we believe that the racial profiling and the brutality and the killing will come to a definitive end? To be someone's property is to live in a most degraded state, robbed of agency, autonomy, bodily sovereignty – to be an object and less than human. Viola Desmond did not win in court. But she was vindicated. Nancy Morton did not win in court. But she was vindicated. Estena Mundle did not win in court. And we fight on.

It is time to move beyond symbolism, beyond words, to action. True victories for freedom and equality cannot be won through tidy court processes or reliance on our current legal systems. They must be won from mass movements, building power from the ground up. We can't replicate the systems of oppression that we purport to fight. We have to acknowledge the past, speak truth, and name oppression. But that is not enough. We have to confront and expose the cancerous effects of a neo-liberal agenda that has taken deep root in every aspect of our lives. We must expose the horrendous toll that capitalism has taken on people and the planet. But that won't be enough to save us, because we could end up with a world that is socialist but sexist, more fair but not free, a world that speaks a language of inclusion embedded in a grammar of deceit.

What must be done to overcome the challenges? We've offered no end of possible solutions: fewer police, more social services. Respect Indigenous sovereignty. Honour the treaties. Reparations for slavery and its after-effects. Education for liberation! Feminism! Socialism! Imagining freedom and inventing ways to get there is actually not the hardest part. It's changing consciousness. If you've read this essay to this point and thought I was talking only about freedom for Black folks, for queer folks of colour, with a nod to freedom for Indigenous folks, then something is missing. While speaking of my own community, I speak of us all. There is no revolution without a change in consciousness. Until you see your freedom as inescapably, inextricably, bound to mine, we're doomed.

When Viola and Estena and Nancy stood for justice, they did so for the common good. They made life better for *all* of us. Each time we collectively understood that those aspects of humanity which were maligned and exploited needed to be honoured instead, we moved one step closer to truly valuing the substance of life itself. The struggles of Black people have always been for ourselves *and* the common good. And yet, we have often been the last or the least to benefit from our collective struggles. Affirmative action, for example, has most benefited White, middle-class, cisgendered, straight women.

We must rally around leadership from groups such as Idle No More and BLM–TO. If we address the needs of the most oppressed among us and fight to free them, then it follows that all of us will be free, because we will have eradicated all forms of domination. What stops us as a whole community from rallying behind the very clear vision and demands of those who have been most negatively impacted by systems of oppression? Even among progressives, many are still so anchored to myths of superiority and inferiority. Until we gain a deep understanding of the interconnectedness of all life, our collective survival is in jeopardy. Resistance and the imagining of a better future have sustained us thus far. We must protect and feed that spirit of resistance while we dream of better days.

NOTE

This chapter is based on a speech delivered at "The Evolving Meaning of Blackness in Canada" symposium, York University (18 February 2017).

REFERENCES

Ahmed, Sara. 2012. *On Being Included: Racism and Diversity in Institutional Life.* Durham: Duke University Press.
Bank of Canada. 2016. "Viola Desmond Chosen as the Bank NOTE-Able Woman to Be Featured on New $10 Bank Note." News Release, 8 December. https://www. bankofcanada.ca/2016/12/viola-desmond-chosen-as-bank-note-able-woman/.

11

NEVER DONE
The Struggle for Health Care

Pat Armstrong

Poll after poll confirms that medicare is Canada's best-loved social program. Indeed, it is central to Canadians' identity. Based on consultations with thousands of Canadians and a wide variety of research reports, the Commission on the Future of Canada's Health Care System (2002, xv) concluded that "Canadians remain deeply attached to the core values at the heart of medicare and to a system that has served them extremely well." This attachment is not surprising, given that medicare allows any Canadian a choice of doctor and hospital care that is free at the point of service. It has increased access to health-care services, especially for the most vulnerable, and provided many with decent paid work. But this support does not mean it is safe from attacks by those who seek to privatize the system. What it does mean is that those attacks are often hard to see, camouflaged as support for the public system rather than as an attempt to undermine it.

Canada's public health-care system is vulnerable to the privatization of the ownership and delivery of services in part because the current structure is complex. The system is based on public payment for services, making it what many in the United States call a single-payer system and those in the United Kingdom talk about as a separation of purchaser and provider. In other words, it is a public insurance plan. For the most part, governments do not deliver services directly, but rather pay others to provide the care. Provinces and territories are primarily responsible for health care, but a significant portion of their money comes from the federal government. The Canada Health Act, the legislation that is the basis of medicare, requires that, in order to receive this federal funding, provincial and territorial services must be universal, accessible, comprehensive, and portable from jurisdiction to jurisdiction. Extra billing for services covered by public insurance is prohibited. The public insurance plan must also be administered by a non-profit agency. Although some jurisdictions prohibit for-profit hospitals and/or private insurance plans from covering services already covered by public plans, there is no such prohibition in the Canada Health Act. However, historically almost all the hospitals were non-profit and responsible to local organizations, while most doctors in private practice were paid directly by the government. They were not required to make a profit for shareholders, but rather could focus on public service. It is important to note that the Canada Health Act explicitly covers only doctors, hospitals, and some dentists for medically necessary services, a limitation that has become increasingly important, as more people have chronic illnesses, and more care can be provided outside hospitals.

In short, for-profit services have lots of room to expand, especially when it comes to services provided outside hospitals and doctors' offices. The fact that governments did not in the main deliver these services has contributed additional space, in part because those seeking to privatize could argue that the system is already private. For-profit firms were anxious to fill the space. As profits began declining in the corporate sector, publicly funded services offered a particularly attractive place for investment, because both customers and payment were guaranteed. Indeed, the Canadian health-care system has been described as an unopened oyster, ready for consumption by the for-profit sector supported by neo-liberal governments that believe markets, the drive for profits, and corporate managerial practices are more efficient and effective.

Today we hear not only about the need for cost savings, but also about the economies required to deal with an aging population that will increase demand for health services. In addition, we hear that for-profit services can offer more choices and quicker services, in the process reducing the wait times that are so often talked about in the media. International and national comparisons of wait times are very difficult to make, because different things are measured in different ways (Viberg 2013). However, the data we do have suggest that, when it comes to hip replacement, knee replacement, cataract surgery, hip-fracture repair, and radiation therapy, three out of four Canadians received their procedure within the recommended wait times, although Canadians seem to wait longer to see a doctor than in other countries (CIHI 2017a). It should be noted that most doctors are in private practices, paid on a fee-for-service basis by the government, and thus control their own access. Moreover, the number of doctors per patient has increased significantly (CIHI 2017b), suggesting that it is decisions by doctors that may be the main problem. And research on Cancer Care Ontario (2017) shows that government strategies to coordinate services have been quite successful in reducing wait times for care.

As the Romanow Report (2002, xv) made clear, "medicare is as sustainable as Canadians want it to be," and other research has shown that the aging population is unlikely to bankrupt the system, especially if we pay attention to the health of older people (CHSRF 2011). Nor is there much evidence to support the claims that a parallel private system would reduce wait times, in part because a parallel system takes care providers out of the public system and focuses on the least-complicated patients, and when complications happen, as they often do, the patients and costs are shifted to the public system (CHFI 2005). At the same time, such a system does increase inequality and bureaucracy. A mainly private system is even worse in terms of both access and cost, as the experience of the United States clearly shows. Health expenditures per person in the United States are twice those in Canada (CIHI 2018), although Canadian medicare covers everyone for doctor and hospital care, while in "2017, 8.8 percent of people, or 28.5 million, did not have health insurance at any point during the year" in the United States.

In spite of this evidence, we have witnessed significant moves toward the privatization of our public system. Privatization of ownership for care services began several decades ago, and it has been accompanied by other forms of privatization that are hard to see. With neo-liberal tax reductions contributing to rising public debt, the federal government cut health-care payments to the provinces and territories. The provinces and territories in turn cut services and applied new managerial strategies taken from the for-profit sector, strategies that were promoted as the means to save medicare by making care more efficient and effective. They significantly reduced the number of beds in acute-care hospitals, reduced patient stays by both redefining necessary hospital care and by shifting to day surgeries, and closed many psychiatric and chronic-care hospitals. Although the Canada Health Act makes it clear that all necessary costs are included when patients are in the hospital, this no longer applies when patients go out the door. As a result, the costs of care were shifted to the patient, and the work of care was too often shifted to women who were not paid to do it.

Some of these developments reflected new technologies and new ideas about care that could improve services. Some were supported by community organizations. For example, a variety of women's health groups argued that childbirth was not an illness, and hospital stays should be avoided or at least significantly reduced for women giving birth. In many jurisdictions, they successfully campaigned for midwifery care. Similarly, part of the disability community fought to have psychiatric hospitals closed and replaced by care in the community, arguing that institutionalization was inhumane. Governments supported these progressive arguments, using them to justify reforms. However, few new public services emerged to replace old ones, wait times increased, and there was no prohibition against either billing for the services outside the hospitals or against the for-profit sector delivering these services. The result was more space for private care and private payment, along with more unpaid care work in and outside the home.

In addition to creating space by reducing access to public services, governments also developed affirmative-action plans for for-profit delivery. Some introduced competitive bidding for services paid for by the government, but the conditions of bidding favoured large corporations. Some of these services were part of larger, non-profit organizations, such as hospitals. Contracting out food services is one example. Others were entire services, such as MRIs or long-term residential-care homes. Public-private partnerships were another strategy for privatization. For example, corporations have financed, built and managed hospitals, based on long-term contracts from the government. Contrary to the rational for going this route, such partnerships do not save money, reduce risk, or create great buildings suited for the purposes of care (Whiteside 2016). What they can do is leave the government responsible if the company goes bankrupt, take decision-making out of the hands of the community, and put the focus on making profits rather than on providing care.

The consequences of these market strategies are particularly negative for those who do the paid health-care work, most of whom are women. The largest proportion of health-care spending goes to staff, and the focus is on reducing those costs. Staff has not increased to fill the demand, and those who enter health services have more complex needs, pushing everyone to work harder and faster. More of the work is part-time and casual, further increasing the strain. Violence and bullying have increased. Reflecting these conditions, the rates of absences due to illness and injury are highest in the health sector (Statistics Canada 2018), and highest for those at the bottom of the hierarchy. A significant proportion of those at the bottom are employed by contracted services, and many are from immigrant and/or racialized communities (Armstrong et al. 2008). At the same time, the move to day surgeries and care at home, as well as the long wait times for a place in a publicly subsidized nursing home, means more unpaid care work, most of which is also done by women.

In sum, privatization promoted by those seeking profits from care and by those who believe that markets should determine all, and that governments should stay out of the way, has multiple negative consequences. Privatization contributes to inequality, while serving to undermine support for the public system. Yet it is precisely this support that has been critical to maintaining what we have, as well as pressuring for reform and expansion of the public system to fill the gaps in care. The Canadian Health Coalition (CHC), which brings together unions and community organizations, provides one example of how to organize resistance while moving toward an expansion of public services.

The coalition's strategy, like that of many organizations struggling for better care, has three basic components. First, research is essential. In the case of demands for pharmacare, for example, studies by people such as Steve Morgan and others (2017) demonstrate that a public system for the coverage of essential drugs could both increase access and lower costs. But it is not enough to have the research. This research needs to be shared, and shared through means that can be understood by a broad audience. These researchers on pharmacare have worked with unions and health coalitions across the country to bring the information to a wide variety of organizations in multiple venues. However, sharing the knowledge is not enough either. It needs to be combined with organized resistance that pressures governments to take action. The Canadian Health Coalition has organized demonstrations, lobbied governments, issued presses releases, and published op eds. It can claim to have had no small part in moving the House of Commons Standing Committee on Health (HESA) to study a national pharmacare program. In turn, HESA directed the Parliamentary Budget Office (PBO) to report on the costs of creating universal pharmacare, resulting in a report that reinforced the research showing the substantial savings that could come with a national public drug plan (CHC 2017). Some provinces have already moved in this direction. The coalition's latest innovative strategy on privatization is an animated video called "Why Does Private Health Care Lengthen Wait Times?" Available on Youtube, it has had thousands of hits. While public meetings tend to be attended mainly by older people, these videos are being watched and downloaded by younger generations. As is the case with the CHC, we need to constantly develop strategies to reach a variety of audiences if we are to keep and expand a public system based on need not greed.

REFERENCES

Armstrong, Pat, Hugh Armstrong, and Krista Scott-Dixon. 2008. *Critical to Care: The Invisible Women in Health Services.* Toronto: University of Toronto Press.
Canadian Foundation for Health Care Improvement (CFHI). 2005. "Myth: A Parallel Private System Would Reduce Waiting Times in the Public System." http://www.cfhi-fcass.ca/SearchResultsNews/05-03-01/5bda3483-f97b-4616-bfe7-d55d0d66b9a0.aspx.
Canadian Health Coalition. 2017. "New PBO Report Finds Lack of National Pharmacare Program Comes at Steep Costs for Taxpayers." News release, 28 September. http://www.healthcoalition.ca/.
Canadian Health Services Research Foundation (HSRF). 2011. *Better with Age: Health Systems Planning for the Aging Population.* http://www.cfhi-fcass.ca/sf-docs/default-source/planning-for-the-aging-population-files/AR_Briefing_ENG.pdf?sfvrsn=0.
Canadian Institute for Health Information. 2017a. *Perspectives on Wait Times in Canada.* https://www.cihi.ca/en/land/in-focus/perspectives-on-wait-times-in-canada.
– 2017b. "Canada's Doctor Supply has Grown Faster than the Population for the Past Decade." https://www.cihi.ca/en/canadas-doctor-supply-has-grown-faster-than-the-population-for-the-past-decade.
– 2018. "National Health Expenditure Trends, 1975 to 2018: Briefing Deck." https://www.cihi.ca/en/search?query-all=per+capita+cost+comparisons&Search+Submit=.
Cancer Care Ontario. 2017. "Safer Cancer Care for Ontarians." https://www.cco health.ca/en/news-media/Safer%20Cancer%20Care%20for%20Ontarians.

Commission on the Future of Health Care in Canada (Romanow Report). 2002. *Building on Values: The Future of Health Care in Canada – Final Report*. Ottawa: Government of Canada.

CTV News. 2012. "Poll: Canadians Are Most Proud of Universal Medicare." 25 November. https://www.ctvnews.ca/canada/poll-canadians-are-most-proud-of-universal-medicare-1.1052929.

Morgan, S.G., W. Li, B. Yau, and N. Persaud. 2017. "Estimated Effects of Adding Universal Public Coverage of an Essential Medicines List to Existing Public Drug Plans in Canada." *Canadian Medical Association Journal* 189, no. 8 (27 Feb.): E295–E302. doi: 10.1503/cmaj.161082.

Statistics Canada. 2018. "Labour Force Survey Estimates (LFS), Work Absence Statistics of Full-Time Employees by Sex and National Occupational Classification (NOC)." Table 279-0040. http://www5.statcan.gc.ca/cansim/a26?lang=eng&retr Lang=eng&id=2790040&&pattern=&stByVal=1&p1=1&p2=31&tabMode=data Table&csid=.

United States Census Bureau. 2018. "Health Insurance Coverage in the United States: 2017." https://www.census.gov/library/publications/2018/demo/p60-264.html.

Viberg, Nina, Birger C. Forsberg, Michael Borowitz, and Roger Molin. 2013. "International Comparisons of Waiting Times in Healthcare – Limitations and Prospects." *Health Policy* 112: 53–61.

Whiteside, Heather. 2016. *Public-Private Partnerships*. Halifax: Fernwood.

12

THE DEATH OF OBJECTIVITY AND THE RISE OF THE "ALT-RIGHT"

Margaret Reid

Introduction

The idea that news media should serve as a public good is multi-faceted. Not only does this idealized vision of the media mean that the production of news should not be entirely determined by market relations, but it also means that the media should fulfill the role of accurately informing the public about matters of public importance, while also holding those in positions of power to account. That being said, the media has rarely been separated from market relations, and this is true now more than ever. Discussions of the threat of fake news in the wake of the 2016 presidential election and the rise of "alt-right" media organizations have certainly signalled that what can be profitable does not even have to be accurate. It is no secret that the news media industry in Canada is in a state of transition. A recent deal between Postmedia and Torstar will see more than thirty newspapers (mainly in Ontario) shut down in the coming months, and 290 employees will lose their jobs (Watson 2017). This is just one example among many in Canada as organizations struggle to compete for digital advertising revenue, most of which now goes to Facebook and Google (Pew Research Centre 2016). News organizations are increasingly becoming beholden to the digital news cycle in attempts to maximize page views. This struggle for survival by news media organizations can often supersede the public's need for contextualized and investigative journalism. This is particularly important in the context of the nascent visibility of the "alt-right" in Canada and abroad. We need media organizations that attempt to investigate, understand, and contextualize these groups, and not just when violence breaks out and it becomes part of the news cycle.

The Right on the Rise

The rise of the "far right" or "alt-right" comes at a time of vast demographic changes in Canada, the United States, and many countries around Europe. According to the 2016 Canadian Census data (Statistics Canada 2017), 51.5 per cent of Toronto's population now identify as visible minorities. Increasingly, the majority status that was historically held by those of white, European heritage is being challenged by migration patterns around the world. These demographic changes have happened concurrently with immense economic depression for the working class, which is characterized by wage stagnation, the rise in precarious working conditions, and job losses for workers in North America and Europe as transnational corporations engage in a race to the bottom, looking for the cheapest labour and maximum profits. The rallying cry in the face of these changes and challenges is to blame immigrants and people of colour for the social ills that are plaguing society, rather than the policies and politics of neo-liberal capitalism. The "far right" tends to reject mainstream conservatism and views multiculturalism as a threat to white nationalism.

However, the ascendance of the "far right" is not just about demographic changes and depressing economic conditions. This movement has been gaining steam in online communities since well before Brexit in the United Kingdom and the 2016 presidential election in the United States, and has been alive and well in Canada for quite some time. However, it has just recently become hyper visible. There is evidence that white-supremacist and neo-Nazi groups have been on the rise in recent years (Perry 2018). Groups that used to reside on the fringes have been given a form of legitimacy as a result of the institutionalization of these ideas vis-à-vis the Trump presidency. The newly established Canadian Nationalist Party is attempting to officially register the party, and seeks candidates for the next federal election, running on a platform that states, "We must maintain the demographic status of the current European-descended majority" (Nationalist 2017). The emergence of a conspicuous White nationalist populous is related to those in positions of power elevating the narrative that immigrants are to blame, as well as overstating and misunderstanding the threat of terrorism. Trump's calls to build a wall on the US-Mexico border and his several attempts to institute a ban on immigration from Muslim-majority countries are evidence enough that one does not need to publicly identify oneself as a White nationalist to espouse ideas and propose policies that work to those ends. Though the "alt-right" has not yet enjoyed electoral legitimacy in Canada, it is important that we do not stand idly by while this becomes a reality.

Beyond the realm of political power, digital-first media organizations like Breitbart, a US based "alt-right" news site, perform the ideological work of discounting mainstream media organizations and their "liberal bias," while presenting themselves as refreshing and much-needed alternatives to "fake news" and the supposed politically correct culture of the liberal media. The "alt-right" emerges as a resistance to what is perceived to be the tyranny of political correctness and "liberal feelings." As Breitbart contributors Milo Yiannopoulos and Allum Bokhari (2016) argued,

> The alt-right is a movement born out of the youthful, subversive, underground edges of the internet. 4chan and 8chan are hubs of alt-right activity. For years, members of these forums – political and non-political – have delighted in attention-grabbing, juvenile pranks. Long before the alt-right, 4channers turned trolling the national media into an in-house sport.

The rise of the "alt-right" began with the culture wars online, but is now being used to justify very problematic policy priorities.

The Death of Objective Journalism?

The news-media ecosystem is currently undergoing what some might call an identity crisis. The era of so-called "objective" journalism is rapidly becoming a distant memory. The media ecology that used to exist was one characterized by high levels of media concentration and convergence and significant barriers to entry for emerging news-media organizations. The rise of "objectivity" in the media emerged alongside these trends. This era was marked by an elevated focus on politically neutral, professional journalism, which was best achieved by striving for "objectivity." Media organizations wanted to reach mass markets rather than particular groups (Skinner, Compton, and Gasher 2005), and the way to do that was to at least feign objectivity. Historically, news was highly partisan, and this was not seen to be a problem as long as there was diversity of ownership as well as diversity in the perspectives being disseminated (McChesney 2008). Now, as a result of digital technologies, barriers to entry have been significantly reduced, and there has been a steady rise in digital-first news media organizations, in which there is more of a focus on niche audiences, rather than on trying to be everything to everyone. Citizens are left to sort through the rubble of clickbait and decontextualized journalism in efforts to find trustworthy information, so that they may make informed decisions about their lives.

No longer are we living in an era where politicians need to provide their public-relations material to news organizations for them to dissect. In Donald Trump's case, he has little need for the mainstream media, but only his own Twitter account, which he can use to communicate with the American people and to denounce news outlets like CNN and the *New York Times* as fake news when they report unfavourably on his presidency. Further, websites like Breitbart, whose executive chairman served as Trump's chief strategist before returning to his role at Breitbart, are being given press-room credentials in the White House as if they had journalistic credentials or integrity. Some media organizations that are still trying to aim for the widest possible readership, like the *New York Times,* have even opted to interview Steve Bannon. The *NYT* interview featured softball questions, while Steve Bannon joked about being "behind enemy lines" and went on to present himself as a reasonable guy and champion of the American working-class interests who is sick and tired of the tenured political class. Bannon was given an unchallenged opportunity, before the wide audience of the *NYT*, to distance himself and Trump's policy efforts from white supremacy. However, White supremacist is not a name that groups give to themselves; it is a name they earn. News media organizations have a responsibility beyond presenting information; they must also contextualize it.

There has been a rise in all sorts of niche news publications online. The Rebel Media, Canada's answer to Breitbart, emerges as a powerful voice for the "alt-right." This online publication, founded by Ezra Levant in 2015, has promoted narratives that denounce Islam, while claiming to uphold "Canadian values." The Rebel has used freedom of speech as a tool to critique

M103, a non-binding motion that attempts to denounce Islamophobia and unfounded hatred toward Muslims in Canada, claiming that it was the "Liberal's first step towards outlawing criticism of Islam" (Goldy 2017). The message disseminated by this outlet is clear: "Canadian values" are in fact white, Christian, European values. The construction of Canadian identity around whiteness is also done more subtly by the media, a fact that is attested to by Sheps's (2018) work on hockey culture in this volume. Freedom of speech is becoming the bargaining chip of the "alt-right" against the left, and is being used to justify antisemitism, Islamophobia, and intolerance toward other marginalized groups.

The biggest threat posed by media organizations like The Rebel Media is that they are propagating fear and hatred by generating stereotypes and falsehoods about marginalized groups in Canadian society, and this has the potential to affect the treatment of those groups. As Perry's (2018) essay in this volume illustrates, hate-crime incidents that were racially or ethnically motivated are on the rise in Canada. Violent hate crimes also rose by 16 per cent, from 487 in 2015 to 563 in 2016 (Statistics Canada 2016, 2017). There is also the threat that this site will begin to be given some sort of institutional legitimacy by politicians, as has been the case with its American counterpart. Importantly, Ezra Levant publicly attempted to distance his website from the "alt-right" and white-supremacy movements after a wave of its contributors (including Levant's co-founder) left the site in the wake of the sympathetic treatment given by one of their contributors, Faith Goldy, to the "Unite the Right" movement of White supremacists in Charlottesville, after participants became violent with counter-protesters. Conservative politicians, including Conservative MPs Michael Chong, Peter Kent, and Conservative leader Andrew Scheer, have also distanced themselves from the site in the wake of ties to white nationalism (Goldsbie 2017). While this does signal a small victory, Rebel Media was promoting white-supremacist values long before Charlottesville; it was only now that these views became undeniable and it was no longer tenable for groups on the right to be openly affiliated with it. Despite the hit the organization took to both its subscriber base and from over three hundred advertisers pulling out (Tencer 2017), The Rebel claims to sustain itself from its subscriber base, which means it is not going anywhere soon. The organization is not relying solely on advertising revenue, which is increasingly becoming a bleak and somewhat unsustainable model for many news organizations.

Other news-media organizations are struggling as a result of dwindling advertising revenues, and it must be considered that marginalized communities are often not in positions to pay for news media. If the media landscape is shifting toward niche, segmented audiences, this may mean that their interests will not be represented as often as the interests of more-lucrative audiences. However, there are some thriving organizations that don't claim to be objective and that wish to prioritize marginalized communities, while striving for and engaging in fact-based reporting. Take Buzzfeed, for example. This American-based site, known for its clickbait-style journalism, has now developed a news wing in Canada and has opened an office in Toronto. Buzzfeed, which has a predominantly young readership, has embedded anti-oppression in its editorial mandate:

> We firmly believe that for a number of issues, including civil rights, women's rights, anti-racism, and LGBT equality, there are not two sides. But when it comes to activism, BuzzFeed editorial must follow the lead of our editors and reporters who come out of a tradition of rigorous, neutral journalism that puts facts and news first (Hilton 2016).

While news organizations need not be "objective," they must be credible. Neither Breitbart nor The Rebel Media have editorial policies or ethical standards. There is no transparency to the supposed "journalism" that they are engaged in producing. Let's stop calling it journalism. Journalism ought to be based on facts. These organizations may have a right to exist, but they do not have a right to be considered legitimate news organizations that are to be taken seriously.

Conclusion

The rise of the "alt-right" signals a war on intellectualism, and in many cases a war on evidence. This is why media organizations must take their role in the covering of "alt-right" movements very seriously, and this is what will ultimately strengthen a resistance movement in Canada. Covering the "alt-right" movements does not mean providing them with equal weight. It requires dissecting the origins of these movements, contextualizing how these narratives are impacting marginalized groups in Canada, and providing solutions-based journalism, rather than reporting a steady diet of horror to the populous. This requires elevating progressive voices that are peacefully mobilizing in opposition to the "alt-right." This means that media organizations must avoid sensationalism at the expense of analysis. News-media organizations must do better in asking tough questions and engaging in rigorous, facts-based journalism. News organizations must resist trends toward investigating and covering "alt-right" groups only when controversy erupts and this becomes "good for business."

Better reporting and fact gathering alone, however, will not solve this crisis. The broader problem is one of ideology. Education and better development of media literacy and critical thinking will be vital in countering the "alt-right." But education, like journalism, is also under attack as a public good as it becomes increasingly marketized and defunded. To build a resistance to these movements, we need to fight for better publicly funded education and support for non-profit media organizations.

REFERENCES

Bokhair, A., and M. Yiannopoulos. 2016. "An Establishment Conservative's Guide to the Alt-Right." Breitbart, 29 March. http://www.breitbart.com/tech/2016/03/29/an-establishment-conservatives-guide-to-the-alt-right/.
Goldsbie, J. 2017. "A Growing List of People Who Have Cut Ties with The Rebel." *Canadaland*, 14 August. http://www.canadalandshow.com/people-who-have-cut-ties-with-rebel-media/.
Goldy, F. n.d. "Freedom to Offend: Support Free Speech, Not Sharia!" The Rebel, 20 November. https://www.therebel.media/freedom-to-offend-free-speech-not-sharia#petition-form.
Hilton, S.O. 2016. "The Buzzfeed News Standards and Ethics Guide." Buzzfeed, 9 December. https://www.buzzfeed.com/shani/the-buzzfeed-editorial-standards-and-ethics-guide?utm_term=.taOLO65d8#.wvoX7Zqlo.
McChesney, R. 2008. *The Political Economy of Media*. New York: Monthly Review Press. http://www.thepoliticaleconomyofmedia.org/.

Skinner, D., and M. Gasher. 2005. "So Much by So Few: Media Policy and Ownership in Canada." In *Converging Media, Diverging Politics: A Political Economy
of News Media in Canada and the US*, edited by D. Skinner, J. Compton, and
M. Gasher, 51–75. Lanham, MD: Lexington Books.

Perry, B., and R. Scrivens. 2016. "Right Wing Extremism in Canada: An Environment Scan." Public Safety Canada. https://www.publicsafety.gc.ca/cnt/ntnl-scrt/
cntr-trrrsm/r-nd-flght-182/knshk/ctlg/dtls-en.aspx?i=116.

Pew Research Centre. 2016. "State of the News Media Report 2016." Pew Research
Centre. http://assets.pewresearch.org/wp-content/uploads/sites/13/2016/06/3014
3308/state-of-the-news-media-report-2016-final.pdf.

Statistics Canada. 2017. "Police-reported Hate Crime, 2016." https://www.statcan.
gc.ca/daily-quotidien/171128/dq171128d-eng.htm.

– 2017. Toronto, C [Census subdivision], Ontario and Ontario [Province] (table).
Census Profile. 2016 Census. Statistics Canada Catalogue no. 98-316-X2016001.
Ottawa. Released 29 November, 2017, accessed November 29, 2017. http://www12.
statcan.gc.ca/census-recensement/2016/dp-pd/prof/index.cfm?Lang=E.

Tencer, D. 2017. "Rebel Media Has Lost 300 Advertisers in the Past 3 Months."
HuffPost, 17 August. http://www.huffingtonpost.ca/2017/08/17/rebel-media-has-
lost-300-advertisers-in-past-3-months-group_a_23081721/.

Watson, H.G. 2017. "Torstar and Postmedia Swapped 41 Newspapers and Are
Closing Most of Them." J-Source, 27 November. http://j-source.ca/article/torstar-
postmedia-swapped-41-newspapers-closing/.

13

STAY CALM, BE BRAVE, AND WAIT FOR THE SIGNS

Janice A. Newson

In the late 1990s, *The Dead Dog Café* aired on CBC radio. It was a wickedly biting comedy created by the acclaimed Indigenous writer Thomas King on the injustices and stupidities endured daily by the First Nations people of Canada and their communities. No matter how bleak, relentless, and soul-crushing were the situations they depicted, the leading characters spiritedly chanted at the end of each episode, "Stay Calm! Be Brave! Wait for the Signs."

Their chant could be a mantra for anyone dispirited, alarmed, over-whelmed, or paralyzed in the face of what many, including the editors of this collection of essays, refer to as "the new political climate." We can debate whether we are, indeed, in a "new" political climate or a heightened version of conditions we have been confronting for some time. In either case, it has not emerged suddenly, without advance warning – or, especially, without resistance.

For some time, people have been struggling individually and collectively against social, political, and economic forces that have led to the current situation, as is so well illustrated in the essays by Bernie Farber and Len Rudner, Tim McCaskell, and Kikélola Roach. Many saw this political turn, or something like it, coming and tried to sound the alarm. It is not surprising, then, that these people especially are among the dispirited, alarmed, overwhelmed, or paralyzed. *Dead Dog Café*'s kind-hearted and energetic mantra may not only sustain their spirits but also offer some strategic guidance on how to respond to this political moment.

I came to a *Dead Dog Café* moment around the end of the 1990s, having been active for several decades in the struggle to reclaim the university as a public-serving institution. When I began my academic career, the shared consensus was that universities served a two-pronged public-serving purpose: to create and widely disseminate knowledge addressing the social, political, and economic needs of all Canadians; and to nurture a well-informed, critical-thinking citizenry to sustain a flourishing democratic society.

Signs that this consensus was breaking down became visible as the 1970s unfolded. Governments began to impose fiscal retrenchment on public-sector institutions, including universities, leading to a series of changes over the next three or four decades – organizational, economic, and political – which reflected, as well as contributed to, a "shift to the right." By the end of the 1990s, universities no longer had their sights set on advancing democratically oriented, public-serving knowledge projects. They had transformed into flourishing knowledge businesses, instruments of neo-liberal economic agendas and private-sector growth.

This transformation did not happen without a struggle, however. Across the country, departments, faculties, and academic senates became the front lines of struggles to preserve academic integrity and retain collegial control over academic affairs in the face of budget-cutting and ballooning administrations. As these struggles persisted and intensified, many faculty associations pursued union status, the idea having taken hold that collective agreements would, in the current climate, shield their members from arbitrary and unilateral changes to their terms and conditions of employment and protect their collegial roles from administrative expansion. I increasingly invested energy in this unionization strategy, convinced that strong and vigilant academic unions provided the best means, politically and culturally, for preserving the university's public-serving mission.

For a time, these struggles met considerable, if limited, success. Collective bargaining, active engagement in collegial bodies, and student-led campaigns against underfunding all helped to set limits on administrative overreach and mitigate the academic damage caused by underfunding. However, by the early 1980s, powerful political and economic agents were advancing a profoundly changed agenda for higher education: namely, that universities should solve their underfunding problems by acquiring new sources of funding from private-sector partners and, in exchange for these funds, provide corporate clients with access to cutting-edge research to help them compete in the increasingly globalized economic order (Currie and Maxwell 1984).

The late Howard Buchbinder and I began to track this unfolding agenda in policy documents and in the infrastructural changes taking place beneath the surface of local campuses. We gave talks to faculty associations, presented papers at conferences, wrote articles in newspapers and magazines, and spoke at public gatherings across the country, alerting our colleagues and the wider public to a new corporate agenda that posed serious threats to the university's public-serving mission. Encouraged by Garamond Press, we published our concerns in *The University Means Business: Universities, Corporations, and Academic Work* (Newson and Buchbinder 1988).

Nevertheless, over the 1990s and into the 2000s, governments – Liberal, Conservative, and N D P – rolled out successive waves of neo-liberal policies that enabled the implementation of this agenda. Publicly funded research councils re-oriented grant programs to facilitate university-corporate collaboration. University brochures and websites embraced corporate language to attract clients, highlighting the ways in which their institution's teaching and research programs contribute to private-sector growth. A corporate ethos increasingly pervaded campus culture. By the early 2000s, universities' role in disseminating social knowledge and nurturing a democratic citizenry was, in practice, overwhelmed by their engagement in producing market knowledge and growing wealth.

One might expect that the academic community – faculty members in particular – would rise to challenge this profound reconceptualization and reconfiguration of the academic life-world. There are several reasons why, in my view, they have not. I want to highlight two in particular.

First is that an important change in academic decision-making began to take place in the mid-to-late 1980s, whereby the established practice of determining academic objectives and priorities through face-to-face debates in collegial bodies was supplanted by new documentary-based forms of decision-making. Documents such as five-year academic plans became the means of determining everything, from resource allocation, to curricular content, to hiring priorities, to teaching formats.

This new form of decision-making seriously weakened collegiality as a resource for derailing the neo-liberal agenda. Rather than being vehicles for resisting corporatization and asserting the university's public-serving mission, the role and authority of collegial bodies were arrogated to these new documentary processes, turning collegial bodies, in effect, into rubber stamps of proposals that university managers largely initiate and/or control. It is hardly surprising that faculty members participate less and less in these bodies as a meaningful or rewarding investment of energy.

A second reason that the neo-liberal transformation of academic life has not been widely resisted is that, beginning in the mid-1990s, the federal government substantially increased its allocations to academic research as part of an innovation agenda. University administrations and academics alike, after decades of underfunding, were notably enthusiastic about this increased access to funds to support research programs and initiatives. There was a catch, however. These new funds were to be channelled through programs – some already existing and some new, such as the Canada Research Chairs and the Canada Foundation for Innovation programs – that embedded neo-liberal objectives into the everyday operations of universities. These included building private-public partnerships, enhancing corporate-style competitiveness within and among institutions, and commercializing academic activities (Polster 2002; Guppy et al. 2013).

Elsewhere in this volume, Alan Sears has highlighted a wide range of neo-liberal social policies that have seriously diminished the economic and political lives of marginalized communities. But it is a politically confounding complexity of neo-liberalism that it creates not only losers but also winners, sometimes side-by-side in the same neighbourhood or workplace. Academic life in the 1990s and early 2000s aptly exemplifies this double edge of neo-liberalism. While the new funding programs provided some faculty members with competitive opportunities to advance their professional and scholarly careers, others, especially those who held part-time and short-term contracts, became increasingly subjected to cost-saving and precarious employment conditions.

In spite of the fact that increased financial resources were obtained at the expense of advancing neo-liberal objectives, a buzzy productiveness began to replace demoralization and acquiescence to declining conditions, as many faculty members redirected their work to fit into the new funding programs and priorities. It was not that they were unconcerned about the increasingly corporatized operations of their own university. Indeed, many were. But there was a painful irony in the unfolding scene. While less able to shape their institution according to their sense of the university's public mission, many faculty members shifted to these new opportunities as the only game in town for pursuing professionally rewarding and meaningful activities. By so doing, their energy increasingly was harnessed to a neo-liberal version of the university's mission.

It was this shift that led to my *Dead Dog Café* moment. I could no longer sense that an active struggle for the public-serving university was under way or even possible. Moreover, I could not see a way forward for this struggle or my continued role in it. I am not ignoring several noteworthy challenges to corporatization, such as the Quebec student strike in 2010, which rapidly escalated into a widespread mobilization of the Quebec public against the destructive effects of neo-liberal policies on people's lives. Yet, even with these efforts, the transformation of public universities into neo-liberal knowledge businesses has continued unabated.

Thankfully, the words that had been sitting for some time on my kitchen island cracked through my inertia: "Stay Calm, Be Brave, and Wait for the Signs." They said, take a take a step back and resist the impulse to try to come up with a new plan of action. If a way forward can't be seen, perhaps conditions for a way forward are not yet in place. Perhaps the moment calls for waiting, reflecting, and watching.

But waiting, reflecting, and watching does not mean doing nothing: it means drawing lessons from the history of this struggle and preparing to press forward whenever an opening appears or can be created. For the present, it is critically important to keep alive the idea and, to the extent possible, the reality of a public-serving university, even from inside the confines of these flourishing knowledge businesses (Newson 2004, 2010).

Several colleagues, whose views I greatly respect, question whether the contemporary university in its current state is any longer a viable place for doing progressive work. I have sympathy for this view and have sometimes adopted it myself: the real-time functioning of the neo-liberal university is the problem more than the solution.

However, the events of the past two years or so have put a foot in this door. A friend (who, incidentally, never graduated from university) recently said to me that there is no better argument for higher education than the election of Donald Trump as president of the United States. Her comment suggests to me that, true though it is that the still-publicly-funded university has been seriously diverted from serving the public good, the public good that it *should* be serving remains – at the very least, to provide an uncompromised intellectual and moral bulwark against "fake news," conspiracy theories, and divisive politics.

But in order for the university to be a site for restraining moves to the right, a concerted collective effort must be undertaken to reinstate its public-serving mission. Suggestions developed by Claire Polster and me in support of this effort can be found on the "Social Kinesis" page of my website, www.janicenewson.ca. Here I will briefly outline two of them.

First, we need to expand conceptions of activism to encompass a wider practice of "social kinesis," which includes *any* intervention that *deliberately* aims to effect a change in social patterns and practices. Activism often equates with confrontational strategies, such as protests, demonstrations, strikes, rallies, sit-ins, and the like – all of which have their place. Social kinesis encourages us to conceive ways of disrupting neo-liberalism and corporate thinking where and when they are at work, organizing the day-to-day, routine activities of faculty members, students, staff, and administrators and shaping their perspectives on, and decisions about, things to be done and decisions to be taken. Contesting corporate language used in discussions, presentations, and reports, or interrogating the neo-liberal assumptions underlying a planning document or performance indicator are good examples. Though less dramatic, such interventions are as "activist" as attending a protest or giving a speech at a rally. In a very real sense, they are forms of "direct action."

Second, concerned faculty, students, and staff need to re-occupy collegial bodies with the intent of working together to recover a *meaningful* role for collegial influence in university decision-making. To do this, we need to become well-versed in "rules of order" and how the decisions of a given collegial body relate to the wider decision-making structures of our universities. Regrettably, it can no longer be assumed that even senior faculty members have this knowledge, let alone young faculty who have not had the opportunities available to earlier generations to be mentored on these matters.

Certainly these recommendations will require people to realign their priorities and redirect their time and energy. But I say to those who choose to become involved in this immensely important undertaking, "Stay Calm. Be Brave. Wait for the Signs." And then, seize the moment!

REFERENCES

Currie, Stephanie, and Judith Maxwell. 1984. *Partnership for Growth*. Toronto: The Corporate-Higher Education Forum.

Guppy, Neil, Edward Grabb, and Clayton Mollica. 2013. "The Canada Foundation for Innovation, Sociology of Knowledge, and the Re-engineering of the University." *Canadian Public Policy/Analyse de Politiques* 39 (1): 1–19.

Newson, Janice. 2010. Recovering the University as a Collective Project. In *Academic Callings*, edited by Janice Newson and Claire Polster, 250–8. Toronto: Canadian Scholars Press.

– 2004. "Disrupting the 'Student as Consumer' Model: The New Emancipatory Project." *International Relations* 18 (2): 227–39.

Newson, Janice, and Howard Buchbinder. 1988. *The University Means Business: Universities, Corporations, and Academic Work*. Toronto: Garamond Press.

Polster, Claire. 2002 (August). "A Break from the Past: Impacts and Implications of the Canada Foundation for Innovation and the Canada Research Chairs Initiative." *Canadian Review of Sociology and Anthropology* 39 (3): 275–300.

14

CHALLENGING AND DEFEATING THE RIGHT
Beyond Trumpism and the Peterson Cult

Neil McLaughlin

Standing up to and fighting back against the authoritarianism unleashed on Canada's doorstep by the election of Donald Trump requires a broad-based movement of the democratic left, liberals, and principled conservatives. My remarks for *We Resist* will thus focus primarily on missteps some left-wing Canadian academics, journalists, and activists have made so far in the Trump era. Intellectual efforts to oppose Trumpism are essential as Canadian intellectuals mobilize against the antidemocratic forces that are gathering influence worldwide. In this essay, I will play the role of a friendly internal critic of this vital resistance.

The challenges we face are partly reflected in the rise to fame in 2016 of University of Toronto psychology professor Jordan Peterson for his stated opposition to laws enforcing the use of gender-neutral pronouns. Peterson's over-the-top rhetoric about the role of Marxism and post-modernism in higher education has contributed to an escalation of attacks on liberal and left professors. This new extremist climate was partly created by the strategies of Canadian far-right provocateur Ezra Levant and the new dynamics of social media.

This is an old story of anti-left bias on campus, but there is a new organizational and social-media dynamic at play. Canadian universities are largely public, unlike the elite private universities that dominate the higher-education system in the United States, where many of the current cultural wars occur. Politics in Canadian universities were generally far less polarized and politicized in the 1960s. We were certainly less successful at undermining our own Apartheid-like settler-colonial structures and laws than Americans managed to be in their civil-rights revolution for African-Americans. It is therefore understandable now that Canadian radicals want to push for radical politics on campuses, focusing on inclusion and diversity and challenging the moderate liberal and centre-right intellectual consensus of our nation. But our public universities are less well-funded and are potentially more open to populist pressures from the far right than are elite American Ivy League universities. Arising in response to the Trump-like movements and sensibilities that are spreading in the hard-right flanks of the Conservative Party, Maxine Bernier's People's Party of Canada, the Ford government in Ontario, and the Rebel Media crowd, are real threats to our resistance efforts.

To unpack and develop this point, we must compare the two major right-wing critics of the academy in each country, American David Horowitz and Canada's Ezra Levant. David Horowitz, a former Communist and Black Panther sympathizer in the 1960s, is now the institutional and ideological leader of the Campus Reform movement in the United States. Bringing the most extreme anti-Muslim voices into the mainstream as a shameless Trump apologist and almost-unhinged Obama hater, Horowitz (2006) is the architect of the infamous Islamo-Fascism week on American campuses and author of *The Professors: The 101 Most Dangerous Academics in America.* Horowitz's influence in Canada, however, flows less from his writing and more from the role model he created for Ezra Levant, Canada's very own extremist and the person most responsible for attacking radical students and professors in this country.

The David Horowitz of Canada, Levant published his short-lived magazine, the *Western Standard,* featuring his own list of Canada's most "nutty" professors on the left (O'Neill 2006). We often underestimate Rebel Media "Commander" Levant because of his obvious propensity to shoot himself in the foot with careless research and libellous charges against ideological opponents. It is easy to hope that he has now been marginalized in Canadian politics, because the Sun News Network, for which he worked, went out of business a few years ago. Further, his online Rebel Media empire went into a financial and political tailspin in the summer of 2017 in the wake of the Charlottesville neo-fascist rally and a series of lawsuits against him by his former British correspondents, who were linked to the extremist English Defence League. It would be a mistake, however, to underestimate Levant's ability to be the comeback kid of the ultra-conservative cause. In fact, after the collapse of Sun News Network, Levant entered his most successful period of activity. Rebel Media was growing, and Levant was instrumental in the rapid rise of Jordan Peterson in the global social-media world after Peterson's controversial anti-PC YouTube videos.

Levant had previously spent many years trying to unite the Canadian right behind the most extreme versions of conservative ideology. He had been unsuccessful in moving beyond the mostly aging White male audience for Sun News Network until he teamed up, informally but successfully, with Jordan Peterson in the fall of 2016. Inspired by Levant's critique of the Canadian Human Right Commission, Peterson shared with Levant a strategy of promoting conservative ideas through a "free speech" frame. This strategy was key to their popularity on the far right. Despite their very different politics, Levant and Peterson were allied during the dramatic events of 2016–17, Canada's campus-free-speech wars, up to and including the Lindsay Shepherd incident. Shepherd, a teaching assistant at Wilfrid Laurier University, was disciplined in an Orwellian manner after a tutorial in which she showed a debate from *The Agenda* between Peterson and another University of Toronto professor.

It is a major political and intellectual error, however, to dismiss Peterson as a right-wing extremist. In his heart, Peterson is essentially a centre-right intellectual with classical liberal convictions, whose obsession with Marxist academics, postmodernists, and feminists verges on the paranoid. He is more opportunistically attracted to fame than to joining the White nationalists. Now far more famous than Levant, Peterson no longer needs the Rebel network as he once did. Now we are seeing him distance himself from the most appalling of the far-right White nationalists on his massive Twitter feed, especially after he disinvited the extremist ethno-nationalist Faith Goldy from a rescheduled "free speech" event he held in the fall of 2017, an event that Ryerson University had cancelled earlier that year.

Peterson uses attempts to shut him down to build support for his brand and message. Political people opposed to Levant's goal of the Trumpification of Canada must be strategic. Attacking Peterson as though he were Levant will help build support for the right, not undermine it. Leaving open space for dialogue with Peterson and his followers may encourage him to continue moving to the centre-right, something that limits the further damage he can do to democracy and to the academy in Canada. Time will tell. But instead of thinking of Peterson as an academic Levant, a better way to think about him is as a cruder and less-progressive version of Jonathan Haidt, the co-author of a famous 2015 *Atlantic* article (and now book) entitled "The Coddling of the American Mind." Haidt's essay helped jumpstart the current debate on trigger warnings and political correctness on campus; his goal is the political diversification of the American academy, not its destruction. An opponent of the extremist movement in his country, Haidt represents a voice for the moderate centre, not for Trumpism or for white nationalism. Peterson and Haidt have known each other professionally for years, and if Peterson were to morph into a Canadian version of Haidt, he would remain a political adversary of liberals and the left. But at least he would not be bringing young Canadians in contact with White supremacists and dangerous reactionaries, as he was doing irresponsibly since late 2016 and early 2017.

We can't, of course, influence Peterson much, but the left-liberal and academic response to Peterson has been a flawed strategy based on a misreading of who he is. Attempts to stop Peterson from speaking, to fire him from his job, or to ban his interaction with students in the classroom are backfiring by creating more, not less, popular support for Trumpism in Canada. Such strategies push Peterson – and, more importantly, some of his followers – to the right. On my own campus at McMaster University, for example, a small group of activists effectively shut down Peterson's talk in the spring of 2017 by chanting and blowing horns, an action captured on smart-phone videos that then went viral. This protest polarized the campus, created more support for right-wing critiques of the university in Canada, and did nothing to enlighten students about how protecting transgender rights would expand democracy and human rights. This incident, along with the Lindsay Shepherd controversy at Laurier, reinforced Peterson's fame around the world and further polarized the debate about the state of Canadian universities in precisely the ways that Horowitz and Levant desire.

What is the best alternative path then for left-wing intellectuals and progressive academics to resist the spread of Trumpism in Canada? We need to stand up in a principled way for the rights of all speakers on campus, as long as they abide by Canada's hate-speech laws. Twelve years ago, I stood with academics, students, and staff at McMaster to defend the rights of Palestinian students to use the "Israeli Apartheid" language the McMaster University senior administrators at the time were trying to prohibit. Hate-speech laws are again being used inappropriately, this time against Peterson, by campus left-liberals, in contrast to their leverage by the right against Palestinian activists a decade ago. Neither incident involved hate speech as defined by Canadian law. In each case, political opponents of ideas should respond with peaceful protests, educational videos and op-eds, debates, or principled silent avoidance. It is naive to think we can interpret regulations and laws to silence those ideas we are offended by without setting in motion a dynamic that will allow these same regulations and laws to be used against Indigenous, progressive, Muslim, and critical voices in turn.

Moreover, there is simply no practical way to successfully defend left-wing ideas and anti-racist activists, Indigenous scholars, and feminist intellectuals on campus without being willing to work critically with university administration to defend the rights of all political and legally defensible viewpoints on campus. University administrators should not be given the power to decide who gets to speak on campus outside of narrow limits proscribed by law – hate speech, incitement to violence, libel, and slander – because over time they will abuse this power. Ironically, it is the principled conservatives – perhaps a laughable concept for some – who occupy an important place in challenging Trump's efforts in the United States today. Centrist and conservative journalists like David Frum, as well as the FBI, military leaders, and CIA staffers are playing a valiant role in trying to stop Trump's efforts to make the United States an authoritarian mafia state instead of just a democratic imperial bully.

The left in Canada and Indigenous activists have a far better chance of succeeding in a political climate if our adversaries are David Frum, Jonathan Kay, or the likes of Jonathan Haidt, and not David Horowitz, Ezra Levant, and Donald Trump. When we are dealing with the followers of Peterson, one major goal should be to assert a radical politics, but in ways that make it easier for the people who disagree to join moderate – not extremist right – groups. This needs to be done simultaneously with building movements of the left that reflect majority support for progressive social and foreign policy and for decolonization. More radical strategies should be done together with grassroots attempts to build bridges, for example between Muslim and Jewish women, as outlined in Kowalchuk's and Levine-Rasky's account of an organization that creates personal bonds between women who agree only on opposition to anti-Muslim bigotry and antisemitism. We need both broad coalition politics and principled militant resistance. Our resistance will certainly have to take seriously the critique of the conceptions of the "common good" that discount Indigenous rights, as articulated by Watts in this volume, as well as Palmater's powerful analysis of the similarities between centrist, even left, liberalism, and the right when it comes to pipelines and land. And we also have to work to build democratic majorities for radical change.

To do so, we must put aside some of our academic jargon and professional privileges and get outside the academic ivory tower to engage the public on vitally important political issues. We must convince Canadians of the need to protect LGBT rights, anti-racism and decolonization efforts, and broader union and democratic socialist values. The academic and intellectual left in Canada must put aside some of our abstract theories and the impulse to hide behind claims of "expert knowledge," a tendency rooted in the neo-liberal university critiqued by Newson in this volume.

We live in dangerous times, but there is also space opening up for radical change. Perry (in this volume) is correct that the far right is growing in Canada, and the militant anti-fascism stressed by both Day and Wood must be part of the strategy we need to support and promote. But we also need to meet and defeat the politics of Trump, Horowitz, and Levant through both mass politics in the electoral realm and intellectual debates on campus and in mass media. With these tools, we convince people that the left is not afraid of the arguments of our adversaries, because we have a vision and the practical knowledge required to build a more equal, just, and democratic society.

REFERENCES

Horowitz, David. 2006. *The Professors: The 101 Most Dangerous Academics in America*. Washington, DC: Regnery Publishing.
Lukeanoff, Greg, and Jonathan Haidt. 2015. "The Coddling of the American Mind." *Atlantic*, September. https://www.theatlantic.com/magazine/archive/2015/09/the-coddling-of-the-american-mind/399356/.
O'Neil, Terry. 2006. "Canada's Nuttiest Professors." *Western Standard*, 25 September.

15

THE MULTICULTURAL MYTH
Don Cherry and the Rise of Nationalism in Canadian Hockey

Stephen Sheps

Few sports seem to capture the hearts and minds of a nation the way that hockey does in Canada. Canadians obsess over hockey. At every level, from minor midget and peewee all the way through to the major junior and professional levels, many Canadians consume hockey voraciously. Hockey in Canada is as close to a universally beloved institution as baseball in the United States. Every year, hundreds of thousands of Canadians watch the World Junior Hockey Championship, a tournament that pits the top teenage Canadian men against the best teenage players from the rest of the world, while *Hockey Night in Canada* remains the highest-rated program on the CBC. Indeed, few would argue that hockey holds a special place in Canadian culture, serving as something of a binding agent for any and all Canadians.

The sport is seemingly ubiquitous and tied so deeply to the Canadian identity that it is referenced extensively in citizenship documents for new immigrants and has been used as a tool for socialization and acculturation for children across the country. On the surface then, it would seem that the game is as multicultural, open, and tolerant as the image the country wishes to project to other nations. However, when one digs a little bit deeper, we can start to see the cracks in the narrative, particularly in the way that hockey is portrayed in the media, and the culture of the sport that is not nearly as open or tolerant of others as it would appear. In spite of recent efforts at both the grassroots and national levels to encourage diversity within the sport, players of colour have been framed as "outspoken" or "lacking character," regardless of their skills or contributions both on and off the ice; Indigenous players, coaches, and management are virtually non-existent at major junior and professional levels (Valentine 2012); and players from other countries, regardless of age or skill level, are often rendered as Other by players, coaches, leagues, and mainstream sports media outlets (Cantlon 2018; Vecsey 1998). These representations in turn have created a fan culture informed by settler-colonial discourses, intolerance, and xenophobia, rather than one that embraces the perceived multicultural national narrative that Canadians present to the world.

In 2009, Chris Hanna of the Winnipeg-based anarchist punk band Propagandhi wrote a song called "Dear Coach's Corner" as a way of working through the disconnect he was feeling about the game he loves and the creeping influence of militarism, xenophobia, and a particular form of Canadian nationalism found in hockey broadcasts and throughout NHL arenas across the country (Propagandhi 2009). The lyrics were based on questions his niece asked while watching a game that featured yellow ribbons, tributes to the troops, and soldiers rappelling from the rafters, and the hyper-nationalist discourse regularly presented by Don Cherry on *Hockey Night in Canada* – the so called "Canadian Way." In a subsequent interview, Hanna referenced the discomfort he has with the NHL "mirroring the NFL in the States to get a captive audience of part of the population to mindlessly nod their heads at military adventurism overseas, especially to a whole nation of children watching on TV. I consider it a form of child abuse" (Mcleod 2009). While Hanna's comparison of the NHL and NFL is apt up to a point, particularly in terms of how the games are presented as an extension of militarism, patriotism, and nationalism, the differences in athletes' responses across the major professional sports in the two countries could not be more different. The so-called "Canadian Way" is embodied by a certain type of player as much by what they say (or do not say) as by who they are. It is built upon more than a century of using athletics to create an idealized Canadian citizen (Field 2012).

Though Hanna's song debuted nearly ten years ago, the ideas presented in his critique of populist-nationalism, militarism, and the ways in which Don Cherry and other hockey media personalities view Canada's role in the world is just as necessary and vital today. While Cherry himself is more a symptom than a cause, he embodies a mainstream perspective in Canada that has shifted ever rightward, one that espouses a populist rhetoric about the culture of the game and Canada's place in the world. When one considers his prominent position on the CBC's weekly hockey broadcast, he has something of a captive audience. The impact he has on the way younger players are socialized, as well as the types of discourses presented in hockey broadcasts, speaks to an increased emphasis on populist-style nationalism. The issue is less about what Cherry says, but rather about what his point of view represents and how it is used to socialize young players. In addition to the socialization process, the rhetoric Cherry espouses presents a new reading of the narrative about Canada's game and Canadian values that unsettles the widely held belief in liberal multiculturalism (McCurdy 2014; Gretz 2013). Ironically, while hockey is often viewed as Canada's game, it does not appear to be a particularly multicultural sport (Valentine 2012).

The predominant aspect of the Canadian national narrative is that it is a multicultural, ethnically and racially diverse, and remarkably tolerant nation-state. The narrative is reinforced through the official policy of multiculturalism built into the Charter of Rights and Freedoms, as well as the Multiculturalism Act of 1988. As a sport both produced and consumed nationally, hockey is a part of the narrative of the nation, but it also tends to run counter to it in a variety of ways. Indeed, the policy and the practices of citizens are often contradictory rather than complementary.

Every national narrative has its own set of mythologies. Hockey has been historically framed as Canada's national pastime, a game that all Canadians grow up playing – on the streets, at neighbourhood and community rinks (both indoor and outdoor), in organized children's, youth, adult, and recreation leagues around the country, as well as an event watched with friends and family (Brownlee 2017). Canada's 1972 win against the Soviet Union in the Canada-Russia summit series is viewed by many as Canada's defining moment during the Cold War, while the Stanley Cup playoffs is so popular in Canada that, despite the lack of Canadian teams in the playoffs and the fact that no Canadian team has won the Stanley Cup since 1993, ratings in Canada have not noticeably declined. Despite the Canadian NHL teams' recent history of limited success, sport media outlets, such as Yahoo's "Puck Daddy" blog and TSN, produced articles breaking down the "likeability" of playoff teams based purely on the number of Canadian players on each roster. These articles speak to emergent trends toward a more populist-nationalist rhetoric in Canadian sport coverage by mainstream media outlets aside from Don Cherry, which contribute to the ever-rightward shift in the discourse. Beyond the role of sport media in the process of socialization and acculturation, hockey is viewed as an essential component of what it means to be a Canadian citizen. Indeed, hockey is so deeply embedded in the Canadian national imaginary that it is referenced no less than twenty-six different times in the *Discover Canada* guide to citizenship for new immigrants (Canada 2012).

Taking this issue a step further, one must consider the challenge presented to new immigrant families within Canada about what sports to play. Historically, sport was viewed as both a site of acculturation and resistance for new immigrants, a space where children could be well integrated into new communities via play, as well as a site for old traditions to be maintained (Field 2012). Given hockey's prominence in Canada's immigration literature, one would assume that the sport would be as multicultural as the literature and policy documents suggest. However, there are several barriers to entry that cut across the intersection of race and class; hockey is a particularly expensive and time-consuming sport, one that requires a certain socio-economic position to allow kids to play in organized leagues. Beyond the financial challenges, White players predominantly play the sport, while players of colour and Indigenous players are significant minorities in both amateur and professional hockey. In 2016, it was noted that 93 per cent of NHL players are Caucasian. Hockey Canada, however, has only recently begun to address this gap, working with grassroots organizations across Canada to ensure that the game is more accessible and inclusive. A few examples of the diversity initiatives include its support and funding for women's hockey and sledge hockey, in addition to its co-sponsorship of the NHL's "You Can Play" and "Hockey Is for Everyone" programs. Agencies like the Hockey Canada Foundation have also recently started to address the ethno-racial gaps on the ice, creating more inclusive local and regional organizations and founding programs for hockey in Indigenous and Inuit communities. However, as necessary as these steps are, the culture of the game and the way it is represented in the media continue to lag behind.

To many, Don Cherry is a symbol of the quintessential Canadian identity, one that runs counter to the official narrative of multiculturalism. Cherry described a tournament win in 2015 against Russia using Cold War discourse, championing the virtues of Canadian players, their style of play, and their preparation habits, including something as seemingly innocuous as wearing suits to the rink, as a mark of Canadian superiority. The emphasis is on intangibles rather than skill sets. Cherry speaks about leadership, heart, and character – particularly among English Canadians – as qualities that other nationalities ostensibly lack.

One of Cherry's primary topics of conversation is the so-called "Canadian Way" in hockey. This is often couched in rhetoric around Canadian superiority in the sport, starting from the way young players are developed in Hockey Canada's system (Gretz 2013; Mahiban 2018). In a recent interview after the 2017–18 World Junior Hockey Championship tournament, a Canadian gold-medal victory against Sweden, Cherry stated (cited in Cantlon 2018):

> Our kids dress up after every game, they go to practice, and they dress up with shirts and ties. We look good, and we are the best. I know we're not supposed to say that in Canada, you know, that we are the best, because we're supposed to be second best all over the world. We are the best. I know our left-wing media hates to hear that because you read about how great the Swedes are. We dress good, we have good code, we have good sportsmanship, we are the best; we're different than other people.

On the surface, these ideas could simply be read as the ramblings of an out-of-touch celebrity, but the fact that they have been as prevalent over a sustained period demonstrates that the discourse has been rendered normative. It adds a level of uncertainty to the common perception or belief that Canada is as tolerant and multicultural in practice as it is in theory.

Superficially, there is nothing particularly offensive about Cherry's comment, but when placed into context, it speaks to a pattern of similarly populist-nationalist rhetoric that he has espoused for a number of years, from his critiques about European players' behaviour and "lack of character," to his constant vilification of Russian hockey players. Cherry has even gone on record to assert that the Canadian Hockey League, a major junior-development-league network for sixteen- to twenty-year-old players with leagues in Eastern Canada, Ontario, the West, and some US cities, should be made up of Canadian players exclusively (Gretz 2013; Mahiban 2018). European- or Russian-born players should not take spots away from good Canadian boys, Cherry urges, particularly goalies.

When one examines Cherry's views combined with his weekly national platform on the CBC and his outsized personality, it is easy to see how his form of populist nationalism is less about Don Cherry the former player, coach, and media personality and more about how media shapes general public discourse through language, symbols, and the presentation of ideology. While he continues his constant references about the need to support the Canadian military and his simultaneous critiques of the cultures of other nation-states, his role as an ambassador for the sport places him in close contact with young players and prospects nationwide; younger players view him as an embodiment of the so-called "Canadian Way" he espouses.

To paraphrase comments Cherry often makes, such as "Don't act like Ovechkin or these soccer-playing goofs, act like Joe Thornton, act like Steve Yzerman, act like Joe Sakic," he implicitly suggests that the "Canadian Way" is a culture based upon white, settler-colonial values (Broken Mystic 2009). This is similar to Claude Denis' "whitestream" concept, which positions whiteness, hegemonic masculinity, and capitalist values at the centre of Canadian society – and anything else on the outside (Denis 1997). While those particular comments of Cherry's are nearly ten years old, the results speak to an institutional practice that normalizes the "Canadian Way" discourse in hockey media, a legacy that builds upon a one-hundred-year old history of similar policies and practices designed for athletics to teach the "Canadian Way" (Field 2012). Jamie Cleland's research into racism in football in the United Kingdom provides an important perspective that could be applied to the context of Canadian sport. In a 2014 article, Cleland suggests that fan racism in UK football:

> [r]emains prominent in the virtual conversations taking place and tends to focus on national identity, belonging, and whiteness, as well as a resistance toward the Other (in particular Muslims) who are often blamed for social problems … The continued reference to non-Whites as being un-British even though they were born here supports the claim by Modood (2007) that communities seeking to be culturally different are often forgotten in the pursuit or expectation of a homogenous host culture containing discourse about the superiority of whiteness and its continued importance in symbolizing national identity and belonging (Cleland 2014).

Given the rise of explicitly white-nationalist organizations in Canada in recent years, "Canadian Way" rhetoric espoused by commentators such as Cherry could be used as another of the many tactics by the far right to prey upon the insecurities so many feel as a result of neo-liberal restructuring and the rise of precarious labour in Canada.

The NHL has not yet had a moment like the NFL or NBA, in which players have been compelled to openly address the shifting socio-political climate in Canada. For the most part, Canadian professional hockey players speak in clichés and broad generalizations, preferring not to engage with the media, even when the social issues are brought up in interviews. This silence extends to racialized players as well as White players, as the ostensible "Canadian Way" referenced by Cherry and others is rooted in a sense of "honour" and "knowing our place."

Like all national narratives or myths, the Canadian narrative is filled with contradictions. While the purpose of this essay is not to vilify Don Cherry the man, it calls into question what Don Cherry the character represents and how the ideology to which he contributes is easily passed on from generation to generation of young players. Sport is a primary agent of socialization and acculturation. Given the cultural value that is placed on hockey, and the value systems and structures found in the game, in addition to how these values are reinforced in the media coverage of the sport, resistance to these narratives will need to come from within the game in order to drive change. The culture of the sport is a reflection of the conservative mentality of the nation's more populist base, which has been connected both symbolically and symbiotically to the athletes. Until the players begin to see a reason to speak, it is unlikely that they will be the drivers of change that athletes in other nations have become.

Postscript

You people … you love our way of life, you love our milk and honey, at least you can pay a couple bucks for a poppy or something like that. These guys paid for your way of life that you enjoy in Canada, these guys paid the biggest price (Strong 2019).

Don Cherry was fired for the culturally insensitive comments he made on 9 November 2019, in which he accused immigrants – phrased as "you people" – of not caring enough about Remembrance Day and Canadian veterans' sacrifices. He devalued immigrants and immigration, effectively suggesting that certain people are not "Canadian" enough in his eyes. Given his history of defining what he believes to be the "Canadian Way," his words were ugly, but not shocking. Yet it wasn't just what Cherry said that made the network decide to fire him; it was about saying things that were much worse over his thirty-eight-year history on Canada's national broadcaster during a program that has been described as an essential component of Canadian cultural citizenship (Scherer and Whitson 2009).

Throughout his career, Cherry has said awful things about Russian players, Europeans, Francophones, Indigenous Canadians, and just about anyone who does not look or think like he does (Dallaire and Denis 2000; Scherer and Whitson 2009; Norman 2012). In 1990, when interviewed for *The Fifth Estate,* he claimed:

> Canadians are ticked off at the foreigners coming over earning the dough … I just say what I think, and that's the way I think. You can say it's bigotry if you want; I don't think it is … Canada first, and Canada only. That's what I am. A nationalist. I want to start a new power, the nationalists (Arthur 2019).

These comments made nearly thirty years ago demonstrate a pattern in Cherry's behaviour that is unchanging and only growing more extreme. Don Cherry represented a certain kind of cultural hegemony, rooted in traditionalism, overt nationalism, and a vocal fear of outsiders. Given this lengthy history, Cherry's final tirade was hardly a surprise. He was fired because he had to be. People had finally grown sick of enabling and defending him, hiding him, shielding him from criticism. The public outcry was finally too much for the network to bear. I won't miss him.

REFERENCES

Arthur, B. 2019. "It Really Should Be Game Over for Don Cherry This Time after Toxic 'You People' Rant." *The Star*, 10 November. https://www.thestar.com/sports/hockey/opinion/ 2019/11/10/it-really-should-be-game-over-for-don-cherry-this-time-after toxic-you-people-rant.html.

Broken Mystic. 2009. "Don Cherry's Xenophobic Remarks on Ovechkin Should Not Be Tolerated." 22 April. https://brokenmystic.wordpress.com/2009/04/22/don-cherrys-xenophobic-remarks-on-ovechkin-should-not-be-tolerated/.

Brownlee, R. 2017. "Everybody's Game." Oilersnation.com, 19 January. https://oilersnation.com/2017/01/19/everybody-s-game/.

Canada 2012. "Discover Canada: The Rights and Responsibilites of Citizenship." Ministry of Citizenship and Immigration. Ottawa: Ministry of Citizenship and Immigration.

Cantlon, K. 2018. "Puck Daddy." Yahoo Sports, 1 January. https://sports.yahoo.com/don-cherry-thoughts-dress-team-sweden-032535409.html.

Cleland, J. 2014. "Racism, Football Fans, and Online Message Boards: How Social Media Has Added a New Dimension to Racist Discourse in English Football." *Journal of Sport and Social Issues* 38 (5): 415–31.

Dallaire, C., and C. Denis. 2000. "If You Don't Speak French, You're Out": Don Cherry, the Alberta Francophone Games, and the Discursive Construction of Canada's Francophones." *The Canadian Journal of Sociology* 25 (4): 415–40.

Denis, C. 1997. *We Are Not You: First Nations and Canadian Modernity*. Peterborough: Broadview Press.

Field, R. 2012. "Sport and the Canadian Immigrant: Physical Expressions of Cultural Identity within a Dominant Culture, 1896–1945." In *Race and Sport in Canada: Intersecting Inequalities*, edited by J. Joseph, S. Darnell, and Y. Nakamura, 29–56. Toronto: Canadian Scholars Press.

Gretz, Adam. 2013. World Juniors: Don Cherry Isn't Taking Canada's Loss Very Well. CBS *Sport*, 4 January. https://www.cbssports.com/nhl/news/world-juniors-don-cherry-isnt-taking-canadas-loss-very-well/.

Hanna, C. (Composer). 2009. Dear Coach's Corner. [Propagandhi, Performer] *On Supporting Caste*. Winnipeg, MB: Smallman Records.

Mahiban, D. 2018. CBC, 25 January. http://www.cbc.ca/sports/hockey/nhl/don-cherry-not-happy-europeans-canadian-hockey-league-1.4503819.

McCurdy, B. 2014. "Cult of Hockey." *Edmonton Journal*, 28 December. http://
edmontonjournal.com/sports/hockey/nhl/cult-of-hockey/don-cherry-rips-
nail-yakupov-yet-again-calls-him-a-little-coward.

Mcleod, D. 2009. Interview. sb Nation, 2 November. https://www.silversevensens.
com/2009/11/2/1105762/interview-with-propagandhi.

Norman, M. 2012. "Saturday Night's Alright for Tweeting: Cultural Citizenship,
Collective Discussion, and the New Media Consumption/Production of Hockey
Day in Canada." *Sociology of Sport Journal* 29 (3): 306–24.

Scherer, J., and D. Whitson, 2009. "Public Broadcasting, Sport, and Cultural
Citizenship: The Future of Sport on the Canadian Broadcasting Corporation?"
International Review for the Sociology of Sport 44 (2–3): 213–29.

Strong, G. 2019. "Don Cherry Not Apologizing for Coach's Corner Poppy Rant."
cbc, 11 November. https://www.cbc.ca/sports/hockey/nhl/don-cherry-fired-
coaches-corner-1.5355764.

Valentine, J. 2012. "New Racism and Old Stereotypes in the National Hockey
League: The 'Stacking' of Aboriginal Players into the Role of Enforcer." In *Race
and Sport in Canada: Intersecting Inequalities*, edited by J. Joseph, S. Darnell,
and Y. Nakamura, 107–38. Toronto, on: Canadian Scholars Press.

Vecsey, G. 1998. "Sports of the Times; First Swedes Took Hit for Future." *New York
Times*, 16 January. Retrieved 11 December 2015. http://www.nytimes.com/1998/
01/16/sports/sports-of-the-times-first-swedes-took-hit-for-future.ht.

16

NEUTRALIZING STATE SECURITY THROUGH EXPOSURE AND DIRECT ACTION

Matthew Behrens

The most bizarre Halloween I ever spent involved trick-or-treating for secret evidence at the Canadian Security Intelligence Service (CSIS). The spy agency had been refusing to say why five Muslim men were being held indefinitely behind Canadian prison walls, without charge or access to bail, under a draconian process known as the security certificate,[1] which allowed any refugee or permanent resident to be disappeared on the basis of secret "national security" allegations that could never be challenged by detainees or their lawyers.

For the first time in its history, CSIS was on complete lockdown for five hours on 31 October 2003, as seventy-five individuals dressed in a variety of spy-themed costumes, from pipe-smoking, Sherlock-Holmes–style detectives to paper-bag-wearing ghouls channelling the ghost of Igor Gouzenko, paraded around the huge perimeter of the futuristic, *architortural* structure in Ottawa's east end. A large "counselling couch" was deposited at the front gates, with a trained therapist offering free therapy to spies afflicted with irrational fear of Muslims. Others proffered detailed plans on how to turn Canada's spy agency into Canada's pie agency (with a special recipe using Northern Spy apples as part of the transition to more socially useful purposes).

The protest, part of a national day of action focused on CSIS human-rights abuses – from racist and religious profiling to pressuring individuals in targeted communities to spy on their neighbours – emerged from a grassroots campaign that, while primarily focused on the cases of what became known as The Secret Trial Five, also questioned the core assumptions undergirding a Canadian state security apparatus operating on hyperdrive after 11 September 2001. During many post-9/11 years of intense fear and caution, few groups were willing to speak out for and walk with the families of those who were arbitrarily designated to be threats and cast outside the realm of due process.

Despite being protected by hundreds of Ottawa police, RCMP officers, undercover videographers, and some very hungry-looking police dogs, worried spies peeked out from behind the closed curtains of their office windows at the motley gathering, which looked more like a Renaissance fair than a state security alert. Thankfully for CSIS, this outbreak of democracy came to a close when an obvious entry point to the grounds was breached by an elderly Korean War veteran and three others. If CSIS were such a bunch of security geniuses, they wondered, why was the sliding electric fence, closed to prevent our access, planted a good eighteen inches off ground level?

When we arrestees sought disclosure to fight our trespassing charges in court, we were told by a befuddled Crown lawyer that the case had been dropped for reasons of "national security confidentiality."

The Halloween demonstration was organized by Homes not Bombs, a non-violent direct-action group whose Campaign to Stop Secret Trials in Canada has spent the past eighteen years working to abolish the security-certificate process and the deportation to torture that inevitably results when a certificate is upheld. The certificate represents a two-tier justice that springs from legislation declaring any such case can be upheld by anything not normally admissible in a court of law. The traditional equation of a "state security risk" with those who are "foreign" to Canada places those subject to this Kafkaesque, star-chamber nightmare very low on most political agendas.

But our campaign, working with small groups of allies across Canada, shifted the focus from alleged terror threats to something more accurate and specific: repression based on racist assumptions, resulting in years of solitary confinement, permanent damage to reputations and livelihoods, and family breakup. The campaign's operating principles are anathema to state security agencies: consistent exposure of their criminality; pointed questioning of the need for such institutions, which exist to protect power and privilege; humanizing of those who, through security-threat designation, lose the rights and recognitions associated with being human; and refusal to be afraid.

The campaign employed tactics that are hallmarks of actions by Homes not Bombs. Creative, theatrical, humorous elements saw everyone from

Santa Claus to the Easter Bunny resisting secret trials, while hundreds of demonstrations featured black-hooded individuals in orange jumpsuits, the still-jarring universal symbol of the war of (not on) terror. We opposed wholesale the so-called anti-terror legislation, refusing to tinker with a fundamentally flawed system. Also critical was how the relative privilege of core campaign organizers – almost all from outside targeted communities – provided a safer space for the wives and children of detainees, and for those suffering behind bars.

Word also got around fast among those in targeted Arab, Muslim, and South Asian communities that ours was a campaign that would take on the cases few others would touch. We also advocated for those rendered overseas to torture based on false information created by the RCMP and CSIS, refugees whose cases were too problematic for most NGOs, and others who had run afoul of state security agencies. Also crucial was the small handful of truly dedicated lawyers who appreciated that political and community support were key parts of these epic legal battles.

The campaign saved lives and placed a serious restraint on the exercise of one of the most draconian powers authorized by parliament. Whereas Federal Court rubber-stamping of security certificates normally meant swift deportation, the Secret Trial Five are all still in Canada, with three cases dismissed and two still fighting deportation to torture. Following two days of historic hearings in 2006, the Supreme Court unanimously concluded that security certificates were unconstitutional. While some two dozen certificates were issued from 1991 to 2003, CSIS issued only one new certificate between 2003 and 2018, a reflection of a different political climate.

Frustrated CSIS officials were clearly vexed by this modest-but-powerful resistance. They spoke publicly of "judicial jihad" when courts that traditionally provided an automatic seal of approval began to ask a few questions. One CSIS director complained that the Secret Trial Five had been turned into "folk heroes," because grandmothers and grade-school students alike sent scores of monthly cards and letters to the detainees. Diligent grassroots work opened the doors enough to have major media outlets interview all detainees during their time behind bars, when hunger strikes lasting as long as 155 days became the focus of significant parliamentary debates and cabinet conferences.

Each detainee was clear: if you have a case, charge me in open court, share the evidence, and if I'm convicted after a fair process, throw away the key. But CSIS knew its cases would never pass the more rigorous scrutiny of criminal court proceedings. Indeed, access-to-information requests revealed CSIS's admission that if information gleaned from torture had to be excluded from security-certificate cases they would collapse. While the revised security-certificate process passed in 2008 remains fundamentally unjust, the addition of security-cleared lawyers (special advocates) helped reveal that, in two cases, CSIS knew – but had withheld from judges – that their secret informants had lied.

While the Secret Trial Five's continued presence in Canada is worthy of celebrating, the costs remain huge, from PTSD and permanently scarred reputations to communities fearful of one of their own, over whom the term "suspect" will always hang.

The ongoing work of the secret-trials campaign yields certain lessons about the value of questioning authority and taking the time to thoroughly analyze the outrageous policies and practices of state security agencies; it also emboldens Homes not Bombs, which has always been dedicated to tackling the interrelated tentacles of violence represented by a nation that pours over $20 billion annually into war at home and abroad. We also work to support women who are behind bars because they have defended their right to live in the face of male violence; try to open church doors to provide sanctuary for refugees who face deportation to situations of grave injustice; and build solidarity with communities of land defenders attempting to stop cultural genocide, such as the Labrador Land Protectors at Muskrat Falls.

Underlying our work is a clear understanding that we ourselves have been designated a threat to state security, which we humbly accept as a badge of honour. Why wouldn't it be a given that we pose a threat to a state based on genocide and colonial dispossession of Indigenous lands, one that operates solely to create and maintain a gross economic and social inequality, in which "acceptable" levels of poverty and homelessness, pollution and environmental degradation are simply standard operating procedure?

A cursory overview of Canadian history reveals that crimes of the past (think residential schools, mass internment, persecution based on sexual orientation) are not aberrations or mistakes, but logical outcomes of a very violent system that views as the gravest of threats the growth of grass-roots democracy.

When we organized a number of Ontario-wide educational caravans to stop Canadian involvement in torture, the RCMP engaged in a cross-country consultation with many of its divisions on how best to handle this street-level protest, which they filed and surveilled under "Criminal Act by Terrorists – Protest/Demonstrations/Marches." At least a dozen of our vigils made it onto the infamous list of demonstrations monitored as threats by the Government of Canada Operations Centre.

This core operational principle of governments was documented in the report *The Crisis of Democracy*, produced by a group of North American, European, and Japanese academics and industrialists (the Trilateral Commission), who, investigating how to reduce the power of the social movements of the 1960s and 1970s, famously wrote that the dangers to "democracy" as they defined it come "not primarily from external threats ... but rather from the internal dynamics of democracy itself in a highly educated, mobilized, and participant society ... There are also potentially desirable limits to the indefinite extension of political democracy" (Crozier et al. 1975, 115).

In other words, governments and their corporate masters rely on a quiet, accepting population to enforce policies that benefit the rich few and exploit the many. The conclusion here is simple: people protesting war and inequality were suffering from an "excess of democracy," which had to be reined in through a conscious application of economic austerity and lowered expectations, defined thusly: "The effective operation of a democratic political system usually requires some measure of apathy and noninvolvement on the part of some individuals and groups" (Crozier et al. 1975, 114).

Recognizing how little it takes to shake the fragility of power (why else would so many billions be poured into state surveillance of every single thing we do, if not for the fear of democracy?), Homes Not Bombs continues to promote non-violent direct action as an incredibly powerful tool that can restrain state power. During 2018, we organized two direct actions to bring the faces of those most at risk from the Muskrat Falls megadam directly into the House of Commons. Thirty of us were arrested and banned from Parliament Hill. In January, a small group of us put the massive Global

Affairs bunker on lockdown for three hours when we tried to deliver to Chrystia Freeland a ready-to-sign letter cancelling the $15-billion Saudi weapons deal.

Equally important is recognizing that everything we have witnessed in the past two decades – arbitrary imprisonment without charge based on racist profiling, renditions to torture, spying on communities, extrajudicial executions – is nothing new, and in fact has long been directed first and foremost against Indigenous peoples.

Ultimately, the history of security states is the history of people's resistance to them, in particular social movements led by women, Indigenous people, racialized communities, labour, anti-war groups, and more. Undergirding them is a lesson we have learned and hope to continue sharing: a refusal to be afraid springs from the recognition that we have more power than we know, and that the exercise of that power may well be the key to resisting a system that, absent our direct intervention, has our species slated for extinction.

How best to exercise that power is an evolving question, but clues can be found among those who are deemed the greatest risk to state security: Indigenous land defenders, those who reject electoral politics as a one-trick pony, communities that self-organize, organizers who embrace the radicalism that gets to the root of problems as a means of hammering out transformative solutions. Knowing our history and celebrating and sharing our victories is as important as a willingness to discard old organizing models that reinforce the very systems of domination that require disarming. As the late resister Daniel Berrigan reminded us, "A revolution is interesting insofar as it avoids like the plague the plague it promised to heal" (cited in Marsh and Brown 2012).

NOTE

1 Under the *Immigration and Refugee Protection Act* (IRPA), CSIS can initiate a "security certificate" that results in the arrest and indefinite detention of permanent residents or refugees who have committed no crime. The basis for the certificate is secret; the standard of proof is the lowest of any process in Canada; and IRPA dictates that "the judge may receive into evidence anything that, in the

opinion of the judge, is appropriate, even if it is inadmissible in a court of law, and may base the decision on that evidence." Those who lose certificate cases often face deportation to torture.

REFERENCES

Crozier, Michel J., Samuel P. Huntington, and Joji Watanuki. 1975. *The Crisis of Democracy: Report on the Governability of Democracies to the Trilateral Commission*. New York: New York University Press.

Marsh, James, and Anna Brown. 2012. *Faith, Resistance, and the Future: Daniel Berrigan's Challenge to Catholic Social Thought*. New York: Fordham University Press.

17

DISRUPTING PROTEST AND DISTRUSTING THE POLICE

Lesley J. Wood

On 21 January 2017, militant protesters attempted to disrupt the inauguration of Donald Trump. They marched en masse, filled the streets, used spray paint, smashed storefronts, pushed past police lines, and destroyed a limousine as they confronted the arrival of the right-wing president. Two hundred and thirty protesters were charged with felony and riot, charges that carry up to a decade in prison and a $25,000 fine (Lennard 2017). They were wildly outgunned. For the event, the DC police spent over $300,000, of which $42,000 went for less-lethal munitions (140 Stinger Rubber Ball Grenades, 140 Rubber Baton Rounds, and 20 smoke bombs) (National Lawyers Guild 2017). This is the latest chapter in a widespread trend of militarization of police, and its attempt to pacify protest. Such policing is exacerbating a crisis of legitimacy in the state and in the police, and shaping movements themselves. Normally, felony charges are not laid en masse. Mara Verheyden-Hilliard, from the Partnership for Civil Justice Fund, argued that arrests "simply based on proximity or shared political views at a march" set a troubling precedent. It implies that, if a participant or a provocateur commits an illegal act at any demonstration, then "the entire demonstration can be subject to indiscriminate force and large groups of people can be suddenly arrested without notice or opportunity to disperse, and face life-altering charges" (Lennard 2017). Eventually, those charges were dropped.

Police attempts to maintain control are not new. The police are an armed institution, given extensive powers in an unequal system rooted in the emergence of the modern capitalist state. Today they use a model of repression that has been described as "strategic incapacitation" (Gillham, Edwards, and Noakes 2013). This model combines less-lethal weapons, specialized units, spatial control, and intelligence gathering to manage protest. In Canada, the G20 protests of 2010 in Toronto represented a high (or low) point of this strategy. Leaders at that summit justified maintaining the existing economic system after the global economic crisis, defending themselves with over one billion dollars' worth of security (Wood 2014). Police surrounded the venue with a security wall, brought officers from over fifty police agencies into the city to join an integrated security unit, infiltrated movement meetings and social events, pre-emptively arrested organizers, and then, after some protesters smashed shop windows, kettled, arrested, and detained over a thousand people. Ontario Ombudsman André Marin described it as "the most massive compromise of civil liberties in Canadian history" (Bugajski 2010).

This militarization is institutionalized in even the largest agencies. In 2015, amid widespread protests against the racist police killing of Eric Garner, the NYPD commissioner formed a special tactical unit called the Strategic Response Group. It was "designed for dealing with events like our recent protests, or incidents like Mumbai or what just happened in Paris." Although he later retreated from his conflation of protests and terrorist threats, his language was not accidental (Gould-Wartofsky 2015). In Baltimore after the police killing of Freddy Gray, local police launched a full-scale offensive against protesters. They used what they described as a "military counter attack vehicle" known as a Bearcat, SWAT teams armed with assault rifles, shotguns loaded with lead pellets, barricade projectiles filled with tear gas, and military-style smoke grenades. They also employed "Hailstorm" or "Stingray" technology, originally used in warfare to conduct wireless surveillance of enemy communications. Such tools allow officers to force cellphones to connect to their systems, to collect mobile data, and to jam cell signals within a one-mile radius (Gould-Wartofsky 2015).

Despite, or perhaps partly because of, such a strategy, the protests against racist police brutality accelerated. In 2016, hundreds of protesters were arrested in New York, Chicago, St Paul, Minnesota, and Baton Rouge, Louisiana, after police killed two Black men, Philando Castile and Alton Sterling, in separate incidents (Fantz and Visser 2016). The battleground goes beyond the streets. In 2017, a leaked FBI counter-terrorism report identified a new domestic threat – Black Identity Extremists (Cosme 2017). Such a category underscored the way that intelligence and police understand and categorize activists who challenge racial inequality. The movement is framed as an enemy. Indeed, during the fall of 2017, police in St Louis, Missouri, chanted the well-known activist slogan, "Whose streets? Our Streets!" while they cleared the streets of anti-racist police brutality protesters.

This language of terrorism was also used against the Standing Rock protesters who were challenging the building of the Dakota Access Pipeline. TigerSwan, a US military and State Department contractor, hired by the builders of the pipeline, Energy Transfer Partners, described the anti-pipeline movement as "an ideologically driven insurgency with a strong religious component" and "compared the anti-pipeline water protectors to jihadist fighters" (Brown, Parrish, and Speri 2017). This echoes an earlier RCMP intelligence report, which described anti-pipeline activists, noting, "There is a growing, highly organized and well-financed anti-Canada petroleum movement that consists of peaceful activists, militants and violent extremists who are opposed to society's reliance on fossil fuels" (McCarthy 2017). As Behrens (2019) and Palmater (2019) note in this volume, presenting Indigenous water defenders as terrorists justifies a militarized approach that pre-empts and contains dissent (Ljunggren and Williams 2016).

This militarization is most likely to occur when the security budget is significant, the event is high profile, and protesters refuse to co-operate with the police or are seen as "threatening" because of race, ideology, age, or organizational form. The trend of making intelligence and threat assessments central to police strategy emerges from an emphasis on cost cutting that pushed for "intelligence-led policing strategies," combined with the context of the war on terror.

But this expanding logic of "total security" is contributing to an ongoing problem of legitimacy for the police. The roots of this lie in the crisis of capitalism and the neo-liberal state, which offers little for the marginalized or impoverished sections of society. Indeed, the main task of the neo-liberal state seems to be promoting and protecting the concentration of wealth, and increasing inequality (Murakami Wood, this volume). Police are called on to defend this arrangement, at the same time that global elites are increasingly globalized and unaccountable. They do so using the tools at their disposal. As an institution which has a tendency to be violent, corrupt, and racist, policing also tends to undermine its own support. Every time a middle-class college kid is arrested and beaten; every time social media circulates video of police shooting a young Black man on camera; every time a corruption scandal is revealed, support for the police is weakened among increasing sections of the public.

This crisis of legitimacy is highlighted by social movements. This became more visible in 2013, when Patrisse Cullors, Alecia Garza, and Opal Tometi founded #BlackLivesMatter as they organized against the acquittal of George Zimmerman, who had shot and killed Black teen Trayvon Martin (Black Lives Matter n.d.). That July, protests in over a hundred cities focused attention on anti-Black racism, on the inadequacy of the justice system, and, most clearly, on the police themselves. The following week, in Toronto, police officer James Forcillo shot and killed Sammy Yatim on a streetcar, and a video circulated. Within twenty-four hours, a Facebook page, "Sammy's Fight for Justice," had almost six thousand "likes." Hundreds of people marched and, in the face of public outrage, Toronto police suspended the officer, who was later convicted of attempted murder.

This movement against racist police violence accelerated when Mike Brown was shot and killed in 2014 in Ferguson, Missouri. Across the United States, Canada, and beyond, protests against racist police brutality shut down highways and shopping malls, marched and mobilized (Maynard 2017). As Trump campaigned, national networks linked local activists through the Movement for Black Lives, Showing Up for Racial Justice, Avaaz, and networks of Occupy activists. As Trump's campaign continued, these formations made the links between police and political neglect of missing and murdered Indigenous women and rape culture, between Bill C51 and immigrant detention, against carding, between police in schools and the police targeting of racialized communities, between those working against the prison industrial complex and those working to support immigrants. In the courtroom, legal opposition has become emboldened. In the Trump era, the American Civil Liberties Union, the National Lawyers Guild, the Canadian Civil Liberties Association, and the provincial law unions have challenged both the weapons and the logics of militarized policing. Inquiries and lawsuits challenge the racism and violence, and the restrictions on civil liberties.

The combination of militarized police and strong movements against them puts pressure on the relationship between political authorities and police agencies. In New York City, at the height of the wave of anti-police-brutality protests, two officers were killed, and, frustrated with the mayor's response, NYPD officers turned their backs on him. In Montreal, police arrested the mayor, and in Toronto, they almost did. The length of time that police chiefs last in office is declining (Hall 2015). In Toronto, the chief responsible for the G20 didn't have his contract renewed. Instead, apparently partly in response to accusations of racism, a new chief was chosen between two Black senior officers. Tension between mayors and police leadership is increasing.

This leads the police to a conundrum. Public confidence in the police in the United States is at the lowest it has been since 1993 (Jones 2015). In Canada, racialized communities show diminishing trust in police. In the United States, numbers of police recruits have declined (Libaw 2017). Morale is low. Police budgets, which have ballooned for twenty years, are now being questioned. "Law and order" is no longer a magic spell. There are inquiries, class-action lawsuits, and threats of oversight. While real constraints on policing are limited, many voices are calling the role of the police into question.

In 2014, *Rolling Stone* magazine published an article, "Policing Is a Dirty Job, but Nobody's Gotta Do It: 6 Ideas for a Cop-Free World" (Martín 2014). New York City criminologist Alex Vitale recently published "The End of Policing" (Vitale 2017). In 2014, Toronto criminal lawyer Peter Rosenthal argued in a local newsweekly that most police should be disarmed (Rosenthal 2014). The chasm between police and the public is wider than it has been in the recent past. When widely supported movements challenge the police, there is new momentum to shrink the power of police, and to handle questions of security in other ways. To defend their undocumented residents from arrest and deportation, many cities are declaring themselves Sanctuary or Solidarity cities. Movements are monitoring the police in their communities and at their demonstrations. School boards and community agencies are removing the welcome mat. In November 2017, the Toronto District School Board heeded the critique that having armed police in the schools reinforces racism and hampers the learning environment and thus ended the School Resource Officer program. While alternatives to policing are still nascent, movements, particularly those led by Black and Indigenous activists, are replacing aspects of the criminal justice system with restorative and transformative justice initiatives.

As Chris Dixon notes, movements operate simultaneously within the existing system, against the existing system, and beyond the existing system

(Dixon 2014). In this way, we must build the power of ordinary people to control their own lives, lifting up the voices of those most affected by injustice. Resisting racialized and militarized policing means both continuing to protest, and building alternatives that reduce harm and injustice and build power in ways that lead away from the police and violence. At a moment when the police work to neutralize and demonize street protest, defending the space is crucial. That space allows us to breathe and stretch, and build the relationships which will allow for grounded, dynamic, and just worlds to grow.

REFERENCES

Black Lives Matter. n.d. Herstory. https://blacklivesmatter.com/about/herstory/.

Brown, Allen, Will Parrish, and Alice Speri. 2017. "Leaked Documents Reveal Counterterrorism Tactics Used at Standing Rock to "Defeat Pipeline Insurgencies." *The Intercept*, 27 May. https://theintercept.com/2017/05/27/leaked-documents-reveal-security-firms-counterterrorism-tactics-at-standing-rock-to-defeat-pipeline-insurgencies/.

Bugajski, Tomasz. 2010. "Ombudsman's G20 Report Cites Civil Liberties Violations." blogTO, 7 December. http://.www.blogto.com/city/2010/12/ombudsmans_g20_report_cites_civil_liberties_violations/.

Cosme, Shante. 2017. "Black Lives Matter Co-Founder Patrisse Cullors on Mass Incarceration: 'Our Everyday Lives Are Criminalized.'" Complex, 17 November. http://www.complex.com/life/2017/11/patrisse-cullors-justice-la-blm-interview.

Dixon, Chris. 2014. *Another Politics: Talking Across Today's Transformative Movements*. University of California Press.

Fantz, Ashley, and Steve Visser. 2016. "Hundreds Arrested in Protests Over Shootings by Police." CNN, 4 August. https://www.cnn.com/2016/07/10/us/black-lives-matter-protests/index.html.

Gillham, Patrick F., Bob Edwards, and John A. Noakes. 2013. "Strategic Incapacitation and the Policing of Occupy Wall Street Protests in New York City." *Policing and Society* 23 (1): 81–102.

Gould-Wartofsky, Michael. 2015. "5 Tools the Police Are Using in Their War Against Activists." *The Nation*, 5 May. https://www.thenation.com/article/5-tools-police-are-using-their-war-against-activists/.

Hall, Rob. 2015. "3 Harsh Realities of Being a Police Chief." Policeone.com, 3 December. https://www.policeone.com/chiefs-sheriffs/articles/49533006-3-harsh-realities-of-being-a-police-chief/.

Jones, Jeffrey. 2015. "In U.S., Confidence in Police Lowest in 22 Years." Gallup.com, 19 June. http://news.gallup.com/poll/183704/confidence-police-lowest-years.aspx.

Lennard, Natasha. 2017. "How the Government Is Turning Protesters into Felons." *Esquire*, 12 April. http://www.esquire.com/news-politics/a54391/how-the-govern ment-is-turning-protesters-into-felons/.

Libaw, Oliver Yates. 2017. "Police Face Severe Shortage of Recruits." ABC News, July 10. http://abcnews.go.com/US/story?id=96570&page=1.

Ljunggren, David, and Nia Williams. 2016. "Canada Energy Companies, Police Scramble to Protect Pipelines." Reuters, 14 October. https://www.reuters.com/ article/us-usa-canada-pipelines-threat/canada-energy-companies-police-scramble-to-protect-pipelines-idUSKBN12E2C4.

Martín, José. 2014. "Policing Is a Dirty Job, But Nobody's Gotta Do It: 6 Ideas for a Cop-Free World." *Rolling Stone*, 16 December. https://www.rollingstone.com/ politics/news/policing-is-a-dirty-job-but-nobodys-gotta-do-it-6-ideas-for-a-cop-free-world-20141216.

Maynard, Robyn. 2017. *Policing Black Lives: State Violence in Canada from Slavery to the Present*. Halifax and Winnipeg: Fernwood Books.

McCarthy, Shawn. 2017. "'Anti-Petroleum' Movement a Growing Security Threat to Canada, RCMP Say." *Globe and Mail*, 17 February. https://www.theglobeand mail.com/news/politics/anti-petroleum-movement-a-growing-security-threat-to-canada-rcmp-say/article23019252/.

National Lawyers Guild, DC Chapter. 2017. Press Release: DC Police Spent over $300,000 in Weapons, Ammunition to Use against Inauguration Day Protesters. https://dcnlg.wordpress.com/.

Rosenthal, Peter. 2014. "Disarm Most Police Officers: Peter Rosenthal's Big Ideas." *Star*, 27 February. https://www.thestar.com/bigideas/experts/2014/02/27/disarm_ most_police_officers_peter_rosenthals_big_ideas.html.

Vitale, Alex. 2017. *The End of Policing*. Brooklyn and London: Verso Books.

Wood, Lesley J. 2014. *Crisis and Control: The Militarization of Protest Policing*. London and Toronto: Pluto Press/Between the Lines.

18

BUILDING A MOVEMENT OF RESISTANCE
TO THE FAR RIGHT

Carolyn Egan and Michelle Robidoux

On 11 August 2017, neo-Nazis gathered in Charlottesville, Virginia, with the stated intention of showing their strength and spewing their bigotry. It was absolutely chilling to watch them march in a torchlight parade, chanting "Jews will not replace us," "blood and soil." It was no accident that it brought to mind the horror of the Ku Klux Klan.

We are seeing the growth of the far right across the globe: Golden Dawn in Greece, the National Front in France, Britain First in the United Kingdom, the Alternative für Deutschland in Germany – and Canada is not immune. The Proud Boys, the Sons of Odin, and the Canadian Nationalist Party are all gaining members. At the time of writing, Quebec's anti-Muslim group La Meute has over seventeen thousand Facebook followers (La Meute Publique n.d.). Though these groups are still relatively small, they are moving from the margins to the centre and attempting to push the political dialogue sharply to the right. Islamophobia, anti-Black racism, and bigotry of all sorts are becoming even more rampant since the economic crisis of 2008. This chapter will concentrate on the growth of racism against the Muslim community and how we can fight it.

The Global Context and Canada

We believe it is important to situate this phenomenon in a political context. Since 9/11, anti-Muslim sentiment has grown, aided and abetted by government policies and actions. Through the wars in Afghanistan and Iraq, fuelled by a colonial legacy and imperialist designs, Western governments have demonized Muslim nations and the people who inhabit them. At the height of Canada's involvement in the occupation of Afghanistan, then–Chief of Defense Staff General Rick Hillier said of the forces Canada was fighting, "These are detestable murderers and scumbags, I'll tell you that right up front. They detest our freedoms, they detest our society, they detest our liberties" (Anonymous 2005 [2013]). This is a clear indicator of the views of the military leadership. It is, of course, nothing new. We need only remember the torture and murder of Shidane Arone, a young Somali man, by Canadian paratroopers stationed in Mogadishu on a "peacekeeping" mission in 1993.

It is ironic that we were told Canada had invaded Afghanistan to "liberate" Muslim women, while the Canadian government was enacting policies at home that took away their right to personal autonomy, by banning the wearing of the niqab during citizenship ceremonies. Women have always been victimized by war. The numbers of those who died as "collateral" damage and the vicious harassment to which Muslim women have been subjected on the streets of Canada have a direct connection to government Islamophobia. Imperialism and war are no friends of women at home or abroad.

The Conservative government under Stephen Harper ratcheted up the rhetoric, taking a strong pro-war stance and putting forward policies demonizing the Muslim community as part of the "war on terror." This in no way diminishes the negative legacy of the Liberals, who are also culpable. We have witnessed csis complicity in the deportation of Canadian citizen Maher Arar to Syria, where he was tortured and imprisoned, only to later be exonerated. Canadian agents assisted US forces in interrogating Omar Khadr at Guantanamo, for which he was later compensated ten million dollars. Security certificates have been used by both Liberal and Conservative governments to imprison Muslim men without trial in the name of fighting terrorism.

In 2015, the Conservatives put forward the Zero Tolerance for Barbaric Cultural Practices Act, clearly targeting the Muslim community. There is no doubt they were enacting policies to divide people one from another, build distrust, and increase xenophobia as they moved the neo-liberal agenda forward in the interest of the 1 per cent. They were attempting to maintain power by speaking of "old stock" Canadians, differentiated from newer immigrant populations. In her failed bid for the leadership of the

Conservative Party, Kellie Leitch, a former cabinet minister, was particularly vehement about the need to maintain "our values."

This attempt to whip up anti-Muslim sentiment did not go unchallenged. A bus chartered by Women Working with Immigrant Women, a racialized women's organization, brought people to Leitch's constituency office in rural Alliston, Ontario. They picketed, put anti-racist placards on the walls and windows of her office, and had positive discussions with her constituents, including high-school students who joined the rally. Signs appeared on lawns in the riding, stating of Leitch, "Not My MP." The Liberals won the 2015 federal election, but there are still Canadian troops in Iraq and an ongoing inability to deal with Canada's colonial legacy and the travesty of missing and murdered Indigenous women.

In Quebec, before the 2014 provincial election, the Parti Québécois tried to inflame xenophobic feelings by putting forward a Charter of Values that would have enshrined the "traditional values" of the majority and targeted religious minorities. The party was defeated. But in 2017, with Bill 62, the "Act to Foster Adherence to State Neutrality," the provincial Liberal government banned anyone wearing a niqab from accessing public services, including the transit system. This was done in the name of women's equality and *laïcité*, or secularism, while a large crucifix still hangs in Québec's National Assembly. This was an absolute travesty, which unfortunately followed in the footsteps of similar legislation in France. There, schoolgirls were banned from wearing the hijab to school in 2004, followed by more repressive measures, including the recent "burkini" fiasco. In response, non-Muslim women in Montreal covered their faces and rode the subways in solidarity, and transit workers have refused to be "niqab police." The law, vigorously protested by Muslim organizations and the Canadian Civil Liberties Association, was later blocked in the courts and was subsequently shelved when the Liberals lost the provincial election in 2018. But, worryingly, a poll found that 87 per cent in the province, as well as a majority in English Canada, supported the legislation (Shingler 2017). And as Howard's essay in this volume observes, the governing Coalition Avenir Québec's Bill 21 – the Act Respecting the Laicity of the State – passed into law in June 2019, is even more limiting of religious expression than its predecessor Bill 62.

Quebec is not more racist than the rest of Canada. One of the corner-stones of the Quiet Revolution was breaking the control of the Catholic church in so many areas of everyday life. This left a strong tendency to oppose any encroachment by religion on public life, particularly in the older generation. This has unfortunately led to a confusion in many people's minds about the difference between state-enforced religion and the right of individuals to religious freedom, including the display of religious garb, such as a turban, yarmulke, or niqab. Today, this confusion is compounded by a constant ratcheting up of anti-Muslim bigotry. And, of course, racist activities are taking place in every province, not just in Quebec. The widespread practice by Canadian police forces of "carding" racialized people is a case in point.

It is very important that progressives get this right. In France, many in the feminist movement and the left have supported regressive measures, such as banning the hijab, niqab, or burkini, ceding ground to the fascist National Front, which was a major contender in the last round of French elections. The Socialist Party, among its many failings (including attacks on labour rights and the implementation of austerity and budget cuts) supported these racist restrictions. Jean-Luc Mélenchon, the presidential candidate on the left in the last election, has taken very problematic positions on Muslim women wearing the niqab or burkini. In the intense climate of Islamophobia in France, this is a disaster. France's Muslim community has opposed this, and others have fought back as well, including feminist intellectual and activist Christine Delphy (2015), who has been a strong and consistent voice against Islamophobia from the government and the right, but also from the left and the women's movement.

There is a toxic mix of racism and sexism at work. Secularism should mean the separation of church and state, not the denial of religious freedom and the targeting of vulnerable populations. It is up to a woman to choose whether or not to wear a hijab or niqab, not the role of the state to impose a position. Anything else maintains women's oppression.

The Trump Election: Repression and Resistance

The victory of Donald Trump has emboldened the right and the far right in both the United States and Canada, shifting the political terrain and giving confidence to bigots and racists. The neo-liberal agenda has been wreaking havoc with the poor and the working class for some time, and the Republican victory has taken this even further. Scapegoating is rampant, and the most vulnerable in our society – racialized and Indigenous communities, women, LGBTQ people – are under renewed attack. Racism and misogyny are coming from the highest levels of government, and the forces of the far right are raising their banners in city squares, boldly marching in the streets and holding meetings on university campuses.

On Sunday, 29 January, just over a week after Trump's inauguration, six Muslim men were massacred while praying in their Quebec City mosque. Alexandre Bissonnette, a student influenced by far-right ideas, attacked what he saw to be the "enemy within." Though this was an isolated incident, it speaks to a virulent atmosphere of hate. In Ontario, the Quran was ripped apart during a school-board meeting in Peel Region outside Toronto, as demonstrators shouted anti-Muslim slogans. In Halifax, Proud Boys attacked Indigenous activists at a ceremony opposing colonial statues. In this case, in addition to being members of the white nationalist group, they happened to be members of the Canadian Armed Forces.

Whether it be Charlottesville, Toronto, or France, the far right finds the fault lines and tailors its message of hate to the circumstances – whether it be defending Confederate statues, attacking Jews, Black people, or Muslim communities. The old adage of divide and rule is in play.

But it doesn't have to be this way.

Solidarity

The Trump victory has had a measurable impact in emboldening the right – but it has also produced inspiring mobilizations of solidarity. Trump's inauguration took place on 20 January. On 21 January, sixty thousand demonstrated in Toronto against racism and misogyny in both countries. On 27 January, Trump instituted his "Muslim ban." It was met with mass protests at airports across the United States. Cab drivers in New York went on strike, refusing to pick up fares at the airport. On 28 January, the American Civil Liberties Union (ACLU) won an injunction against the ban. On 29 January, in response to the attack on the Quebec City mosque, thousands gathered in vigils across the country. In Toronto on 30 January, over a thousand people came together for a candlelight procession to an east-end mosque. On 3 February, an estimated eighteen hundred east-end residents gathered in solidarity at another local mosque.

On 15 February, a mass meeting of a thousand supporters of the right and the far right took place in Toronto. The meeting, which featured prominent Conservative MPs Kellie Leitch, Chris Alexander, and Brad Trost, was organized to oppose a parliamentary motion against Islamophobia (Motion 103). Two days later, participants from that rally blockaded Masjid Toronto, a downtown mosque, chanting anti-Muslim slogans. When the word got out on Facebook, there was an immediate response from local residents, trade unionists, and activists, who quickly arrived at the mosque with signs and messages of solidarity.

Trump's policies and the actions of his European counterparts gave the far right in Canada confidence. They started mobilizing monthly at city halls across the country. They also began gathering at the border points in Quebec where refugees were crossing. This provoked discussions among progressive organizations – including labour, community, and women's groups – about how to respond. The women's movement in Toronto has had an anti-racist perspective for many years, led by women of colour. The International Women's Day Committee organized in the past under themes such as "No to War: From Oka to the Gulf," in solidarity with Indigenous women at the standoff at Oka with Canadian Forces, as well as the war in Iraq, making the connections between the fight for women's liberation and against imperialism and colonialism. This history and the present conjuncture led the committee to organize International Women's Day in 2017 under the banner "Stop the Hate, Unite the Fight, Build the Resistance." Diverse women spoke on a wide range of issues, making the links, and eleven thousand marched through the streets of the city. It was the biggest IWD action in decades, outnumbering any mobilization of the right, and pointed the way forward on how best to respond. It allowed women from every background, as well as their supporters, to become a part of the movement against bigotry and hate. It was an exhilarating day in freezing temperatures and showed the government and the right that we will not accept these attacks.

On 21 March, the Day for the Elimination of Racial Discrimination was celebrated by the labour movement and anti-racist groups, which came together to fill City Hall chambers with speakers from Indigenous, Muslim, Black and Asian communities. Shortly afterwards, a public Iftar dinner in the same chambers, sponsored by a major union and the National Council of Canadian Muslims, brought Muslims and non-Muslims together to break their fast during Ramadan.

In Toronto's east end, community members, along with anti-fascist networks and a number of other groups, organized a counter-protest against a threatened fascist rally in a local park, stating clearly that they will not allow this bigotry to go unopposed. In Vancouver, a rally of four thousand completely shut down a handful of neo-Nazis who were attempting to mobilize an anti-Muslim demonstration.

These are just a few examples of the type of broad-based mobilization we need in order to build an ongoing movement of resistance to the far right and racism at every level, and to strengthen the common good in Canada. Large numbers prevent the far right from occupying public space, which they are trying to do in the name of freedom of speech. If it is clear that the majority rejects their views and takes a strong stand against them, their forces will lose confidence and become demoralized. Today there is real suffering, anxiety, and uncertainty; people want something very different from the world that is. As we build this movement, we must also present an alternative vision of a society without racism, sexism, oppression, and exploitation.

The threat of the far right has to be taken seriously. Marine Le Pen of the National Front was one of the two runoff candidates for the presidency of France. There are now neo-Nazis sitting in the Bundestag in Germany and Austria for the first time since the Second World War. Sixty thousand supporters of the far right recently marched in Poland. We cannot allow this to develop further in Canada and Quebec. Working together, Muslim organizations, trade unions, women's groups, and community activists must build a strong, accessible movement that can stop the growth of this right-wing cancer and be part of building a better world.

REFERENCES

Anonymous. 2005 [2018]. "Gen. Hillier Explains the Afghan Mission." *Globe and Mail*, 16 July. https://www.theglobeandmail.com/opinion/gen-hillier-explains-the-afghan-mission/article1331108/.

Delphy, Christine. 2015. *Separate and Dominate: Feminism and Racism after the War on Terror*. London, UK: Verso.

La Meute Publique. n.d. In Facebook [Group Page]. https://www.facebook.com/
   groups/942237742559979/.
Shingler, Benjamin. 2017. "Amid Criticism, Quebec Explains Rules of Its Face-
   Covering Ban." CBC News, 17 October. https://www.cbc.ca/news/canada/
   montreal/quebec-face-covering-guidelines-bill-62-1.4368594.

19

LGBTIQ REFUGEES, ABUSE, AND UNITY MOSQUES
A Queer Muslim Perspective

El-Farouk Khaki

"Queering" is grounded in a praxis that calls us to continually and simultaneously consider the intersections of race, class, gender, embodiment/
disability, environmental issues, interspecies realities, animal rights,
colonisation, cultural representations, sexualities, spiritual practices …
prison-industrial complex, etc. These are not and cannot be treated as
peripheral considerations in the context of Sacred Arts, Sacred Activism,
and Sacred Scholarship.
(Sheikh Ibrahim Farajaje 2014)

I am the imam and, with Dr Laury Silvers and "artivist" Troy Jackson, the
co-founder of El-Tawhid Juma Circle, a gender-equal, LGBTIQ-affirming
mosque movement. I am also ordained as a reverend by the Clergy Support
Memorial Church. My spiritual activism, liberation theology, and ministry
focus on gender, sexuality, and minority issues. Gender and LGBTIQ issues
are directly linked to my own journey of reconciliation of my intersection-
alities as a racialized immigrant, feminist, and gay Muslim man, in tandem
with my legal work representing refugees. Since starting my refugee and immigration law practice on April Fool's Day 1993, I have represented refugee
claimants from over 110 different countries, the majority of whom have
sought protection due to their sexual orientation, HIV status, gender iden-
tity/expression, and/or gender. Two years earlier, in 1991, I started "Salaam:
A Social/Support Group for Lesbian and Gay Muslims" as part of my own
search for community, reconciliation, and healing as a racialized gay Muslim man.

I began my law practice and my queer activism at a time when our rights
were nascent, and part of the growing societal discourse and social visibility
of LGBTIQ people in Canada. Inclusion of sexual orientation in human-
rights codes did not guarantee inclusive or progressive interpretations, while

trans people had no explicit protections. We were politically expendable across the political spectrum, as evidenced when, in June 1994, the Ontario NDP left our rights and dignity up to a free vote with Bill 167, a law that would have given same-sex couples similar benefits, rights, and obligations as those enjoyed by hetero-married and common-law couples. The legislation did not pass, thanks to New Democrat MPPs who voted against their own party's bill, and the Ontario Liberals, who withdrew their support at the last minute. Canadian queers have had to fight for our rights through the courts at every step.

In 1994, the refugee claim of José Ortigoza, a gay-identified Venezuelan, propelled the issues of LGBTIQ rights and refugee protection into media – and our – consciousness. Ortigoza was detained by Canadian immigration authorities who feared he would illegally enter the United States to join his American partner. The quintessential good neighbour, Canada spent thousands of tax dollars to detain a refugee claimant to protect the integrity of America's borders. Evidently, LGBTIQ rights were not easily seen as human rights, and there was little publicly available information. A special request by the local Amnesty International (AI) office to the AI London Secretariat resulted in a two-page response that was crucial in securing refugee protection for Ortigoza. Almost two dozen individuals from the federal public service and diverse refugee, human-rights, and LGBTIQ organizations observed the proceedings at some point over the course of eight sittings. Media coverage informed Canadians and particularly members of the LGBTIQ communities that refugee protection was available to those fearing persecution due to their sexual orientation/gender identity or expression (SOGIE), resulting in an increase in such claims in general, including in my office. The Ortigoza case highlighted the need for training, and eventually guidelines, on SOGIE claims for Refugee Board decision-makers.

While Canada has been at the forefront of interpreting the refugee definition to be inclusive of gender, sexual orientation, gender identity/ expression, and HIV status, Refugee Board decision-makers have not all been enlightened. Bigotry manifest in decisions suggested bisexuals can (and ergo should) avoid harm by choosing an opposite-sex partner, and that queer people could/should avoid persecution by being "discreet." This later notion underscores the erroneous belief that non-heterosexual sexual identity is defined solely by sexual acts.

Similar to trends in other Western countries, Canada's refugee determination and immigration systems have been victims of right-wing and xenophobic shifts that have demonized immigrants and refugees and tightened or restricted access to would-be immigrants and refugees. Concurrently, many legal-aid bodies throughout Canada have either eliminated or drastically reduced funding for refugee and immigration cases. Over the past twenty-five years, refugee advocates and lawyers have had to regularly lobby Ontario Legal Aid against the elimination or reduction of funding or services for refugee and immigration matters.

With clients from all continents except Antarctica and Australia, I began to see patterns in how LGBTIQ people were perceived and treated around the world. Gay men, for example, are often seen as less than "real" men, effeminate, penetrated, and therefore like women, and therefore inferior. Lesbian women are often seen as disruptive to the foundation of society and the "natural order" for not knowing "their place" as wives and child-bearers, and for refusing to be penetrated. For defying social norms and patriarchal expectations, LGBTIQ people are often seen as transgressive, and unworthy of dignity and respect. The advent of the HIV/AIDS pandemic served to confirm for the haters that homosexuality was a curse, for which illness was simultaneously punishment and cure. Due to extremely limited information on HIV/AIDS-related stigma and discrimination and its impact on people's day-to-day life, affidavit evidence and an expanding Internet were essential to exploring the intersection of human rights, sexuality, and HIV/AIDS. My practice soon expanded to the representation of HIV-positive heterosexual female clients, who were often seeking protection from gender-based violence (GBV), including domestic violence, forced marriage, and female genital mutilation, and eventually to non-HIV-positive female clients fearing GBV.

My experience and observations of the human condition have brought me to the conclusion that, universally, religion vested in patriarchy is used as a vehicle for spiritual violence – violence against the *spirit* of the individual – denying the full divine agency and the full humanity of others, and of women and LGBTIQ people in particular. It affirms cis-hetero male normativity as the sole image of God, and any deviation as a perversion of that image, as something less than human. The denial of an individual's full equality as an agent of the Divine easily translates into a denial of their civil and political rights. If God denies your equality, then it follows that humans can and ought to as well.

This is in complete negation of the Quranic declaration that God is closer to us than our own jugular vein – an articulation of *tawhid* and horizontal reciprocity. Muslim theologian Dr Amina Wadud's exegesis of *Tawhid* [Divine Unity] emphasizes the unity of all human creatures under One Creator on the basis of *horizontal reciprocity or interchangeability*. Wadud (2005, 28) believes that, if Tawhid is "experienced as a reality in everyday Islamic terms, humanity would be a single global community without distinction by reason of race, class, gender, religious tradition, national origin, sexual orientation, or other arbitrary, voluntary, and involuntary aspects of human distinction. Their only distinction would be on the basis of their *Taqwa*" [God-consciousness]. Professor Khaled Abou Fadl (cited in Wadud 2005, xi–xii) characterizes patriarchy as an "offence against morality and Islam" that "erases and marginalizes women; and, most significantly, it negates the possibility of true surrender to God" by "displacing God's authority." Referring to despotism and oppression, he declares that, "from a theological point of view, the worst forms are when human beings usurp the role of God, and exploit the name of the Divine in the process of erasing the autonomy and will of other human beings."

The devastation caused by patriarchy is manifest in the lives, beliefs, and aspirations of many of the refugees I have represented. One conversation with a young, Black, African Muslim lesbian is especially illustrative. "Mina" broke down in tears in my office, believing she had disobeyed God when she escaped the physically and sexually abusive marriage her father had forced her into. After he discovered she was lesbian, he brutally assaulted her. I reminded her that God in the Quran tells Abraham to respect and care for his parents, but not to follow their misguided ways. I told her that not only had her father failed in his duty to protect her, he had actually caused her harm. I suggested to her that she was not a bad Muslim for having fled, but maybe her father was for having given her cause to flee.

In the Muslim context, there are few organized spaces where patriarchy and homo/bi- and transphobia are actively challenged and subverted. The dominant post-colonial discourse, among many Muslims and non-Muslims alike, is that sexuality, and in particular non-heteronormative sexuality, and Islam are incompatible and irreconcilable. In May 2009, Dr Silvers, Troy

Jackson, and I responded to the spiritual violence we observed, and had ourselves endured, by starting El Tawhid Juma Circle/Toronto Unity Mosque
for ourselves, for those de-Muslimed (Muslims not seen as Muslim enough),
and those un-mosqued by not having a mosque that reflected their values
and/or beliefs. We believed then, as now, that people can reclaim Islam for
themselves and transform Muslim social reality around gender, sexuality,
and all things that divide us. We are guided by Mevlana Rumi's invitation to
the most stigmatized and maligned in his society and era:

Come, come, whoever you are,
Wanderer, idolater, worshiper of fire,
Come even though you have broken your vows a thousand times,
Come, and come yet again.

In receiving the 2017 Harmony Award for the Toronto Unity Mosque,
President Troy Jackson stated:

We started ETJC (El Tawhid Juma Circle)/The Toronto Unity Mosque
out of necessity and of love. We believed, then and still, that all people
are equal in and before Allah. We wanted a mosque space that affirmed
the dignity of all peoples; where diversity is celebrated not merely tolerated, where women exercise equal divine agency, and where LGBTIQ people are affirmed.

    ETJC is a healing space for those who have experienced religious
trauma in the name of religion, and in the name of Islam in particular.
It is a place to heal, and reclaim their Islam. Many are so incredulous that
such a mosque exists, that we regularly witness tears.

Central to our work is an understanding that Islam is not a monolith,
and that it is possible to embrace tradition while also opening our hearts
and minds to modernity and the whole of humanity. It is a reminder that
Islam is a journey, not a destination, and a living, breathing thing; we give
life to it as it breathes life into our hearts. In an interview with Natasha
Turak, Dr Amina Wadud articulates our collective aspirations in this way:
"My lifelong effort as a Muslim has been to disengage that connection between God and all forms of discrimination. Not just sexism, but racism and

nationalism and xenophobia and homophobia and class elitism, the caste system, apartheid, and everything."

We can and must be the change we want. Our Unity Mosque movement is actively seeking and building coalitions and networks, locally, nationally, and internationally. El Tawhid Juma Circle is a member of the Global Queer Muslim Network (GQMN) and the Alliance of Inclusive Muslims (AIM) that "seeks to challenge theological justifications for hate and supremacism with the progressive values ... inherent in Islam, including human rights and dignity for all." The Toronto Peace Iftar, a Ramadan community meal and celebration, for its fifteenth year brings together Queers and non-Queers, Muslims and non-Muslims alike to break bread. The first Peace Iftar in 2003 included only a handful of non-Queer-identified Muslims. Today, Iftar partners include three non-queer-specific Muslim organizations (the Canadian Institute of Sufi Studies, the Canadian Council of Muslim Women, and UMAH – Uniting Muslims and Allies for Humanity), AIDS service organizations, and others such as Sacred Women International, The 519, and Women's Health in Women's Hands.

As racist, xenophobic, and hateful right-wing movements like the neo-Nazis rebrand themselves as the "alt-right," those committed to a more just and equitable world must also come together out of love. Atrocities continue to be committed in the name of Islam against women, LGBTIQ people, minorities, and others. The majority of sexually dissenting Muslims live in fear in societies where their rights and lives have little, if any, value. While change is slow, change is inevitable. Transformation is possible. The prophet Muhammed, peace be upon him, is reported to have told his followers, "None of you has faith until *they* love for *their sibling* what *they* love for *themselves.*" Cornell West reminds us that, "Justice is what love looks like in public." Our path forward is one of love and justice. It is the path of resisting the forces of fear and prejudice that divide us.

We resist because we must. Because we can. Because the common good is our good.

REFERENCES

Farajaje, Sheikh Ibrahim. 2014. "'Queering' the Study of Islam: And Ain't I a
  Muslim?" Intersectionality and the Study of Islam. Original Facebook post.
  Email from El-Farouk Khaki to Cynthia Levine-Rasky, 12 March 2018.
Turak, Natasha. 2015. Interview with Amina Wadud, American Muslim Feminist.
  Euphrates Institute, 5 February. https://euphrates.org/interview-with-amina-
  wadud-american-muslim-feminist/.
Wadud, Amina. 2005. *Inside the Gender Jihad.* London, UK: Oneworld Publications.

PART THREE

SOCIAL POLICIES IN HOSTILE TIMES

20

EXPOSING THE RIGHT
The Foundations of Right-Wing Extremism in Canada

Barbara Perry

Canadian complacency about our relative lack of far-right extremism (RWE) was shattered on 29 January 2017, when a young man, reputedly inspired by the likes of Donald Trump and Marine Le Pen, opened fire in a St Foy, Quebec, mosque, killing six Muslim men at prayer. This was a sombre indicator that we are not immune to the violence of hatred and bigotry. Throughout the latter part of 2016 and right through to the present, we have sadly seen additional and ongoing evidence of Canadian engagement in right-wing extremist violence. Data from the National Council of Canadian Muslims (2015–17) and B'nai Brith Canada (2016) indicate that anti-Muslim and antisemitic hate crime and hate incidents increased significantly during 2016 and 2017. Veiled Muslim women have reported assaults on the street, in shopping malls, and on buses. Jewish schools and places of worship have been targeted with offensive graffiti. This was substantiated by federal statistics showing a staggering 47-per-cent increase in hate crimes reported to police in 2017 (Statistics Canada 2018).

Equally significant, neo-Nazi, nationalist, and white-supremacist groups have also grown in number and boldness since the beginning of 2017, thanks to the White House's normalization of hate. According to recent media, police, and community-agency reports (for example, from the National Council of Canadian Muslims), and the online and offline activities of such hate groups, it is likely that the number of groups has swelled by at least 25 per cent in 2018. Recent activities, both on the Internet and on the streets, reveal that existing groups have added new chapters across the country (for example, the III%ers, the Hammerskins), and new groups have emerged (such as Storm Alliance and the Proud Boys). Chatter on public social-media platforms and the growth in volume on dedicated websites (such as Stormfront) also suggest that more people are engaging with the movement. It appears we are in the midst of an alarming qualitative and quantitative shift in right-wing activism in most parts of Canada.

Xenophobic flyers have been posted by right-wing groups, containing such slogans as "Tired of anti-white propaganda? You are not alone"; "It's only racist when White people do it"; and, borrowing from Trump's slogan, "It's time to Make Canada Great Again!" The flyers were perhaps the first sign that RWE adherents were coming out of hiding. They suggested, also, that the RWE movement was enjoying newfound "freedom" to hate. Across major Canadian cities, far-right vigilante groups, such as PEGIDA, Soldiers of Odin (SOO), Sons of Odin, and the III%ers have patrolled streets to "protect" Canadian citizens from what they perceived as the "Islamic" threat, seeking to silence and marginalize Muslims through intimidation and a show of force. According to the leader of the Alberta chapter of the III%ers, these armed and paramilitary-trained activists have several mosques under surveillance, on the assumption that "These mosques, from what we've gathered, from our intel, these mosques are fronts for training groups, for terrorist training groups ... We will continue to watch these mosques and monitor these situations" (Lamoureux 2017).

Proud Boys made their first public appearance in Canada on 1 July 2017, disrupting an anti-colonialist protest at the Cornwallis statue in Halifax. Similarly, the Canadian Coalition for Concerned Citizens (CCCC) and the SOO rallied against the federal motion M-103 (adopted March 2017), which was intended to limit Islamophobia and track hate crimes. On 4 March 2017, these groups protested M-103 in Toronto, making the public claim that "Islam Is Evil" and clashing with counter-protesters. Racist and Islamophobic rallies have continued. Ironically, in the tragic aftermath of the Charlottesville rally (12 August 2017), which was punctuated by the murder of anti-racism activist Heather Heyer, Canada's far-right activists appeared to be emboldened rather than disconcerted by the terror that ensued there. Canadian white-supremacist groups seem to have taken that rally as a call to arms. Similar rallies were immediately planned across the country. For instance, the World Coalition Against Islam, the Cultural Action Party, and the Soldiers of Odin, among others, joined forces for a rally in Vancouver in September 2017. While none of these resulted in the sort of violence that characterized Charlottesville, they nonetheless represented a worrying trend toward coalition-building across sectors of the far right in Canada. No longer are isolated groups working alone. Rather, they are collaborating in what appears to be an attempt to "unite the right."

Much of the blame for the rise of the right across the United States and Canada has been laid at the feet of Donald Trump. His endless vilification of Muslims, of Mexicans, and of immigrants generally fed into a simmering dissatisfaction among White males in particular. The social-media borders are porous, and through these platforms Canadians also have been fed a steady diet of Trump's hyperbole. His Twitter feeds reach us; his sound bites have made front-page news in the Canadian media; the extreme-right social-media ecology and forums are accessible here. Yet his sentiments do not fall on fallow ground. The foundations for the building of an active RWE movement had been laid by Canadian politicians over at least the past decade. A crucial backdrop to the uptake of Trumpism in Canada is provided by reactionary trends at federal, provincial, and municipal levels of government. Most notably, the "Harper years" were characterized by a retreat from human rights, the elimination of hate-speech protections, fear mongering and hate, anti-immigrant rhetoric, and restrictions on immigrants and refugees to Canada. Especially pronounced was Harper's vilification of Muslims. After the "terrorist" attacks in Quebec and on Parliament Hill in 2014, Harper introduced Bill C-51, with the claim that "Violent jihadism is not just a danger somewhere else. It seeks to harm us here in Canada" (Janus and Johnson 2015). During the 2015 election campaign, Harper ratcheted up his Islamophobia, depicting Muslim culture as contrary to Canadian values. He called Islamic culture "anti-women," declared the wearing of the hijab "offensive," and said that "We do not allow people to cover their faces during citizenship ceremonies" (Chase 2015). Conservative Party leadership hopeful Kellie Leitch followed suit, raising the twin spectres of a "barbaric cultural practices" tip line and a screening of immigrants for "Canadian values."

Provincial patterns also provided settings ripe for the uptake of far-right xenophobia. In particular, since the mid-1990s Quebec has been the province where Islamophobic politics is most pronounced and divisive. This is evidenced in multiple ways, from long-standing attempts to bar Muslim women and girls from wearing hijabs to school, to twenty-first-century polls that expressed a growing public opinion in Quebec that immigration from Islamic countries should be reduced, to the creation of a Statement of Values in Herouxville in 2007 and in Gatineau in 2011 aimed at banning people from publicly wearing religious symbols and attire.

The Parti Québécois (PQ) and its previous premier, Pauline Marois, were especially prone to this position. In 2012, the PQ proposed a Charter of Values to ban religious expression in the public sector (with the obvious exception of the large crucifix mounted on the wall of the Quebec legislative assembly). While the charter was "dressed in the guise of narratives of gender equality and secular values" (Ameli and Merali 2014, 68), it actually targeted Muslims. Far from backing a ban on symbols of Christianity, Judaism, or Hinduism, most PQ leaders and supporters focused on removing the hijab from public space. This became institutionalized under Bill 62 in October 2017. Though this was subsequently halted by a Quebec Court, in June 2019 the new government of the CAQ passed even harsher legislation, Bill 21, which bars face coverings for those receiving any provincial services – including transportation, medical care, and library lending. The bill, "An Act Respecting the Laicity of the State," further marginalizes and stigmatizes Muslim women in particular. It can only exacerbate the trend whereby covered women are overrepresented as targets of hate crime.

Cumulatively, the normalization of hatred and bigotry in mainstream politics has rendered a broader permission to hate that has shaped parallel forms of hate on the street. Yet this has not gone without considerable resistance in Canada. Harper's defeat in 2016 and Leitch's dramatic loss of popularity signal repudiation of their narratives. That anti-racists far outnumber racists at far-right rallies is a welcome indication that more people stand against hate than for it. This was also evident in the aftermath of the mosque shootings in St Foy, Quebec. Even in that province, the signs of solidarity and community building were heart-warming. Multi-faith and multicultural marches and vigils marked the losses, reminding Muslims that they did not stand alone.

Although powerful, public rallies and marches are insufficient for countering the deep-seated bigotry that seems to permeate contemporary culture. While the sites of effective intervention are many and varied, I would like to highlight just three: education, media, and political leaders. Youth continue to be uninformed about the darker sides to our history, leaving them vulnerable to the narratives of loss of white privilege, threats of cultural "takeover" by immigrants, inter alia. As a corollary, they are also largely unaware of the threat posed by far-right extremists, either in terms of recruitment tactics or impacts on communities. In the current context, it is imperative that educators take the opportunity to discuss and decon-struct the hate-filled narratives that are so pervasive. It is, in part, complacency about Canada's ability to fully realize the core values of inclu-sion and equity that has allowed the creep of right-wing sentiment. We must learn to be more self-reflective and critical about where the chinks in our armour may be.

Until Trump's ascension to political office, mainstream media sources were also silent on the issue of far-right extremism in Canada. That has clearly changed in the months leading up to and following Trump's elec-tion. Between November 2016 and November 2017, I have done more than three hundred related interviews with local, national, and international media. Not a week goes by that there is not a handful of press articles on the activities and ideologies of active right-wing groups. To use a worn adage, knowledge is power. Only if we understand the foundations of far-right narratives can we effectively counter them. Failure to shed a critical light on the dark recesses of the movement allows them to thrive. Exposure reveals them, enabling the necessary critique that lays bare the faulty logic of their belief "systems."

Finally, political leaders have a responsibility to challenge the normaliza-tion of hate. We have seen this in many guises, locally and nationally. When racist and antisemitic pamphlets and flyers began to appear in Canadian cities, local mayors spoke out against them. So, too, have some of them challenged planned racist – a.k.a. "free-speech" – rallies. The mayor of Vancouver, for example, encouraged anti-racist rallies in response to a planned right-wing rally in that city. Perhaps most notable was the federal adoption of MP Iqra Khalid's motion (M103), which condemned "Islamo-phobia and all forms of systemic racism and religious discrimination" (House of Commons 2017). The downside of that, of course, was the resist-ance that it engendered among partisan politicians and far-right extremists, who insisted that the motion – misidentified by many as a "law" – allowed for sharia law, or that it made criticism of Islam illegal. Their wilful distor-tion of the potential scope and impact of the motion was a disingenuous attempt to further vilify Muslims.

Moreover, subsequent events have borne out the limited on-the-ground effects of the motion. It has not been followed up by substantive measures aimed at effectively ameliorating the conditions underlying the xenophobia, racism, and hate that affect so many communities. Our political leaders must be challenged to reach beyond purely symbolic messaging to deploy financial and other concrete resources in the interests of resisting hate. Academics require increased funding to more fully unpack the right-wing extremist movement; community organizers require similar infusions of funds to support anti-racism/anti-fascism education and programming that forms the foundation for community-based forms of resistance. The "common good," insofar as it entails the full recognition of the value and place of all communities, regardless of race, religion, sexuality, or other identity marker, demands concrete action that pushes back against past and present forms of individual and systemic exclusion. Political rhetoric must be followed by actions such as the re-enactment of Section 13 of the Canadian Human Rights Act, the resurrection of Canada's Action Plan on Racism, or the repeal of discriminatory legislation like Quebec's Bill 21, as examples. Provincial and federal legislatures have a responsibility to be leaders of resistance to RWE, not enablers of its spread.

REFERENCES

Ameli, Saied R., and Arzu, Merali. 2014. *Only Canadian: The Experience of Hate Moderated Differential Citizenship for Muslims.* Wembley, UK: Islamic Human Rights Commission. https://www.researchgate.net/publication/281967118_Only _Canadian_The_Experience_of_Hate_moderated_citizenship_for_muslims.

B'nai Brith Canada. 2016. "Audit of Antisemitic Incidents / Audit des Incidents Antisémites." http://www.bnaibrith.ca/audit.

Chase, S. 2015. "Harper's Stance on Niqabs Shows He Doesn't Really Care about Women." *Globe and Mail,* 10 March. https://www.theglobeandmail.com/news/ politics/niqabs-rooted-in-a-culture-that-is-anti-women-harper-says/article 23395242/.

House of Commons. 2017. Iqra Khalid – Private Members' Motions – Current Session. http://www.ourcommons.ca/Parliamentarians/en/members/Iqra-Khalid (88849)/Motions?documentId=8661986%2520.

Janus, A., and A. Johnson. 2015. "Stephen Harper Makes His Case for New Powers to Combat Terror." *CTV News,* 30 January. http://www.ctvnews.ca/canada/anti- terror-bill-gives-new-powers-to-canada-s-spies-1.2213119.

Lamoureux, M. 2017. "The Birth of Canada's Armed, Anti-Islamic 'Patriot' Group."
   VICE News, 14 January. https://www.vice.com/en_ca/article/new9wd/the-birth-
   of-canadas-armed-anti-islamic-patriot-group.
National Council of Canadian Muslims. 2015–17. "Tracking Anti-Muslim Incidents
   Reported Across Canada." https://www.nccm.ca/map/#.
Statistics Canada. 2018. "Police Reported Hate Crime, 2017." The Daily, 29 Novem-
   ber. https://www150.statcan.gc.ca/n1/daily-quotidien/181129/dq181129a-eng.htm.

21

RESISTING OR RECAPTURING SURVEILLANCE?

David Murakami Wood

The Authoritarian Turn

After years of globalization, the early years of the twenty-first century seem to be signalling a reversal. This reversal is not the radical left-anarchist critique offered by the anti-globalization movement of the 1990s. That movement eventually recognized its own proposals as an alter-globalization rather than a complete rejection, a difference emphasized in the slogan "another world is possible." The reversal comes instead from the reactionary right. It is frequently portrayed as populist, authoritarian, sometimes even as fascist, and the commonalities with the 1930s are in many ways obvious. This reaction signals a turn away from the global and the transnational toward the national, and from openness to closure, from progress toward nostalgia, and from ideas of common humanity toward ethnic and cultural difference and hierarchy.

However, the differences are significant too. As I have argued elsewhere (Murakami Wood 2017), the current reaction is a retreat from an almost-completed process of globalization and the emergence of the planetary that also brings with it new disruptions, in particular terrorism, mass migration, and climate change. The scale of the latter problem in particular seems almost unimaginable. Even when the scientific evidence is accepted and the idea of an "Anthropocene" era is normalized, the possibility of effective action to reverse or even mitigate climate change seems itself to presage huge and unwelcome changes to lives and lifestyles. The reaction is a product of social fear and of the structural failure of political economic systems to respond effectively to these massive and complex issues. The reaction is a retreat to the certainties of easy solutions provided by authoritarian father figures, known institutions, the scapegoating of racialized enemies, and the disavowal of the planetary scale itself.

Surveillance Capitalism...

The other main difference from the 1930s is the emerging form of planetary political economic organization: a data-driven, platform capitalism, which threatens to align capital and the state far more closely, with the latter finally taking on the characteristics of the former. This transformation of capitalism is only somewhat delayed and inconvenienced by the present reactionary, authoritarian turn. As activists, we have to understand the character of this emerging political economic order and be prepared to fight this, as well as the reactionary forces, because neither are our friends, and the solutions provided by one are not the answer to the other. How can this be done? Both the emergent planetary system and the reaction share a common basis in surveillance as the key mode of ordering. I suggest here that, in fighting surveillance, we can find ways of opposing both. To do so, we need to understand what the current form of surveillance is and what it does.

From the early 1970s, analysts began to voice concern over the emergence of the computer database as a tool of government. Michel Foucault (1977) shifted the understanding of the origins of this mode of ordering further back to the emergence of modernity itself, arguing that surveillance in societal institutions is an essential part of why we are what we are. The idea of "surveillance society" gained wider academic currency with the work of Oscar Gandy (1993) and David Lyon (1994), and, by the 2000s, this had generated a whole new transdisciplinary field of research: surveillance studies.

Within this field and beyond, attention has returned to the question of data. What Gary Marx (2016) calls "the new surveillance" indicates a change in intensity, scale, reach, intrusiveness, and so on, as well as a change in temporal registers from knowing the past in order to the know the present, to knowing the present in order to know possible futures. Databases are no longer single things located on a single computer in a single location, but distributed, networked, and addressable from multiple locations. The sources of data are no longer hand-typed records and analogue photographs and audio recordings, but the products of multiple and multiplying surveillance devices. The devices are everywhere, in material and virtual space. The data themselves can be anything that such devices capture: video, usage patterns, footfalls, location, purchases, political views, emotions, bodily traces, and more. The data may no longer be about anything in particular in advance of it being collected. Rather, the purposes increasingly emerge from patterns recognized algorithmically in enormous collections of "big data" (Pasquale 2015). Surveillance is increasingly less specific and unusual and more pervasive and normal. Its products are presented as a public good, like security, or a private service, like personalized marketing. Advanced surveillance tools that were accessible only to state agencies a few years ago are available even to individuals; for example, advanced wireless networked surveillance cameras can be ordered on Amazon, and email tracking is now a mere app installation away.

In the immediate term, this makes possible what surveillance studies scholars have warned of for years. The Stasi of the former East Germany, the nadir of the previous wave of totalitarianism, had detailed paper-based files on just one-third of the population (Funder 2002). The prior Nazi regime used punchcard-based IBM Hollerith machines to laboriously compile census data for genocide (Black 2001). Now, pervasive surveillance, networked databases of personal information, real-time tracking, and predictive analytics allow authoritarian power to become genuinely totalitarian, that is, to work on the basis of total knowledge of individuals. But at the same time, the political economy of surveillance appears to be moving in a somewhat different direction. Our lives are lived increasingly in these networked databases. The genius of the most recent iteration of capitalism, what Shoshana Zuboff (2015, 2019) calls "surveillance capitalism," is the commodification of previously unavailable spheres: the social and the intimate. Within online social networks, we produce such personal (meta)data all the time as the by-product of interactions and expressed views and preferences. As Nick Srnicek has argued – speaking against the grain of current depictions of this form of capitalism as a social factory or unpaid labour – this is not "labour" in the classic Marxist sense. The corporate providers of these increasingly central and essential social services do not turn the social into work, rather they commodify this by-product of social interaction, this data exhaust that Zuboff refers to as the "social surplus," and turn it into profit. Jonathan Crary (2013) shows that few areas remain outside this system, one example being the one-third of our life spent in sleep.

... Or Platform Capitalism?

Srnicek, for his part, does not refer to this phenomenon as "surveillance capitalism," but as "platform capitalism." Both terms are accurate, but each sees only one aspect of the whole transformation, however the latter term highlights a further emergent transformation, and one that is at the heart of the need for a dual strategy of opposition to both authoritarianism and capitalist globalism. Surveillance capitalism leads us to consider the mode of ordering, where platform capitalism draws our attention to the organizational, the political. Whereas Foucault argued that state institutions like medicine, education, and hospitals were the main vehicles for the spread of surveillance in the modern period, in the current period, surveillance is also carried out via software systems on distributed networks. The companies that own and operate these platforms are now the largest in the world: Alphabet (Google), Amazon, Apple, Facebook, Tencent (Alibaba), and so on. These platforms themselves are not just "corporations" or "companies" however, but in many ways are increasingly state-like. Their users resemble citizens, and the companies themselves assert, in more or less overt ways, a kind of sovereignty. Platform sovereignty is de facto (derived from reality) rather than de jure (derived from law), but it is there, and if it becomes dominant, it will transform the world of laws in the same way that the Treaty of Westphalia of 1648 confirmed the reality of the emerging international system of nation-states at the beginning of the modern period.

Facebook's CEO, Mark Zuckerberg (2017), recently articulated his particular ambition in this area with an open letter called "Building Global Community," which argued that Facebook can be far more than conversations between friends, but can in fact be a kind of government, or a techno-communitarian organization that can do things better than government (see Rider and Murakami Wood 2018). And we see the movement of platforms into spatial-territorial governance in the "test-bed urbanism" (Halpern et al. 2013) of "smart city" projects like Sidewalk Toronto and Amazon's HQ2, about which more below.

It is important to note that the coming era of platforms will not be simply a matter of corporations taking over conventional government, but also that not all platforms will be based in neo-liberal capitalist corporate logic. In the context of the top-down state-directed form of capitalism operated by China, Tencent is effectively a Chinese state enterprise and China's model for the world. A ruthless combination of the platform and the state, it operates not from the western nation-state model, but from a model of a revived empire, a model that was for much of human history regarded as the most effective and legitimate method of rule. Tencent is part of an empire that relies on the very same collection, sorting, and use of data that social-network companies carry out. And systems like the Chinese state's proposed "Sesame" social-credit system, which will assign a continually up-dated "score" to all Chinese citizens, represent one of the few truly successful extant combinations of surveillance capitalism and totalitarian practice. It may yet become an example to others; it is already being exported to China's extended global zone of influence in Africa.

Oh, Canada

What will happen to other nation-states like Canada is uncertain. The "threats" of terrorism and mass migration have prompted a hardening of borders, and this has made them one of the most important locations for the rendering of vulnerable human bodies as information, through everything from "naked scanners" to the interrogation of social-media activity by border agents. But as Wendy Brown (2014) argued, this in itself may be evidence not of the persistence of the power of the nation-state but of its weakness and decline: borders are one of the few (and certainly the most obvious) areas where nation-states can still make a demonstration of their control, having given up almost everything about the effective regulation of the economy and given in to demands for lower taxes and privatization of much else. Borders are a key location and symbol for the new authoritarian politics: demands for walls and fences to keep "them" out, and for the return of "illegal" migrants to wherever it was where they started their perilous journeys.

In this paranoid climate, citizenship now seems less about rights and more about responsibilities. Citizens are increasingly being asked to identify not just with a nation-state but also with particular government agendas. This makes conventional forms of politics fraught. Signing a petition for peace negotiations may now be portrayed as the support of terrorist organisations, as many progressive academics in Turkey are now finding. Working for human rights, openness, and transparency can be cast as being the tool of some nefarious cosmopolitanism, often associated by the right, in an only-thinly-veiled extension of classic antisemitism, with George Soros.

In this climate, and with the usual simplistic habit of comparing only two possibilities, it seems that a surveillance-driven platform sovereignty can appear as a more liberal and progressive alternative to the authoritarian turn. Combined with the increasing primacy of social media as a means of political debate and action, we are in danger of taking social media itself for granted. Conventional left political parties like the NDP think that they can follow the online campaigning examples of Barack Obama, Bernie Sanders, Jeremy Corbyn, or, in Canada itself, the infinitely Instagrammable Justin Trudeau.

These are mistakes. It is a mistake first of all for social movements to think they can "use" social media in simple ways to organize and fight. The Arab Spring showed that a limited social media-driven revolution to remove particular governments is actually relatively easy. But it also showed the superficiality and ultimate fragility of such media-driven revolts. As Zeynep Tufecki (2017) has shown, the situation was far more complex than either overly optimistic or rejectionist accounts of the role of social media.

But it is undoubtedly a major error to push more power into the hands of platforms as they are currently designed, as alternatives to authoritarian states. What we need are alternative platforms or alternatives to platforms that are capable of providing something like a new bottom-up planetary belonging, that is not a citizenship granted by a planetary capitalist state but something created between people that crosses and effaces old borders. It is inevitable with planetary-scale problems in the Anthropocene that we will have to operate on that level. An immediate localism alone is not possible, except in some post-apocalyptic mode that will have already condemned millions to death and accepted some major measure of disaster. What is needed is what European Green parties have long understood by the term "subsidiarity," the assigning of appropriate actions to the appropriate scale. This means a redistribution both up to the planetary and down to the local (and several scales in between).

This means that we also cannot imagine that Canada has a future as "Canada." The Harper Decade allowed many to imagine that, once Harper himself was removed, Canada could resume its reputation as a "good country." Yet as the false choices offered over state surveillance during the

Bill C59 consultation process showed, the Trudeau government, while more media-savvy, is not that different from Harper's in its pursuit of legislation as legitimation for the illegal and unethical practices of state surveillance agencies. Legitimation, not transparency or accountability, let alone democratic control, is the basic purpose of Bill C59, just as it was with Harper's Bill C51. Unless "Canada" can reinvent itself as a kind of alternative platform itself, say, one which offers a form of social and ecological model, led by Indigenous peoples following the example of the Idle No More movement in Canada or the #NODAPL fight in the USA, then Canada will go the way of all other nation-states. In that sense there are no solutions for Canada alone. Anthropocene social movements must be a true internationalism beyond nation-states. The old state socialist answer of nationalization is another kind of retreat, and one which merely plays into the hands of authoritarians.

Data-Subjects of the World, Unite!

The final irony is that, if we are to repair the damage that capitalism has done, we are going to need the technologies – even the surveillant capabilities – of existing states and platforms that were developed within capitalism in order to measure and manage a return to a stable environment and create a more just society, even one driven ultimately by the values of a new indigeneity or presaged on a longer-term localization. Magical thinking is not going to help, and neither is a retreat to solipsistic and extremely libertarian forms of privacy possible or desirable. This is not to say: (1) that such technologies should be used in the same ways – technologies have many affordances; nor (2) that further developments should cease – particularly with energy systems, this is essential; nor, finally, (3) that this would mean acceding to surveillance capitalism is some way that is more vulnerable than other strategies – capitalism is everywhere, and there is no scale or place or strategy that is not vulnerable. In the end, whatever our aims and ambitions, we need overwhelming numbers; no strategy of resistance or revolution can hope to succeed without them.

However, we might be able to manage the requirements of ecological and social justice and the combined demands of safety, transparency, and privacy in co-operative ways. Indeed, the message of the co-operative so-cialist movements of the nineteenth century that had seemed to have been eliminated at both ends by state communism and free-market capitalism now seems more pertinent than ever. However, we can't return to the self-creation of those movements. The platforms and the technologies are al-ready there, and efforts to create entirely new more "just" or "ethical" platforms and to persuade people to migrate to them, as in the case of Di-aspora or Mastodon, have proven to be elitist failures, popular only within tech communities.

To enable a "platform co-operativism," which could be the basis for a new kind of planetary citizenship, we need to take the platforms that exist, but for that we need to reinvent almost every activist tool that we have. In some cases, particularly where platforms are failing to generate the kind of value expected by investor-capital, combined worker and user buyouts might be possible, after the manner of worker or consumer co-operatives. Twitter is the most obvious target for such a strategy. In others, divestment and refusal might be better: there is really no need for something like LinkedIn outside of the capitalist marketplace. Co-option and user pressure could work with an entity like Facebook, where the owners appear to be genuinely torn between conflicting future pathways, confronted as they are by the revelations of the use of this system to influence elections, as well as just (the intended) purchasing decisions.

But beyond this, there does need to be a redoubled effort toward the cre-ation of truly open platforms and open systems that do not require coding or hacker knowledge as the price of entry. Open-data initiatives opposed to corporate smart cities is one such example, and there is already a fight brewing in Canada between the advocates of the Sidewalk Labs scheme for what amounts to a "Google neighbourhood" on Toronto's waterfront and determined opponents coalesced into the Toronto Open Smart Cities Forum. Ultimately, this is fight for what Henri Lefebvre (1996) called "the right to the city" and, with more of these privatized urban enclaves being presented as encompassing solutions to cash-strapped municipal authori-ties, it's a fight that must be recognized for the precedent-setting conflict that it is.

It's not going to be easy.

REFERENCES

Black, Edwin. 2001. IBM *and the Holocaust*. London: Little, Brown.

Brown, Wendy. 2014. *Walled States: Waning Sovereignty*. Cambridge, MA: Zone
  Books.

Crary, Jonathan. 2013. *24/7: Late Capitalism and the Ends of Sleep*. New York: Verso.

Foucault, Michel. 1977. *Discipline and Punish: The Birth of the Prison*. New York:
  Allen Lane.

Funder, Anna. 2002. *Stasiland: Stories from behind the Berlin Wall*. London: Granta.

Gandy, Oscar. 1993. *The Panoptic Sort: Political Economy of Personal Information*.
  London: Routledge.

Halpern, O., J. LeCavalier, N. Calvillo, and W. Pietsch. 2013. "Test-Bed Urbanism."
  Public Culture 25 (2): 272–306.

Lefebvre, Henri. 1996. *Writings on Cities*. Oxford: Blackwell.

Lyon, David. 1994. *The Electronic Eye: The Rise of Surveillance Society*. Minneapolis:
  University of Minnesota Press.

Marx, Gary. 2016. *Windows into the Soul: Surveillance and Society in an Age of High
  Technology*. Chicago: Chicago University Press.

Murakami Wood, D. 2017. "The Global Turn to Authoritarianism and After."
  Surveillance & Society 15 (3/4).

Pasquale, Frank. 2015. *The Black Box Society: The Secret Algorithms that Control
  Money and Information*. Cambridge, MA: Harvard University Press.

Rider, K., and Murakami Wood, D. 2018. "Condemned to Connection? Mark
  Zuckerberg's Facebook Manifesto and the Authoritarian Turn." *New Media &
  Society* – Online First. https://doi.org/10.1177/1461444818804772.

Srnicek, Nick. 2016. *Platform Capitalism*. New York: John Wiley & Sons.

Tufecki, Zeynep. 2017. *Twitter and Tear Gas: The Power and Fragility of Networked
  Protest*. New Haven, CT: Yale University Press.

Zuboff, Shoshana. 2019. *The Age of Surveillance Capitalism*. New York: Public
  Affairs.

– 2015. "Big Other: Surveillance Capitalism and the Prospects of an Information
  Civilization." *Journal of Information Technology* 30 (1): 75–89.

Zuckerberg, Mark. 2017. Building Global Community. Facebook, 16 February.
  https://www.facebook.com/notes/mark-zuckerberg/building-global-community/
  10154544292806634/.

22

THE WAR ON THE POOR AND THE RISE OF THE RIGHT

John Clarke

There is an over-hasty and stereotypical assumption that the far right is made up of poor White members of the "lumpenproletariat." Historically, racist and fascist movements have certainly drawn from among those embittered and enraged by poverty and unemployment, but they have also been focused on those sections of the middle class for whom economic crisis means a threat to their relative economic privilege. Certainly, if we were to view the base of support for Donald Trump as a kind of pre-fascist formation, the income level to be found there is much higher than is generally supposed (Carnes and Lupu 2017). However, with this qualification in mind, I want to try and take up the question of how the agenda of neo-liberal austerity, and the "war on the poor" that is part of it, creates an anger that can be diverted along destructive paths toward racism, Islamophobia, and hostility to immigrants and refugees, into which even racialized poor people can be sucked. I want also to suggest how movements of social resistance are the primary means by which such poison can be counteracted.

In a country like Canada, when racism sheds its more normal and pervasive forms of coded and implied expression and becomes overt hatred, it is rapidly labelled "extremism." This is a convenient way of focusing on the weeds and not considering the mainstream soil that they grow out of. Yet it is the dominant political agenda that imposes austerity, generates inequality, wages endless war, fuels an international refugee crisis, and generates the economic and social conditions that lay down the basis for the extremism. Moreover, it is the politicians and corporate media whose chorus of "respectable" racism and xenophobia offers the base of support and springboard for those who go further, into overt hate speech and acts of violence. Let's look at the austerity attacks that have resulted in increased poverty and destitution, and then consider how they can be used to feed the objectives of the racist right.

The War on the Poor

The growth of poverty and outright destitution has been an effect of the decades-long neo-liberal agenda. By the 1970s, the postwar economic boom had broken up, and the concessions that had been made to trade unions and those given in the form of improved social programs had cut into the rate of profit for corporations and banks. A counter-attack was unleashed by governments and corporations that included moving jobs to areas with lower wages, implementing social cutbacks, and, in particular, gutting programs like unemployment insurance and welfare so as to create a climate of desperation. The impact of this has been dramatic. In Ontario, only one worker in forty was on the minimum wage as recently as 1997. By 2015, that had risen to one in eight (Tencer 2015). This has been accompanied by the driving down of social-assistance rates to ensure that this supply of low-wage workers was facilitated (Monsebratten 2010). If we consider homelessness to be the sharpest expression of a war on the poor, the impact here has been astounding. The City of Toronto issues a Daily Shelter Census. The figures are doctored and understated, but still quite shocking. In January 2017, an average of 4,366 people a night stayed in the permanent home-less-shelter system. In January 2018, that had gone up to 5,663 a night. The system is so full that a substandard overflow network has been established that provides "winter respite" facilities over and above those of the permanent shelters. In 2017, the numbers forced to use these backup centres were exploding. On 22 December 2017, 572 people used them. By 12 February 2018, that had shot up 810 people, and there is a real fear it will reach 1,000 before the winter is out (City of Toronto n.d.).

Racism in the Face of Poverty

The austerity agenda has been about increasing the ability of elites to profit from the exploitation of workers, and the proliferation of poverty has been a tool in obtaining these results. In such a situation, as can be imagined, the impact on working-class people has not been uniform. Some have maintained living standards, albeit by accepting worse working conditions and putting in longer hours, while others have been forced into poverty and even homelessness. It is hardly surprising that, in this profoundly racist society, those impacts have also been shaped by prevailing racial hierarchies. In Toronto, a vastly disproportionate number of Indigenous people are part of the homeless population. Rates of poverty among racialized and immigrant communities are hugely elevated. Black people face the most egregious treatment in this regard. To this must be added the increased numbers of refugees coming into the city as the Trump administration tightens the xenophobic screws in the United States and his immigration enforcers conduct a reign of terror (Reiti and Sienkiewicz 2017).

Basis for Unity

The dominant ideas and values of those with economic and political power have great force in this society. Poor people facing attack on their meagre living standards are by no means certain to draw the conclusion that the source of their hardship lies within that power structure at the top. They may, to one degree or another and in varying ways, blame each other. Xenophobic notions of protecting "our own" from the claims of outsiders can be part of this. The greatest factor in reinforcing such harmful illusions is passivity in the face of attack, just as united action and resistance are the most potent means of identifying and challenging the real enemies, the architects of neo-liberal austerity.

Building unified resistance in poor communities under attack has several elements. The first is that real solidarity will only be built by making the grievances of those who face the worst attacks of racism and xenophobia the starting point, and not by pandering to the illusions and hostility of those who want to cling to petty privilege. As Toronto's homeless shelters burst at the seams, the influx of refugees, sadly but inevitably, produces resentment. Preposterous allegations of favoured treatment and "queue jumping" abound. This has to be challenged in word and deed. The reality has to be driven home that poverty and homelessness are caused by homegrown developers and bankers, and not by refugees coming to Canada, often because Western governments are exploiting and attacking their countries. Some time ago, I came across a young Indigenous man on the street who was yelling at a Muslim couple. Assuming they were refugees, he was telling them to go home. I told him that this was certainly Stolen Land, and he had more of a right to decide who should be here than me. Then I asked him who he would rather put in a boat: these people or a bunch of cops? He laughed and agreed with me.

Poor people face real challenges and hardships in their lives as they try to access resources that appear all too finite. Divisions will never be overcome among the poor on the basis of hypocritical liberalism. It is very easy for Justin Trudeau to fill his eyes with tears as he tweets "welcome to Canada" nonsense. His brand of fake internationalism comes easily to someone who has never known economic adversity. Poor and working-class people, however, will unite when they are struggling for common goals against a common enemy. Right-wing populism and the far-right movements that draw strength from it will never be countered by the political message of mainstream, "moderate" neo-liberalism. The status quo that this speaks to has failed impoverished people and can't possibly offer an alternative to the false message of the right. That alternative must come from the left. It must challenge the politics of poverty by challenging the politics of wealth. It must confront the austerity of the neo-liberal era by rejecting the capitalist system that has produced it.

The Struggle Is Decisive

It is important to deliver a political message, but it will only be by taking action that communities under attack will draw the really important lessons. As Black Muslim people, Somalis face some of the most glaring forms of racist hostility in Toronto. From 2005 to 2010, the Ontario Coalition Against Poverty (OCAP) took up a campaign to win a benefit called the Special Diet for people on social assistance. We held clinics where medical providers filled in forms, and we mobilized relentlessly to ensure that reluctant welfare officialdom provided the benefits people had signed up to receive. It was the Somali community that played a leading role in winning the Special Diet, with Somali women, organized by OCAP Women of Etobicoke, being the leading force in nearly all the many actions that took place. Solidarity was built into their action.

At this time, OCAP and others are fighting tooth and nail to deal with an unprecedented crisis of homelessness. As I've pointed out, the shelter system is collapsing under the impact of this. We are confronting the austerity agenda at the point of outright social abandonment. Protests and other forms of pressure have had a major impact. The City Council has agreed to keep overflow facilities up and running after they would normally close in the spring. A sustained mobilization, culminating in an OCAP disruption of the council's budget debate, was instrumental in winning a commitment to try and secure a thousand extra shelter bed spaces in 2017. These are fragile gains, and far from the concessions needed to respond to the poverty crisis. However, they have been won by mobilizing people in a struggle for elements of social provision their lives depend on. If you can't find a shelter space, you may be tempted to blame a refugee for your situation, but if that refugee is by your side demanding shelter for everyone, things look very different.

Every month, in the poor Toronto downtown-east neighbourhood, OCAP offers a Speaking Series. After a community meal, a packed room hears a presentation and then engages in discussion. We have tackled issues of racism and Islamophobia and dealt with the refugee crisis. We work to build a sense of working-class internationalism with the diverse and vibrant population of the area that is well placed to appreciate and reinforce this. We will build unity against the right and the system that it grows out of by fighting back and, even more, by building the anti-austerity movement needed to win the fight.

Threat from the Right

Internationally and locally, we can only expect the conditions of neo-liberal austerity and economic crisis to produce even-deeper attacks on working-class people and an intensified war on the poor. The right and the far right have always grown under such conditions, and there is no reason to expect this will not continue to be the case. As vile as it is, the right-wing message offers at least the illusion of a radical alternative. We must be as radical and more so. Our movements must be, and must be seen to be, the means of struggling for that alternative. When it comes to workers' rights, decent income, housing, health care, child care, public transport, and other vital public services, we must show that we can push back the austerity agenda and win real gains. Yet we must also pose an alternative that goes further than this and challenges not just austerity, poverty, and racism but the colonial and capitalist society that produces them. If we are to defeat the Right, we must forget the middle ground and redefine the Left.

REFERENCES

Carnes, Nicholas, and Noam Lupu. 2017. "It's Time to Bust the Myth Most Trump Voters Were Not Working Class." *Washington Post*, 5 June. https://www.washingtonpost.com/news/monkey-cage/wp/2017/06/05/its-time-to-bust-the-myth-most-trump-voters-were-not-working-class/?utm_term=.023953b2b2cf.

City of Toronto. n.d. "Daily Shelter and Overnight Service Usage." https://www.toronto.ca/city-government/data-research-maps/research-reports/housing/housing-and-homelessness-research-and-reports/shelter-census/.

Monsebratten, Laurie. 2010. "Cost of Ontario's 1995 'Welfare Diet' Soars Amid Inadequate Rates." *Star*, 10 October. https://www.thestar.com/news/gta/2015/10/10/cost-of-ontarios-1995-welfare-diet-soars-amid-inadequate-rates.html.

Rieti, John, and Alexandra Sienkiewicz. 2017. "Refugees Fearful of U.S. Immigration Orders Seek Sanctuary in Toronto Shelters." CBC *News*, 23 February. http://www.cbc.ca/news/canada/toronto/refugees-shelters-1.3995021.

Tencer, Daniel. 2015. "Share of Workers in Minimum Wage Jobs Has Grown Fivefold in Ontario: Study." *Huffington Post*, 15 June. http://www.huffingtonpost.ca/2015/06/15/ontario-wages-earnings-ccpa_n_7587844.html.

23

BACK TO THE FUTURE?
Continuity and Change in Migrant Worker Struggles

Aziz Choudry and Mostafa Henaway

> The tradition of the oppressed teaches us that the "emergency situation"
> in which we live is the rule. We must arrive at a concept of history
> which corresponds to this.
> (Walter Benjamin 2003, 392)

There is a long history of looking below the US border to try to explain racism in Canada. This deflects attention away from confronting structural racism and colonialism central to the foundation of our own nation-state's, processes that still have an impact on many people's lives on a daily basis. Such denial tends to overlook how racialized capitalism manifests through labour and immigration injustice and inequality, including what Grace-Edward Galabuzi (2006) calls Canada's "creeping economic apartheid." The increased visibility and media coverage of the far right today must be seen through a critical historical lens in order to effectively understand, challenge, and defeat all forms of racism.

The same month that Trump took office in the United States, amid aggressive pseudo-populist rhetoric and policy measures of his administration, a White nationalist Quebec university student murdered six Muslim men and injured many others in an attack on a mosque in St Foy, Quebec City. These forms and expressions of politics and violence do not erupt out of nowhere, nor do they merely leap northwards across the border. This means that in Quebec, as in Canada more generally, we must go beyond acknowledging earlier periods of high-visibility, right-wing extremist activity (e.g., the Heritage Front, white-power skinheads, fascist organizing in the 1980s and 1990s), to face the depth, prevalence, and impact of racism in what are purportedly more-respectable sections of Canadian politics. They exist within the federal Conservatives (remember Harper's Conservative

Party 2015 election pledge to launch a "barbaric cultural practices" hotline?), the Bouchard-Taylor Commission on "reasonable accommodation," and the engineered moral panic about Quebec identity, and Quebec City's *radio poubelle* ("trash-talk radio"). Indeed, various forms of "respectable racism" are deeply embedded in the national fabric of Canada, as feminist anti-racist scholars like Sunera Thobani (2007) and others remind us. Moreover, the way in which global capitalism works to discipline and divide workers and render them vulnerable on capital's terms has echoes of earlier periods of entrenched unjust and exclusionary immigration/labour policies, from the late-nineteenth- and early-twentieth-century head tax on Chinese people, to the struggles of Caribbean women domestic workers in the 1970s and 1980s, who insisted: "good enough to work, good enough to stay" (Leah 1999), to the restrictions placed on many temporary foreign workers today.

Meanwhile, as in previous eras, and in many countries, the latest wave of nationalist, racist, and pseudo-populist politics seeks to divide and rule communities already fractured by years of social and economic upheaval and growing inequality. Free-market policies have atomized communities and dispossessed many people of livelihoods and futures, and in some cases have led to an electoral shift away from a political establishment associated with these policies. These political agendas attempt to divert attention away from the real causes of today's social and economic problems. Fighting against racism and xenophobia means struggling against free-market capitalism.

Legacies of Earlier Struggles

The history and foundational nature of racism in Canadian society is rarely appreciated beyond what are presented as unfortunate past episodes, or chapters of history. Moreover, equally long histories of anti-racist and anti-colonial resistance, and their lessons for today, are often overlooked. We want to draw attention to Ramirez and Chun's (2016, 88) question: "What impact do the histories of resistance and struggles by racially subordinated groups of workers, histories that go unrecorded and often exist as fleeting memories, have on current struggles to bring about a more just and emancipatory world?" These are important not simply for historical interest. The histories of the struggles and contributions made by those viewed to be at the margins of society, including their political ideas and visions, are too rarely made part of the histories of movements and social and political change. In turn, understandings about the scope for strategies and resistance overlook these perspectives and experiences – they are not part of what is usually taught and learned about working-class struggles, except as an addendum or afterthought. Failing to acknowledge the critical roles that marginalized groups of workers and activists have played in challenging dominant positions in labour and the other struggles in Canada on broader questions of social justice (racial, economic, gender, immigration justice, for example) runs the risk of distorting our current understandings of agency and horizons of possibilities for struggle and political action. Instead, we often take an ahistorical perspective on racialized migrant (and immigrant) workers and marginalized communities, one which views them as passive victims of exploitation and not as agents in resisting and challenging their conditions. In recalling these longer histories of resistance, we might reflect on how useful this analysis might be for understanding the current moment, as a tool for contemporary organizing, and in turn how this might strengthen struggles that move beyond reactive responses.

Migrant-Worker Organizing Today

With this in mind, we highlight the importance of contemporary migrant-worker organizing in Canada in the context of the continuing and evolving history of restrictive immigration policies and of social, political, and economic change as a result of the restructuring of global capitalism. The restructuring of the global economy has entailed a direct assault on people's livelihoods across the globe – on trade unions, increased competition, and downward pressures on workers' wages and conditions. The free flow of capital and structural adjustment policies has laid the ground for both producing – and generating increased demand for – migrant workers (Choudry and Hlatshwayo 2016).

Most temporary foreign workers in Canada face structural barriers, due to the fact their work permits are tied to a single employer – there is little or no pathway to permanent residence, and these conditions contribute to the formation of a two-tier labour market. Employers are able to wield power over these workers because of their immigration status. These conditions, coupled with the current climate of the defensive nature – and weakened power – of trade unions, means that the organizing of racialized migrant workers has often been through initiatives on the edge of, or outside of, the traditional trade-union movement.

Experiences of migrant-worker organizing also offer activists inside the established labour movement ways to reinvigorate the labour movement with strong anti-racist and immigration-justice politics and community organizing traditions. The types of organizations engaged in migrant-worker organizing are laboratories of struggle, which seek to creatively build the foundations of collective organizing through consistent outreach, democratic organizing, taking the lead from workers themselves, and organizing for structural change. There is much to learn from the organizing already occurring on the ground: migrant farmworker organizing through the grassroots collective, Justicia 4 Migrant Workers (J4MW) in Ontario and British Columbia, the efforts of Migrante Canada, an alliance of Filipino migrant and immigrant organizations in Canada (which in turn is part of a global alliance), to domestic-worker and caregiver organizations like PINAY (Quebec) and the Caregivers' Action Centre (Toronto). Worker centres such as Toronto's Workers' Action Centre (WAC), and the Immigrant Workers Centre (IWC) in Montreal are examples of organizing that seek to build the grassroots power of some of the most marginalized and precarious workers in Canada.

One element shared among migrant-worker organizers has been the rooting of their work in the needs of workers themselves, beyond fighting solely on traditional workplace issues. For example, the IWC has been supporting the organization of temporary foreign workers through a Temporary Foreign Workers Association, founded in 2013 by workers and their allies. Since then, alongside, and based in, individual and collective cases, the work seeks to target the structural causes that limit their organizing for decent working conditions, with precarious immigration status and deportations fundamentally being addressed as workers' issues.

These efforts to organize with migrant workers means struggling to change the system of closed work permits and temporary immigration status. This was highlighted by the Harvesting Freedom Caravan in Ontario in 2016, organized by J4MW with the support of unions and other allies. Marching with hundreds of farmworkers from southern Ontario to Ottawa to demand an end to the current labour regime, the caravan demanded permanent legal status for thousands of migrant workers. As J4MW (2016) states, "For 50 years, seasonal agricultural workers have been the bulwark of agricultural food production, and yet they have no access to secure, permanent immigration status." The work of building such campaigns has meant a type of organizing that is rooted in these communities, and consistent relationship-building in contrast to the type of business unionism that has hampered many trade unions (see Camfield 2011).

Recent organizing efforts have focused on building relationships among workers. A J4MW organizer, Adriana Paz Ramirez, describes the efforts of activists to visit rural communities on a weekly basis, meeting workers in town or in their houses: "The workers were able to go public because of the months creating a relationship, in restaurants, parking lots, talking by phone. People don't just speak up when they feel a huge sense of injustice" (Ramirez 2016, 159). In Quebec, the IWC organizes social activities and workshops to foster connections between migrant workers and organizers. It seeks to challenge racism, labour exploitation, and marginalization by centring the organizing around the experiences and needs of the migrants.

In this work, activists and organizers have tried to support and facilitate worker leadership through education and building skills, so that their struggles and demands are front and centre. Justicia for Migrant Workers contends that it is "a movement that is led and directed by workers themselves" (J4MW 2011). The Temporary Foreign Workers Association in Quebec develops direct leadership by the workers through a membership-based association. This has meant extensive training on labour and immigration rights, as well as on organizing skills, campaign strategy, and integration of leaders into the Precarious Workers Coalition. As WAC's Deena Ladd notes, it is critical that the leadership development be constantly linked to ongoing organizing and campaigns (2016). Such organizing among migrant workers differs from a service provision model that is based on reacting to the needs of government and funders, or workplace organizing that does not address fundamental issues at the core of the injustices faced by migrant workers. While the challenges are immense, broader coalitions are being built, such as the Migrant Workers Alliance for Change, which brings together migrant-worker organizations into a federal coalition with unions. But the continual work of building alliances on the ground – based on anti-racist, working-class perspectives that centre that movement of racialized migrant workers and their demands – is crucial.

Concluding Thoughts

Ramirez and Chun (2016, 101) ask:

> Why after more than forty years in Canada do migrant farmworkers remain at the margins of established political movements and organized labour organizations? How do migrant farmworkers struggle outside of established organizations and social movements? What kind of impact do migrant workers' hidden struggles and daily concerns have on movements that claim (or attempt) to speak for the dispossessed?

These struggles by racialized communities and migrant workers do not just challenge the current face of racism and xenophobia, but can also confront the very foundation of racism and colonialism in Canada. The prevailing economic and political system that rests on these foundations continues to benefit an enriched ruling elite. It also feeds contemporary manifestations of racism and nationalism that mask the structural pillars that have led to such inequalities. For many people today, the words of Swedish-American labour organizer and songwriter Joe Hill, spoken shortly before he faced a Utah firing squad over a hundred years ago, have a renewed urgency and meaning: "Don't waste any time in mourning. Organize!"

History shows us that organizing progressive movements for social and political justice is a vital force in changing the world, including the often-unacknowledged importance of the visions and ideas that are produced in the struggles themselves. Solidarity with migrant workers is central to building a movement that can lead to genuine social justice and transformation. Such a movement needs to clearly connect bosses' undermining of workers' organizing and justice work, to the privatization and downloading of health care, as well as to the role of Canadian corporations, foreign policy, and security policy in countries throughout the global south. These are the forces that exacerbate social injustice, poverty, and land dispossession that contribute to the conditions which drive many migrants to come to Canada. Thus, the struggles of migrant workers today stand at the crossroads of labour rights and the urgent work for ecological justice and against ongoing forms of colonialism and neo-liberal policies that continue to tear up the fabric of the gains made by earlier movements.

REFERENCES

Benjamin, W. 2003. *Selected Writings*. Vol. 4: *1938–1940*, edited by H. Eiland and M.W. Jennings. Cambridge, MA: Harvard University Press.
Camfield, D. 2011. *Canadian Labour in Crisis: Reinventing the Workers' Movement*. Black Point, NS: Fernwood.
Choudry, A., and M. Hlatshwayo, eds. 2016. *Just Work? Migrant Workers' Struggles Today*. London: Pluto Press.
Justice for Migrant Workers. 2016. "Harvesting Freedom." https://harvestingfreedom dotorg.files.wordpress.com/2016/09/harvestingfreedomreachesottawa-media advisoryfinal.pdf.
Ladd, D., and S. Singh. 2016. "Critical Questions: Building Worker Power and a Vision of Organizing in Ontario." In *Unfree Labour? Struggles of Migrant and Immigrant Workers in Canada*, edited by A. Choudry and A.A. Smith, 123–41. Oakland, CA: PM Press.
Leah, R.J. 1999. "Do You Call Me 'Sister'? Women of Colour and the Canadian Labour Movement." In *Scratching the Surface: Canadian Anti-Racist Feminist Thought*, edited by E. Dua and A. Robertson, 97–126. Toronto: Women's Press.
Ramirez, Paz, and J.J. Chun. 2016. "Struggling Against History: Migrant Farm-worker Organizing in British Columbia." In *Unfree Labour? Struggles of Migrant and Immigrant Workers in Canada*, edited by A. Choudry and A.A. Smith, 87–104. Oakland, CA: PM Press.
Ramirez, Paz A., J. Calugay, J. Hanley, M. Henaway, D. Ladd, M. Luciano, C. Ramsaroop, E. Shragge, S. Singh, and C. Sorio. 2016. "Organizers in Dialogue." In *Unfree Labour? Struggles of Migrant and Immigrant Workers in Canada*, edited by A. Choudry, and A.A. Smith. Oakland, CA: PM Press.
Statistics Canada. 2017. "Transition from Temporary Foreign Workers to Permanent Residents, 1990 to 2014." Ottawa: Statistics Canada. https://www.statcan.gc.ca/pub/11f0019m/11f0019m2017389-eng.htm.
Thobani, S. 2007. *Exalted Subjects: Studies in The Making of Nation and Race in Canada*. Toronto: University of Toronto Press.

24

AUSTERITY URBANISM, POPULISM, AND LABOUR

Steven Tufts, Mark P. Thomas, and Ian MacDonald

Since the global financial crisis of 2008, workers have been under attack, as both private capital and governments have implemented programs of austerity, reducing expenditures to cut deficits and boost balance sheets. Although urban and suburban areas continue to drive capitalist economic growth in many parts of the world, austerity measures as a response to the crisis have been acute in cities. In fact, austerity urbanism characterizes much of urban life today, as local economies and states adjust to the con- tradictions of contemporary global capitalism. Austerity urbanism has also coincided with the rise of populism, in its various forms. In many cases, populism on the right has been effective in forging popular support for austerity projects, in particular legitimating attacks on organized labour in the city. We briefly identify some links among austerity urbanism, right populism, and workers in contemporary North America. The discussion concludes with some possibilities for organized labour and a counter-left urban populism.

Austerity Urbanism

Jamie Peck (2012) argues that, following the economic crisis/recession of 2007 to 2009, an intensification of neo-liberal governance emerged in many US cities. As the fiscal stimulus following the crisis ended, state governments soon cut budgets, downsized, and reorganized public services, implemented user fees, and increased revenues from other sources, such as casinos. To- gether, these measures imposed an even greater financial and social disci- pline on cities in a new era of austerity urbanism.

Defining a project as complex and geographically diverse as austerity urbanism is challenging. A number of key pillars have, however, been iden- tified by Davidson and Ward (2018). While often used to describe the US experience, these trends also apply (however unevenly) to the United King-dom, Canada, and other countries. First, there is the downloading of pro-gram delivery and responsibility onto municipalities. This is sometimes accompanied by transitional funding, but eventually there is a reduction in financial support for such programs. The provision of social housing and transit are key examples of areas where higher levels of government con-tinue to regulate but have reduced financial commitments.

Second, there is the privatization of assets and new forms of financializa-tion of urban economic development. These projects can take the forms of deferred taxation schemes (Davidson and Ward 2014) or a range of public-private partnerships. Recently, the bankruptcy of Carillion, a large UK-based construction firm that employed over forty thousand globally, has demon-strated the vulnerability of such shared-cost arrangements (*Economist* 2018). These efforts parallel other neo-liberal privatization initiatives, such as the privatization of Canada's health-care system documented by Armstrong in this volume.

Third, municipal governments have attacked both the wages of public-sector workers and services on which the poor depend. The result is in-creased economic polarization that inevitably has unequal impacts across racialized and gendered groups. Disciplining public-sector workers who provide city services involves several strategies, including layoffs, privatiza-tion, union busting, and the reorganization of work (Ross and Savage 2013; Krinsky 2011). Unions still manage to play a role in shaping urban develop-ment, but often do so unevenly, in ways that further fragment urban work-ing classes (MacDonald 2017).

In order to implement the multi-faceted agenda identified above, mu-nicipalities are required to manage dissent over withdrawal from service provision. As a result, a fourth pillar, extreme revanchism, emerges with increasing investments in policing and local security apparatuses required to control marginalized populations (see Smith 1996). While police are not immune entirely to austerity urbanism, historically they are often the last to feel any impact given authoritarian populist support for law and order.

Austerity urbanism is therefore a constellation of practices that has been born out of earlier forms of neo-liberal governance (see Brenner and Theodore 2002). To implement austerity urbanism as a practice, however, requires significant political power. In the United States, for example, the rise of right-wing populist discourse from the Tea Party to Donald Trump has supported this process. Similar examples can be seen elsewhere, with a most notable recent Canadian example being evident during the term of Toronto's Mayor Rob Ford (2010–14) (Thomas and Tufts 2016a). The right's attack on labour coincides with austerity programs aimed specifically at poor people in the city, as Clarke notes in this volume.

Right Populism and Workers in the City

It is important to acknowledge that right populism and its authoritarian and extremist variations have long historical trajectories, as both Day and McCaskell point out in their contributions to this volume. The current moment of right populism has emerged as an iterative process to facilitate austerity projects. In previous work, we have detailed how different aspects of populism have been operationalized to discursively attack workers and labour unions (Thomas and Tufts 2016b). Across North American cities, right populism is now part of contemporary urban experiences. These are not simply suburban reactions to downtown "elites," although challenging "elites" through common appeals to "the people" is a hallmark of both left and right populism (Laclau 2005). We consider different elements of populism, identified by others (Canovan 1981; Bertlet and Lyons 2000; Mudde and Rovira Kaltwasser 2017) that play out across urban spaces daily.

Producerism is a populist concept, according to which everyone has to be productive in society and generate something of use. "Lazy" city workers who are protected by union contracts and "produce nothing" is one such trope favoured by right populist politicians. Such concepts are intended to create cross-class identifications that fragment the labour movement, delegitimize unions as political actors, and paralyze class mobilization. The public sector is a large source of union members; private-sector unionization rates are much lower than in the public sector in both the United States (6.5 per cent versus 34 per cent) and Canada (16 per cent versus 71 per cent). In the United States, the Supreme Court decision in *Janus v. Afscme* will potentially exempt public-sector workers from paying mandatory union dues, continuing a long process of decline in organized labour (Fletcher Jr 2018).

Racist "scapegoating" and "nativism" are central elements of right populism. Targeting immigrants for "taking jobs" and "ruining our cities" is typical discourse. As Choudry and Henaway discuss in this volume, such attacks both build upon the long history of racism in Canada and reflect current processes to discipline and divide workers in the current era of global capitalism. Attacks on the public services that immigrants and Indigenous communities in cities depend upon are part of austerity urbanism's uneven racialized impacts. Conspiracism and apocalyptic narratives also drive right-populist agendas, with frequent references to "big government" and "big unions" being in league with big corporations and elite financiers. There is also a sense of doom, as urban financial centres brace for an impending crisis (stress from "too many immigrants") and urban infrastructure is perceived as being on the brink of collapse.

Populism also often entails a cult of leadership. In Toronto, the rise of populist Mayor Rob Ford and his antics captured the global stage from 2010 to 2014 (Doolittle 2017). He maintained a following of loyal supporters, even as he plummeted into the darkest corners of a substance-abuse scandal. Ford was also no friend of unions and appealed to Torontonians with promises to end "the gravy train" – a right-populist code that included, among others, unionized municipal workers – at City Hall (Thomas and Tufts 2016a). There are many populist municipal leaders across the United States with a similar appeal.

Lastly, right populism is also characterized by a creeping authoritarianism. In the United States, the rise of Black Lives Matter as a direct confrontation of racialized police killings has spread across urban centres in both Canada and the United States. Police associations, the only unions politicians do not openly challenge, have responded with a populist Blue Lives Matter campaign – a direct attempt to "de-centre" the movement against police violence and abuse of power (Thomas and Tufts 2020). Authoritarian populism continues to drive racist revanchist projects that control austerity urbanism (see Hall et al. 2013).

Importantly, such discourse is not just deployed from above to further the austerity project. Insofar as right-populist ideas are embraced by workers themselves, including unionized workers and public-sector workers, they also reflect a working-class conservatism and individualism that has long characterized North American urban space. Such conservatism among workers has re-emerged with urban austerity and reflects the failure of the labour movement to offer a viable, progressive alternative.

Counter-Left Urban Populism

The rise of right-populist discourse as part of austerity urbanism has also met resistance. From the Occupy movement, to Black Lives Matter, to the Fight for $15 and Fairness, urban space is a new battlefield where the strategies and tactics needed to organize against the right-populist attack on labour are both implemented and debated. Despite progressive suspicion toward populist currents, we feel that it is possible to reorient the most basic sentiments against the "elite" toward a counter-left urban populism to defend workers (Tufts and Thomas 2014). While populism can lead to regressive and even hateful ideologies, distrust of "elites" and those in power is at the heart of much resistance by labour and community groups. Inspiring others by appealing to populist currents and substituting alternate content is possible.

In terms of producerism, there is much to be said about the plight of the "working poor" and how the minimum wage does not allow people to live in high-cost cities. Further, public-sector workers provide services with use value that benefit all. Tasked with reproducing capitalist society in the context of austerity urbanism and revanchism, public-sector workers also find themselves imposing discipline and providing uneven access to degraded public services. Left varieties of producerism in the public sector could constitute an effective response to austerity urbanism. Left bargaining strategies in the public sector must identify contract demands that improve the job quality of public-sector workers in ways that also respond to the needs and demands of the working class for accessible public goods and services. The Chicago Teachers' Strike of 2012 is one example of how bargaining was linked to popular demands for quality education in the city (Brogan 2014), a link also present in the wave of teachers' strikes in the United States in 2018 (Virginia) and 2019 (Los Angeles).

Conspiracism is driven by workers' need to understand their own economic insecurity. The "1 per cent" identified by Occupy plays to this, but it must be tempered with labour education that allows workers to uncover the roots of systemic inequalities and white supremacy. Who are the "1 per cent" if not elites controlling the levers of global capitalism? While some rightfully argue that the "1-per-cent" discourse was problematic in its proximity to antisemitic, anti-globalist rhetoric, "scapegoating" the "1 per cent" was a powerful element of the Occupy movement. Scapegoating the rich as a means to illuminate the causes of economic inequality within capitalism can be part of an effective response to right-populist scapegoating of immigrants and appeals to nativism. To this end, a populist union education program that maps the "1 per cent" and the financial structures of contemporary capitalism, as well as their intersections with the dynamics of white privilege and white supremacy, is crucial.

Narratives of environmental collapse often reflect an apocalyptic neo-Malthusianism. Invoking the apocalypse as a "sense of urgency" in order to inspire transformation of the capitalist economy's relationship to nature is not without merit, but can be demobilizing. Elitist and pro-business discourses of ecological modernization that dominate urban policy fail to speak to average workers and avoid the capitalist root of the crisis. Some eco-socialist responses to the planetary crisis are framed as transitional New Deal–type jobs programs that respond to workers' economic insecurity as well as local environmental deficits that are closely linked to classed and racialized locations in urban space. Campaigns such as Good Green Jobs in Toronto are not without contradiction, but they do have some popular appeal. Similarly, a "Green New Deal" has been advocated by left-populist congresswoman Alexandria Ocasio-Cortez, and a policy document of the same name was promoted by numerous climate justice and environmental organizations in Canada during the 2019 federal election campaign.

Populist leaders are suspect among progressives who tend toward more-horizontal leadership models. Yet, the promotion of left leaders within populist grassroots formations does not inevitably lead to anti-democratic, top-down leadership. Leaders can inspire, and the labour movement should not be afraid to rally behind progressives who manage to connect with workers on key issues. Progressive populist mayors, city councillors, and unionists must not be easily dismissed, nor should they be insulated from criticism from below. In Seattle, the election of left-populist socialist Kshama Sawant to city council has been an example heralded by progressives.

Populism has an authoritarian streak, but also an anti-authoritarian counterpart. Addressing questions of surveillance in urban workplaces and communities and fostering a backlash against practices such as racialized police "carding" have brought changes to policing in New York and Toronto. While unions have financially supported Black Lives Matter and spoken out against racist policing, there is arguably more coalition work to be done here by populist appeals to freedom of mobility for all urban workers.

There are countless opportunities to insert counter-left urban populism into campaigns. Counter-left urban populist campaigns are not always orchestrated, but may seize moments. In Ontario, the Fight for $15 and Fairness campaign brought issues of worker economic security and rights to the forefront. It was anything but spontaneous, as it was planned over months through a coalition of workers' groups, students, and unions. When an increase in the Ontario minimum wage to $14 was implemented on 1 January 2018 (as a step toward $15), it was discovered that Tim Horton's franchisees were rolling back employee benefits, and a populist backlash against the multinational coffee chain quickly surfaced. Here, unions were presented with an opportunity to reach out and organize these almost exclusively non-union workers. Tim Horton's brands itself as a working-people's restaurant. As wealthy franchise owners act to keep workers from realizing the benefits of a mandated wage increase, the company is open to campaigns that effectively capture the "anti-elitist" sentiments of low-wage workers – not only Tim Horton's employees, but also its customers. The election of a Conservative provincial government under the leadership of right-populist Doug Ford in June 2018 resulted in the minimum wage being frozen at $14 per hour; thus, the Fight for $15 and Fairness campaign has continued.

New coalitions can challenge "elite" bureaucrats and planners who decide to cut back urban services. Though urban workers are susceptible to nativist constructions around national identities and borders, it is nevertheless possible to build populist forms of working-class solidarity, based not on where someone is from, but rather on who they are becoming and how they contribute to society as part of a larger working class. Resistance that co-opts rather than dismisses elements of populism may inspire workers to build cities for people rather than simply for elites under conditions of austerity. Failure to do so only cedes populism to the right and further enables right-populist attacks on workers.

REFERENCES

Berlet, C., and M. Lyons. 2000. *Right-Wing Populism in America: Too Close for Comfort*. New York: Guilford.

Brenner, N., and N. Theodore. 2002. "Cities and the Geographies of 'Actually Existing Neoliberalism.'" *Antipode* 34 (3): 349–79.

Brogan, Peter. 2014. "Getting to the CORE of the Chicago Teachers' Union Transformation." *Studies in Social Justice* 8 (2): 145–64.

Canovan, M. 1981. *Populism*. New York: Harcourt.

Davidson, M., and K. Ward. 2014. "Picking up the Pieces: Austerity Urbanism, California, and Fiscal Crisis." *Cambridge Journal of Regions, Economy, and Society* 7 (1): 81–97.

– 2018. "Introduction." In *Cities under Austerity: Restructuring the US Metropolis*, edited by M. Davidson and K. Ward. New York: SUNY University Press.

Doolittle, R. 2014. *Crazy Town: The Rob Ford Story*. Toronto: Viking.

The Economist. 2018. "Where Did Carillion Go Wrong?" *Economist*, 18 January. https://www.economist.com/news/britain/21735047-mistakes-caused-mega-contractors-demise-are-common-outsourcing-industry-where.

Fletcher Jr, B. 2018. "Attacking the Rights of Workers: The US Supreme Court Hides Behind the First Amendment." *Bullet*, 28 June. https://socialistproject.ca/2018/06/attacking-the-rights-of-workers-the-us-supreme-court-hides-behind-the-first-amendment/.

Hall, S., C. Critcher, T. Jefferson, J. Clarke, and B. Roberts. 2013[1978]. *Policing the Crisis: Mugging, the State, and Law and Order*. 2nd ed. London: Palgrave.

Krinsky, J. 2011. "Neoliberal Times: Intersecting Temporalities and the Neoliberalization of New York City's Public-Sector Labor Relations." *Social Science History* 35 (3): 381–422.

Laclau, E. 2005. *On Populist Reason*. London: Verso.

MacDonald, I. 2017. "Introduction: The Urbanization of Union Strategy and Struggle." In *Unions and the City: Negotiating Urban Change*, edited by I.T. MacDonald, 1–26. Ithaca, NY: Cornell University Press.

Mudde, C., and C. Rovira Kaltwasser. 2017. *Populism: A Very Short Introduction*. New York: Oxford University Press.

Peck, J. 2012. "Austerity Urbanism: American Cities under Extreme Economy." *City* 16: 626–55.

Ross, S., and L. Savage, eds. 2013. *Public Sector Unions in the Age of Austerity.*
    Halifax, NS: Fernwood.

Smith, N. 1996. *The New Urban Frontier: Gentrification and the Revanchist City.*
    New York: Routledge.

Thomas, M., and S. Tufts. 2016a. "Enabling Dissent: Contesting Austerity and Right
    Populism in Toronto, Canada." *The Economic and Labour Relations Review* 27 (1):
    29–45.

– 2016b. "Unions Confront Austerity and Populism in Canada." *Antipode* 48 (1):
    212–30.

– 2020. "Blue Solidarity: Police Unions, Race, and Authoritarian Populism in North
    America." *Work, Employment & Society* 34 (1): 126–44.

Tufts, S., and M. Thomas. 2014. "Populist Unionism Confronts Austerity in
    Canada." *Labor Studies Journal* 39 (1): 60–82.

25

ADVOCATING FOR THE COMMON GOOD

Canadian Muslim Women and Their Families

Alia Hogben

As Canadians, as Muslims, and as women we are deeply affected by the political events of the world. We are dealing with the fallout from authoritarian, far-right policies and fundamentalism that have spread all over the world. The hope that democracy would spread to Muslim-majority countries has not occurred; instead there has been an increase of totalitarian regimes. Values such as human rights and freedoms have been suppressed. The current wars in the Middle East affect their citizens the most, including rapes and maltreatment of women and girls. The political changes have led to the rise of extreme conservative policies and practices, not only in Africa and Asia but also in developed democracies such as the United States. The move to erect barriers around countries and to close ranks has resulted in an increase in the division between "them" and "us."

The recent global political environment has focused on Islam and Muslims. This is partly due to the shocking actions of some Muslims and mostly due to the terrible reactions of the West against nations with Muslim majorities. The vengeful acts of aggression by the West, such as the wars in Syria and Iraq, have resulted in thousands of deaths and an increase in refugees from these countries. Refugees have been created because of the lack of stable, democratic governments in countries that have become the killing fields for both their own tyrannical governments and for the West. The increase in the world's refugees has mostly been among Muslims, and the arrival of these people in the West has led to fears and hostility against those seen as outsiders.

The context for us, Canadians, is that many of us are immigrants from countries that have problems of their own, including cultures that are patriarchal and have a conservative interpretation of Islam. This influences family lives in Canada, and the Canadian Council of Muslim Women (CCMW) is often called upon by women to assist with these challenges. We are fortunate that, as Canadian Muslim women, we do have a stable government and the Charter does provide us with protections. However, these protections are often threatened by racism and prejudice from other citizens, but also at times from our elected governments.

The CCMW was founded in 1982, when a group of women sought to mobilize their passion for social justice and faith in order to enrich their communities and work toward the common good of Canadian society. We are committed to Canada, to Islam, and to the welfare of women and their families at a time of turmoil about the faith and about Muslim women and at a time when there are so few national or international groups standing up against these forces. The organization is a member of two international networks, Women Living Under Muslim Laws, and Musawah, a movement to change family laws so that equality of women and girls is integral to relevant legislation.

The organization was founded with the goals of equity, equality, and empowerment of Canadian Muslim women. We are women who believe in Islam, and although we may practise the religion in diverse ways, it is critical that we hold to an interpretation of Islam that allows us to demand equality within Islam. We have continued to assist women and their families to achieve these goals by pursuing integration through active participation and civic engagement. This includes: advocating; completing projects on women's rights and civic engagement; providing educational resources; and providing local workshops across the country. We continuously work with the media to ensure positive public communication. We actively advocate for an interpretation of Islam that is congruent with the Universal Declaration of Human Rights and the Canadian Charter of Rights and Freedoms. Fortunately, there are a number of brilliant Islamic scholars whose work encourages this humane version of Islam in which women's rights are held as an integral part of the faith.

As Canadian Muslim women, however, we find ourselves in a tangled mess of colliding, contradictory, and conflicting forces from various sources. In our work, we face issues from two directions – those that are within Muslim communities, and others such as racism and anti-Muslim prejudice that are directed at Muslims from the society around us. Internal to Muslim communities, the political agenda is closely tied to the everyday life experiences of women and girls. The practice of a patriarchal model of society and the family has been damaging for women and girls. The model of male-dominated families, with assigned roles, has little space for the intellectual or nurturing growth of women and girls. This patriarchal system is upheld by the use of cultural norms, but also by a literal and conservative interpretation of Islam. Women's rights are not on the agenda, and even the term "equality" is denigrated and replaced with terms such as "complementariness of genders."

An unfortunate reality in our lives is that the version of Islam that currently dominates is one espoused and financed by states such as Saudi Arabia. That country's alliance with Wahhabis has a strong conservative message that is propagated all over the world and funded by petrodollars. This is done overtly not only in Muslim-majority countries, but in countries such as Canada. The other source of this interpretation is the Internet. There are hundreds of sites of so-called religious leaders who are strident in their teachings regarding women. Sadly, many women are seduced by these men and accept their interpretations of the religion, even if it is anti-woman. These religious personalities are charismatic and heavily funded, so that money and message go hand in hand. In their world view, if Muslims would return to the halcyon days of Islam, then we Muslims will again be dominant and outshine any contributions of the West. Tragically this view is based on a sense of anomie, of loss and hopelessness, and a search for a strengthened identity. Too many Muslims are living in lands that are turbulent conflict zones, lacking economic stability and with little regard for human rights. The call to Islam as the answer to all their ills becomes powerful.

The emphasis on the *ummah* – community of believers – is a strong and persuasive message for Muslims. The unrealistic belief in the Caliphate as espoused by Daesh is one example. Another example of the *ummah* is when young Muslims hear the siren call that encourages them to fight against the "enemy," which is the West. The manipulation of religion is pervasive, and any democratic change is stalled, because these leaders enmesh religion and politics.

In Canada, due to changes in government policies, there has been an increase in the population of Muslims over the last forty years. The diversity of the newer immigrants from almost all parts of the world has changed the dynamics within Canadian Muslim communities.

There is much heterogeneity among Muslims, of race, culture, ethnicity, as well as religious beliefs. As there is no monolithic Muslim community, we must be careful not to homogenize all Muslims or to make generalizations about us as though we are a cohesive group. Certainly, there are common threads that bind us together, but there are strains that differentiate us as well. The context for these tensions exists as widespread threats to democracy in many areas, including the United States, Europe, and Canada. Some political parties, both in the West and in developing countries, are based on ideology that insists on a separation of peoples by race, colour, religion, or ethnicity. Instead of emphasizing cohesion and common humanity, these groups are threatening all that holds us together.

The new terminology of far-right extremism, such as "alt-right," is part of the rise of white nationalism, which is really an ethnic position of white superiority. Surely, colonialism has shown that any practice of superiority of one race over another is cruel and leads only to suppression of human rights. The recent rise in nativism – an ideology that contends that countries should be inhabited only by "native" groups – conflicts with the right of any other group to live within these states. The white nationalist groups would happily deport all groups except the "Whites."

How has the work of organizations such as the ccmw changed with the rise of political forces like white nationalism that threaten democracy in Canada and the world? The ccmw emphasizes fundamental human rights as articulated in the Universal Declaration of Human Rights and the Canadian Charter of Rights and Freedoms. It is these values that must be the underpinnings of any movement for change or protest. There has to be common ground that includes common values, so that these can work against community fragmentation. Diversity of faith, culture, ethnicity, and race must be recognized but, more importantly, it is our shared values of democracy, equality, equity, and empowerment of all peoples that will bind us together.

One Canadian example of efforts to create change was the struggle of Canadian Muslim women to advocate against the imposition of religious family laws. From 2003 to 2005, ccmw formed a strong movement with many partnerships to fight the use of such laws. Even though we are believing women, we reject religious family laws, since none have women's equality rights embedded in them. Our advocacy succeeded, and the government agreed that no religious family laws can be used in family arbitration.

We succeeded because we were able to form strong alliances with similar groups. However, this was in Canada, where a system of rights and freedoms provided us with a context for change. This may not have been the case if we had had to campaign against a conservative government that had a narrow understanding of "Canadian values" and was anti-immigration, with racist policies and practices. Some recent examples of this emerged in the previous Canadian federal government, whose ministers insisted in calling some harmful cultural practices "barbaric," and wanted to set up a "snitch line," so that people could phone in complaints against each other. Then there is the recent uproar in Quebec regarding a law to ban face coverings such as the niqab worn by some Muslim women. Such a strong reaction about the clothing of a few women can only be described as racist.

What needs to be done to surmount these challenges and to strengthen the common good in Canada? Our experience with the struggle against religious family laws taught us many practical lessons. It required resistance to the widely held view that family laws are sacrosanct and incapable of change. This is especially relevant for religious groups like some fundamentalist Jews, Christians, and Muslims. Another lesson learned is that any movement for change must have an impact on more than one group; our focus was on *all* religious family laws, not just Muslim ones. We learned that diverse people had to be committed to creating change, and that, although there may be differences, we had to have general consensus on our objectives. There had to be agreement about the values and clear goals of what we wanted to achieve. The other critical need is a free press, a democratic institution currently being suppressed by authoritarian leaders. There is also the harsh reality of financial resources. No change can be carried out for a long period without resources, and there are few women's organizations with adequate finances.

In conclusion, any social movement requires passion, commitment, courage, and organization from those who hold similar values. We must remain hopeful and work toward creating partnerships and a movement for change. We must believe in what Margaret Mead stated: "Never doubt that a small group of thoughtful committed citizens can change the world; indeed it's the only thing that ever did."

26

TRUMP
Climate Denial on Steroids

Keith Stewart

After Ron Liepert, a former Alberta energy minister and current federal Conservative member of parliament, called me an extremist for the third time on CBC radio's *The Current*, host Anna Maria Tremonti asked him why he used that label, since "that is the same language we use for ISIS" (CBC 2014). His response was telling: "Because individuals like your guest would like to see fossil fuels eliminated across the world. That is simply not going to happen. He lives in this dream world where somehow airplanes are going to fly with solar power, where transit in his city is going to be powered by renewables from wind. This is just a dream world these extremists live in." To be fair to Mr Liepert, he may truly believe that my call to phase out fossil fuels is an extremist position, because there has been a decades-long campaign to deny the reality of climate change.

As a long-time climate activist, I have been struck by how the denial campaigns of the 1990s were, in many ways, a dry run for today's "alt-right." Understanding climate denial's political strategy can provide useful insights into the contemporary rise of post-truth, anti-science authoritarianism. The parallels and continuity are not an accident. Trump's transition team included at least nine high-profile climate deniers. His picks to lead the EPA and the Department of the Interior question the basic science of climate change (Milman 2016). The former CEO of Exxon-Mobil, the company that was central to the creation and financing of the denial machine (Oreskes and Conway 2010, 247–8), was his pick for Secretary of State.

Trump is a master of chaos, but the method behind his madness becomes a little clearer once you recognize that, when Trump threw out the rulebook of conventional politics, he picked up the denial playbook. Many of the "false news" tricks and post-truth politics that helped bring Trump to the White House were invented and/or refined in the climate wars: unashamedly inventing "alternative facts" in order to advance your interests, creating an echo chamber to repeat those claims, attacking the credibility of the institutions designed to separate fact from fiction, and claiming that the wealthy and powerful are political underdogs besieged by tyrannical ideologues.

This was the *modus operandi* of the denial machine that was created and financed by oil and coal companies (Oreskes and Conway 2010). It proved to be devastatingly effective at delaying action on climate change – often with the assistance of a credulous mainstream media, who are now having these tools turned against them. This strategy was so effective because it was telling (some) people what they wanted to believe. As Naomi Klein argues in *This Changes Everything*, the political right was correct about climate change in one regard: there are no non-radical solutions left. We have waited so long to act (not least because of the success of the denial campaign waged by fossil-fuel interests) that there is no incrementalist policy path that would keep warming below dangerous levels. The level of state intervention required to deal with the world's biggest market failure is completely incompatible with the conservative agenda of shrinking the state. In the face of this challenge to their core values, many on the political right choose to reject the science instead of re-evaluating their commitment to free markets (Klein 2014).

In politics, it is always important to recognize that there are interests at play. When those interests are named Exxon, Shell, or Chevron, the play can get rough. But what I think we can learn from the history of climate denial to better understand Trumpian politics is how those interests deployed motivated reasoning to pursue their policy agenda.

Mainstream environmentalists have wasted a lot of time trying to find the magic words or the one incontrovertible peer-reviewed study to convince conservatives to fight climate change. This hasn't worked (in the United States at least), because rather than being rational individuals who assess evidence independent of context, human beings tend to absorb knowledge socially and resist revising beliefs that constitute our social identities. This is what social scientists call "motivated reasoning": the unconscious tendency of individuals to fit their processing of information to conclusions that suit some end, such as maintaining a valued identity, particularly as a member of a group (Roberts 2016).

We all engage in motivated reasoning to some extent. Scientific institutions and the media – as institutions – are designed to help us overcome
that tendency by establishing standards as to what can be considered
"true." While they do so imperfectly and contain many hidden biases (for
example, see Haraway 1989), these institutions do represent an attempt to
go beyond the tribalism of motivated reasoning in which what is true depends on whether the speaker is inside, or outside, the group. This is why
attacks on science, the mainstream media, and expertise as being "fake"
or biased are core to new-right politics. They want to *encourage* motivated
reasoning by stoking fears and resentments in such a way that the mere
act of presenting counter-evidence is interpreted as an assault on the
group identity.

This cultivation of motivated reasoning is behind the increasingly bitter
partisan divide in politics, but it is difficult to root out because it allows
select interests (such as fossil-fuel companies) to pursue their goals with
limited scrutiny. A key difference in the contemporary era relative to the
1990s, however, is the degree to which security forces and not just think
tanks are being brought to bear in this conflict. The stakes have gone up, as
activism begins to threaten corporate profits and oil and coal companies
now face a serious threat to their business plans from what Naomi Klein
has labelled Blockadia: the loosely affiliated network of social movements
that is confronting the extractive industry everywhere, from Greece's gold
mines to Canada's tar sands (Klein 2014). The long-running battle over tar-
sands pipelines is only the most visible of these confrontations, which are
happening around the world. The success of these strategies has led not
only to national media attention, but also to a powerful response from corporate and state security forces. In effect, the (relative) success of land and
water defenders has led to them being framed as not just wrong or misguided idealists, but as enemies of the state.

In Canada, we saw the Harper government demonize pipeline opponents
as "radicals" (Payton 2012) and "money-launderers," (Paris 2012) whose actions were "treacherous" (Reuters 2011). In co-operation with a Conserva-
tive-linked front group called Ethical Oil (McCarthy, 2014) (the forerunner
of The Rebel News), the Harper government launched an unprecedented
attack on environmental groups through the Canada Revenue Agency, "political activities" audits of environmental groups with charitable status

(Beeby 2014). My own organization, Greenpeace, was listed as a multi-issue extremist organization under anti-terrorism laws, in spite of an unbroken four-decade-long record of non-violence (McCarthy 2012).

The Harper government's anti-terrorism law, Bill C-51, incorporated a controversial definition of "economic terrorism" that included activities such as anti-pipeline blockades. An RCMP "critical threat assessment report" obtained by Greenpeace warned of "a growing, highly organized and well-financed, anti-Canadian petroleum movement" (McCarthy 2015). That RCMP document went on to echo denial talking points, implying that climate change was a mere claim advanced by members of this movement: "Non-governmental environmental groups such as: Greenpeace, Tides Canada and Sierra Club Canada to name a few, assert climate change is now the most serious global environmental threat, and that climate change is a direct consequence of elevated anthropogenic greenhouse gas emissions which, they believe, are directly linked to the continued use of fossil fuels" (RCMP 2014).

This wasn't limited to Canada or to state security forces. During the 2016 Standing Rock protests over the Dakota Access pipeline in the United States, the pipeline company (Energy Transfer Partners) hired a mercenary firm (Tiger Swan) to target the Indigenous-led movement opposed to the pipeline, according to internal documents obtained by *The Intercept* (Brown, Parrish, and Speri 2017a). Tiger Swan, which characterized the water protectors as following "the jihadist insurgency model," employed military-style counterterrorism measures while collaborating closely with police in at least five states. Energy Transfer Partners also paid Tiger Swan to gather information for what would become a billion-dollar conspiracy lawsuit that accused Greenpeace and other environmentalist groups of inciting the anti-pipeline protests (Brown, Parrish, and Speri 2017b).

The attempt to "blame" the Standing Rock conflict on environmental groups is likely an attempt to intimidate and dissuade outside groups with political, cultural, and financial resources from supporting front-line communities, for one of the distinctive shifts within "Blockadia" has been the emergence of new leadership (predominantly women) from Indigenous and front-line communities. These communities are increasingly allying themselves with sections of the environmental movement which – after reflecting on the failure of climate advocacy over the last twenty-five years – have shifted their strategy from traditional lobbying to direct action (such as blockades) to stop extractive projects.

These types of alliances are not easy to build or maintain. Past Greenpeace campaigns, for example, have harmed Indigenous communities. We have apologized and worked with Indigenous communities to craft a policy on Indigenous rights to guide our work (Greenpeace Canada 2017). We are also working with communities like Clyde River to protect their Indigenous way of life (Skura 2015), but there is much still to be done to rebuild trust.

Rather than seeking to manage risks, this powerful new movement seeks to defend core values (e.g., "water is life" was the core principle motivating the resistance to the Dakota Access pipeline). It points out that it is insufficient to do *something* to reduce greenhouse-gas emissions; we have to do *enough*, as informed by the "carbon math" (McKibben 2012) that lays out how much of the oil, coal, and gas needs to stay in the ground if we are to avoid catastrophic levels of warming.

So what can we learn from the twenty-five-year battle against organized climate denial in today's context? Some suggestions:

Don't give the lies unwarranted air time: The media's cultural norm of "show both sides" meant that they gave deniers equal billing with the scientific consensus, as if there were two equally compelling arguments; we are now seeing this with coverage of the far right. For years, I have refused to debate climate deniers because it perpetuates this false sense of balance, and we are going to have to take the same kind of approach with Trump et al. If he is lying, then say it is a lie, not that it is a claim with which some expert doesn't agree.

Show who really benefits: Trump has positioned himself as an outsider, a brilliant businessman who will negotiate a better deal for the little guy. Just as the denial machine went off the rails (in most places) once it was shown to be a creation of the oil and coal companies, we need to show who is really benefiting from Trump's policies. This (accurately) places Trump outside of the "us" (his supporters' social identity) and with the "them" (the 1 per cent), which creates an opening for dialogue.

Love trumps hate: Don't imagine that one more scientific study, media fact-check, or brilliant skewering on a late-night comedy show will dissuade supporters of authoritarian politicians like Trump. The seeds planted by climate deniers and Trump fell on fertile ground because significant numbers of people wanted to believe what they were saying. So, rather than explaining why their fears and concerns are groundless (patronizing), or attacking them (reinforcing the group identity), acknowledge the fear and advance solutions. Empathy won't work for everyone (as with the hard-core racists), but it might work for enough to tilt the scales.

Be prepared for a bumpy ride on the way to a better future: These are extraordinary times, and as the stakes rise, so do the risks. Faced with a resurgence of fascism, it is worth repeating a line from Antonio Gramsci, an Italian writer-activist in the 1930s who tried to understand the rise of fascism while rotting in one of Mussolini's jails. He wrote: "the crisis consists precisely in the fact that the old is dying and the new is not yet born; in this interregnum a great variety of morbid symptoms appear" (Gramsci 1971, 275). We are at a turning point, and the thing that gets me out of bed in the morning is the idea that this concerted attack on land, water, and climate protectors is the last gasp of a dying regime that is striking out because it is cornered and afraid. Those "morbid symptoms" are doing enormous damage, but the response can be what Cory Doctorow calls "the first days of a better nation" (his science-fiction novel *Walkaway* is a must-read for activists in the Trump era) (Doctorow 2017).

Be a good ally: We need to stand together to resist the new authoritarianism and to build a better alternative. Climate change can be a key node for organizing the resistance. Expanding the resistance in the face of the inevitable attacks – rhetorical, legal, economic, and physical – will require a new emphasis on being a good ally and supporting each other in our struggles.

REFERENCES

Beeby, Dean. 2014. "Canada Revenue Agency Accused of 'Political' Targeting of Charities: Charities in First Wave of CRA Audits Were Largely Opponents of Conservatives' Energy Policies." *Maclean's*, 3 August. http://www.macleans.ca/news/canada/canada-revenue-agencys-political-targeting-of-charities-under-scrutiny/.

Brown, Alleen, Will Parrish, and Alice Speri. 2017a. "Leaked Documents Reveal Counterterrorism Tactics Used at Standing Rock to Defeat Pipeline Insurgencies." *The Intercept*, 27 May. https://theintercept.com/2017/05/27/leaked-documents-reveal-security-firms-counterterrorism-tactics-at-standing-rock-to-defeat-pipeline-insurgencies/.

– 2017b. "Dakota Access Pipeline Company Paid Mercenaries to Build Conspiracy Lawsuit Against Environmentalists." *The Intercept*, 15 November. https://the intercept.com/2017/11/15/dakota-access-pipeline-dapl-tigerswan-energy-transfer-partners-rico-lawsuit/.

CBC. 2014. "Keystone XL Pipeline Will Keep Canada from Hitting 2020 Greenhouse Gas Emissions Targets, Say Critics." *The Current*, 14 November. http://www.cbc.ca/radio/thecurrent/keystone-xl-pipeline-and-palliative-care-doctors-on-end-of-life-care-1.2907219/keystone-xl-pipeline-will-keep-canada-from-hitting-2020-greenhouse-gas-emissions-targets-say-critics-1.2907222.

Doctorow, Cory. 2017. *Walkaway*. New York: Tor Books.

Gramsci, Antonio. 1971. *Selections from the Prison Notebooks*. London: Lawrence & Wishart.

Greenpeace Canada. 2017. "Policy on Indigenous Rights." https://www.greenpeace.org/canada/en/policy-on-indigenous-rights/.

Haraway, Donna. 1989. *Primate Visions: Gender, Race, and Nature in the World of Modern Science*. New York: Routledge.

Klein, Naomi. 2014. *This Changes Everything: Capitalism Versus the Climate*. Toronto: Knopf Canada.

McCarthy, Shawn. 2012. "Security Services Deem Environmental, Animal-Rights Groups 'Extremist' Threats." *Globe and Mail*, 16 February. https://www.theglobeandmail.com/news/politics/security-services-deem-environmental-animal-rights-groups-extremist-threats/article533559/.

– 2014. "Greenpeace Asks Elections Canada to Investigate Tory Ties to Ethical Oil." *Globe and Mail*, 8 April. https://www.theglobeandmail.com/news/politics/greenpeace-asks-elections-canada-to-investigate-tory-ties-to-ethical-oil/article17875650/.

– 2015. "Anti-petroleum Movement a Growing Security Threat to Canada, RCMP Say." *Globe and Mail*, 17 February. https://www.theglobeandmail.com/news/politics/anti-petroleum-movement-a-growing-security-threat-to-canada-rcmp-say/article23019252/.

McKibben, Bill. 2012. "Global Warming's Terrible New Math." *Rolling Stone*, 19 July. http://www.rollingstone.com/politics/news/global-warmings-terrifying-new-math-20120719.

Milman, Oliver. 2016. "Trump's Transition: Sceptics Guide Every Agency Dealing with Climate Change." *Guardian*, 12 December. https://www.theguardian.com/us-news/2016/dec/12/donald-trump-environment-climate-change-skeptics.

Oreskes, Naomi, and Erik M. Conway. 2010. *Merchants of Doubt: How a Handful of Scientists Obscured the Truth on Issues from Tobacco Smoke to Global Warming.* London: Bloomsbury Publishing.

Paris, Max. 2012. "Charities Urge Peter Kent to Retract 'Laundering' Accusation." *CBC News*, 4 May. http://www.cbc.ca/news/politics/charities-urge-peter-kent-to-retract-laundering-accusation-1.1213026.

Payton, Laura. 2012. "Radicals Working Against Oil Sands, Ottawa Says." *CBC News*, 12 January. http://www.cbc.ca/news/politics/radicals-working-against-oilsands-ottawa-says-1.1148310.

RCMP. 2014. "Critical Infrastructure Intelligence Assessment: Criminal Threats to the Canadian Petroleum Industry." 24 January. https://www.desmog.ca/sites/beta.desmogblog.com/files/RCMP%20-%20Criminal%20Threats%20to%20Canadian%20Petroleum%20Industry.pdf.

Reuters. 2011. "Canadian MP Says Oil Sands Opponents 'Treacherous.'" *Reuters*, 16 November. https://www.reuters.com/article/us-oilsands/canadian-mp-says-oil-sands-opponents-treacherous-idUSTRE7AF2X220111116?feedType=RSS&feedName=environmentNews&utm_source=feedburner&utm_medium=feed&utm_campaign=Feed%3A+reuters%2Fenvironment+%28News+%2F+US+%2F+Environment%29.

Roberts, David. 2016. "This One Weird Trick Will Not Convince Conservatives to Fight Climate Change." *Vox*, 29 December. https://www.vox.com/science-and-health/2016/12/28/14074214/climate-denialism-social .

Skura, Elyse. 2016. "Clyde Hunters Laud 'Surprising' Greenpeace Partnership." *CBC*, 16 November. https://www.cbc.ca/news/canada/north/greenpeace-clyde-river-nunavut-seismic-testing-battle-1.3318691.

27

TRUMP AND OUR HOSTILE TIMES

Edward C. Corrigan

The election of Donald Trump as president of the United States in the fall of 2016 shocked most pundits, academics, and many voters. Trump lost the popular vote to former secretary of state and former senator Hillary Clinton but, due to the Electoral College system in the United States, Trump won more Electoral College votes and the election. Trump's attack on refugees, immigrants, Mexicans, and Muslims offended many people but struck a chord with alienated and primarily White voters in the American Heartland. This phenomenon, the rise of right-wing populism and direct or indirect appeals to racism is emerging as a trend, not only in the United States but also in Canada and Europe. Some commentators have drawn parallels to the 1930s and the rise of fascism in Europe.

The rest of the world is facing similar problems of appeals to populism, but frequently in the guise of religious extremism and puritanical religious orthodoxy. To some this may represent a simplistic world view, but there is no denying its attraction to people seeking salvation from the world's problems. This view is supported by the rise of the Islamic State and related Islamic movements, including the Taliban in Afghanistan and the existence of the Islamic Republic in Iran and the Wahhabis in Saudi Arabia. Further support is found in the rise of the Hindu nationalist movement in India, Buddhist nationalism in Myanmar, Hamas in Palestine, and the growing power of Jewish religious nationalism in Israel. More evidence is seen in the use of the Christian religion to legitimize political movements and to recruit soldiers in Africa, as with the Lord's Resistance Army headed by Joseph Rao Cony, which wanted to turn Uganda into a Christian theocracy and which was notorious for chopping off the limbs of dissenters.

This rise of religion as a political force has also occurred in Western society and especially in the United States. Religious conservatives were a major factor in Donald Trump's election victory and the Republican Party is, in many respects, now dominated by evangelical Christians and individuals who are anti-Muslim and to a lesser extent anti-Jewish. There are also undercurrents of hostility to Latinos and Blacks, who are perceived as a threat to the dominant White community's social and economic interests.

It is certain that the secular democratic national model, which is the reputed foundation of Western civilization, is being attacked and eroded on the basis of ethnicity and religion. The creation of the Turkish nation-state serves as one example. Built out of the ruins of the Ottoman Empire after the First World War under the leadership of Mustapha Kemal Ataturk, it was, in the view of many social and political commentators, an attempt to imitate the success of the European nation states that had defeated the religiously legitimated Ottoman Empire. The Kemalist attempt to secularize Turkey has not been a resounding success, however. The increasing influence of Islamist views, and the election of Turkish President Recep Tayyip Erdogan and his conservative Justice and Development Party, which derives much of its support from voters who want a greater role for Islam in the governance of Turkey, illustrates this point.

How did these and related dynamics play out in the election of Donald Trump? Virtually every media and political commentator not only got that election wrong, but were wrong on the Brexit vote and other populist conservative elections as well. The media commentators, many with a liberal bias, underestimated the impact of Fox News, conservative newspapers like the *National Post* in Canada, and the role of the Internet in allowing people to find alternative sources of information to reinforce their own political and social views. The proponents of social and religious conservatism built their own infrastructure to disseminate their ideas and views and, while this network grew, it was for the most part under the radar of political and media elites. Who had heard of Steve Bannon and Breitbart News? Almost nobody in the mainstream media and liberal political circles. However, Bannon built an Internet juggernaut and a massive following among a general public that was becoming tired of the constant refrain from the Washington elite. Trump's catch phrases "drain the swamp," "Crooked Hillary," and "Make American Great Again" captured the attention of a large section of the American electorate. Trump's attacks on Mexicans, Muslims, Blacks, and refugees, and his claims about making Mexico pay for the wall, no matter how outlandish and racist, motivated a significant segment of alienated

Americans to come out and vote for an outsider who seemed to have all the answers to complex problems.

The related consequence was that a significant number of voters were not happy to vote for Hillary Clinton and assumed that a buffoon like Donald Trump would never get elected as president. According to this view, there was no urgency to vote, and many did not bother to vote, since the outcome, as the media frequently told them, was a foregone conclusion. Many Democratic supporters were also very unhappy with how Senator Bernie Sanders was treated by the Democratic National Committee (Fox News 2017). Many did not vote for this reason.

Hillary Clinton's failure to campaign in Wisconsin, the choice of where to spend advertising dollars, the get-out-the-vote campaign, and voter-registration initiatives all had a critical impact on the election outcome. With razor-thin margins, it is clear to see how rules on voter identification and who is eligible to vote can determine political outcomes. Many states have restrictions on voters who have criminal records, which affect Black, Latino, and Native Americans disproportionately and disenfranchise millions of probable Democratic Party supporters (Berkowitz 2013). Some elected officials have admitted that laws on the possession of drugs and other crimes were designed in part to disenfranchise Blacks and other groups that tended not to vote Republican (Gumbel 2017). The placement of polling stations and even hours of operation can affect the turnout and the outcome. The state governor controls the state election apparatus, and most states are controlled by Republicans. The Republican Party is well known for its attempts at voter suppression and gerrymandering of districts to tilt the election results in their favour (Editors 2016; Rosenfeld 2012). As the *New York Times* has noted (Editors 2016):

> It's become an accepted truth of modern politics that Republican electoral prospects go up as the number of voters goes down. Conservatives have known this for a long time, which helps explain their intensifying efforts to make it harder to vote, or to eliminate large numbers of people from political representation entirely.

Conservative politicians in Canada are also aware of this "accepted truth," and in some cases have adopted vote-suppression tactics from their

Republican neighbours to the south (Ibbitson 2011). What is important in elections is getting your supporters to the polls and making it hard for your opponents' supporters to vote. Splitting the vote is also a key consideration where there are third-party candidates. A difference of one vote per poll can turn a loss into a win. Micro-targeting of voters to identify what issues will motivate them to vote can also have a decisive impact. There are many other tactics that can influence the outcome of an election. Some are legal, like, for example, gerrymandering. Others are objectionable if not illegal, for example, a "poison poll," where voters are asked their opinion on false information about the candidate (Barber 2006).

The far right has been slowly building social and political infrastructure to support their views and to mobilize their supporters. Many of those on the far right were angry that Barak Obama, a Black man (and in their view a secret Muslim), had been elected president – not once, but twice. This fact brought to a boil the latent racism toward Blacks that unfortunately still exists in the United States. For this segment of the population, there is a spillover toward other minorities, especially Muslims, Latinos, and Jews. These sentiments spurred these individuals to vote for Donald Trump and snub their noses at what they perceived to be the Eastern and California/Hollywood establishments. This helps explain why Trump was silent when addressing the issue of racism and how he courted support from White nationalists.

While the far right was building its infrastructure in the media and in social media, the evangelical Christians were doing the same. They have established elaborate media networks, a powerful presence on social media, and a network of evangelical churches across the United States and in Canada that has millions of adherents. Evangelical Christians have become very politically active and may represent as much as 10 per cent of the population. Trump's choice of Mike Pence – a well-known evangelical Christian and governor of Indiana – as his running mate was an attempt to woo the evangelical Christian vote (Monroe-Kane 2016). Trump was successful in securing the vast majority of the fundamentalist Christian vote, and this strategy was a key component of the coalition he put together to win the US presidency.

Similar considerations apply in Canada. This trend likely began with the election of Stephen Harper, leader of the Conservative Party, in February

2006. Harper, a harbinger of this trend toward social and religious political conservatism, is an evangelical Christian and a member of the Christian and Missionary Alliance Church. According to one author, "The Alliance Church believes Jesus Christ will return to Earth in an apocalypse, won't ordain women, strongly opposes abortion and divorce, condemns homosexuality as the most base of sins and believes those who aren't born-again are 'lost'" (Todd 2011). Today, evangelical Christians are a significant voting bloc in Alberta and the rest of Western Canada. Toronto city council member Doug Ford, brother of Rob Ford, the late mayor of Toronto, won the leadership of the Ontario Progressive Conservative Party in 2018. He won by courting the support of Christian evangelicals and mobilizing his social-network base (Benzie and Rushowy 2018).

Racism and intolerance toward visible minorities are also factors driving politics in Canada (CBC News 2018). According to an Ekos study released in October 2017, about 40 per cent of Canadians reveal some degree of racial intolerance. Ekos reports that "[t]his expression of racial intolerance is strongly linked to economic outlook and social class. Working class, poor, and the pessimistic are most opposed [to visible minorities] ... The biggest divide is partisanship with this indicator of racial intolerance being over four times higher among Conservative supporters than Liberals" (Ekos Politics 2017). Notably, Doug Ford refused to participate in a political debate organized by the Black community (CBC News 2018).

What measures can be taken to turn things around? Primaries, nomination meetings, leadership races, executive elections, voting in local, provincial, and national elections, and campaign fundraising are the key pressure points in the democratic political process. They count in electoral contests. Signing petitions, emails to decision-makers, protests, letters to the editor, and lobbying elected officials after elections have little or no impact, unless they have a real potential to defeat the elected official. It is imperative that individuals who want to have a positive impact and maintain a progressive, environmentally friendly, and tolerant political system understand how politics work and engage the political system in a meaningful manner. It is also important to outsmart and outwork your opponents. As many others have said, democracy is a messy political system, but it is the best one we have. The need to defend a tolerant and compassionate Canada is more urgent than ever.

REFERENCES

Barber, John. 2006. "Brand New Slime, Same Old Smell." *Globe and Mail*, 13 September. https://www.theglobeandmail.com/news/national/brand-new-slime-same-old-smell/article731731/.

Benzie, Robert, and Kristin Rushowy. 2018. "Doug Ford Wins Ontario PC Leadership after Chaotic Party Race." *Toronto Star*, 10 March. https://www.thestar.com/news/queenspark/2018/03/10/tussles-over-ballot-counting-delay-results-in-ontario-pc-leadership-race.html.

Berkowitz, Bill. 2013. "Felon Disenfranchisement: The New Jim Crow." Buzzflash. Truthout, 7 May. http://buzzflash.com/commentary/item/17952-felon-disenfranchisement-the-new-jim-crow .

Carlson, Peter. 2000. "Another Race to the Finish." *Washington Post*, 17 November. https://www.washingtonpost.com/archive/politics/2000/11/17/another-race-to-the-finish/c810a41c-7da9-461a-927b-9da6d36a65dc/?utm_term=.2ee46da0a0af.

CBC News. 2018. "Doug Ford Declines to Participate in Black Community Provincial Leaders' Debate: All Other Provincial Leaders Have Said Yes to April 11 Debate." *CBC News*, 4 April. http://www.cbc.ca/news/canada/toronto/doug-ford-black-community-provincial-leaders-debate-1.4605166.

Cook Political Report Staff. 2016. "Fifty-six Interesting Facts about the 2016 Election." *Cook Political Report*, 16 December. https://web.archive.org/web/2017071 5170550/http://cookpolitical.com/story/10201.

Editors. 2016. "Republicans and Voter Suppression." *New York Times*, 4 April. https://www.nytimes.com/2016/04/05/opinion/republicans-and-voter-suppression.html.

Ekos Politics. 2017. "Open Versus Ordered: Cultural Expressions of the New Outlook." Ottawa, 10 October. http://www.ekospolitics.com/wp-content/up loads/open_vs_ordered_october_10_2017b.pdf.

Fox News. 2017. "Goldberg: New Revelations Prove Bernie Sanders Wasn't 'Paranoid' about DNC and Hillary." *America's Newsroom*, 2 November. http://insider.foxnews.com/2017/11/02/jonah-goldberg-donna-braziles-new-book-proves-bernie-sanders-wasnt-paranoid-about-dnc.

Friesen, Joe, and Bill Curry. 2012. "Prime Minister Harper Unveils Grand Plan to Reshape Canada." *Globe and Mail*, 26 March. https://www.theglobeandmail.com/news/politics/prime-minister-harper-unveils-grand-plan-to-reshape-canada/article542480/.

Greenberg, David. 2000. "Was Nixon Robbed? The Legend of the Stolen 1960 Presidential Election." *Slate*, 16 October. http://www.slate.com/articles/news_ and_politics/history_lesson/2000/10/was_nixon robbed.html.

Gumbel, Andrew. 2017. "America's Shameful History of Voter Suppression." *Guardian*, 13 September. https://www.theguardian.com/us-news/2017/sep/13/ america-history-voter-suppression-donald-trump-election-fraud.

Haaretz, 2018. "Israeli Spies and Ukrainian Honey Traps: The Dirty Tricks Used by Cambridge Analytica, the Firm Behind Facebook Data Breach." *Haaretz*, 20 March. https://www.haaretz.com/world-news/israeli-spies-and-honey-traps- the-dirty-tricks-cambridge-analytica-1.5918177?utm_source=Push_Notification &utm_medium=web_push&utm_campaign=General.

Ibbitson, John. 2011. "Has US-Style 'Voter Suppression' Made It to Canada's Elec- tion?" *Globe and Mail*, 26 March. https://www.theglobeandmail.com/news/ politics/ottawa-notebook/has-us-style-voter-suppression-made-it-to-canadas- election/article613300/.

McDonald, Michael P. 2016. November General Election Turnout Rates. United States Election Project. http://www.electproject.org/2016g.

Monroe-Kane, Charles. 2016. "Trump Chooses Pence, but Should Evangelical Christians Choose Trump?" *Public Radio International*, 16 July. https://www.pri. org/stories/2016-07-16/trump-chooses-pence-should-evangelical-christians- choose-trump.

Rosenfeld, Steven. 2012. "3 Ways the GOP Has Already Disenfranchised Thousands of Swing-State Voters." *AlterNet*, 9 September. https://www.alternet.org/2012/ 09/3-ways-gop-has-already-disenfranchised-thousands-swing-state-voters/.

Todd, Douglas. 2011. "Harper the Evangelical." *Canadian Charger*, 14 April. http:// www.thecanadiancharger.com/page.php?id=5&a=862.

28

FIGHTING (AND WINNING) PROPOSED REFORMS TO CITIZENSHIP LAW

Lorne Waldman

In February 2014 the Conservative Government of Stephen Harper intro-duced the Strengthening Canada's Citizenship Act. Despite its title, the leg-islation was a clear attack on the fundamental values of Canadian society. It introduced measures to strip Canadians of their citizenship if they were convicted of terrorism-related offences. Among other measures that made citizenship harder to get and easier to take away, it lengthened the residency requirement for qualifying for citizenship from three to four years, and in-troduced a process that allowed the government to revoke citizenship with-out a hearing. It was clear that the legislation was going to be a key part of the Conservative government's re-election platform, and that the Harper Conservatives were convinced that playing to the public's concern over "Islamic terrorism" and national security would help it in its efforts to win a new mandate.

The decision of the Harper government to take its hard line toward terrorists – and in particular Islamic terrorists – was reflective of the rise of anti-immigrant sentiment in much of the western world. By 2014, the concerns over the increasing flow of asylum seekers into Europe had created a backlash there. Although there had always been some level of intolerance, the sudden influx of refugees fleeing the civil war in Syria brought all these sentiments to the surface. Right-wing parties were making significant inroads throughout Eastern Europe, particularly in Hungary, where the xenophobic rhetoric was extreme. In all of Western Europe the anti-immigrant parties made gains at the expense of the tra-ditional parties. Given the rise of right-wing nationalist groups, it was not surprising to me and other lawyers who were working to defend the rights of immigrants and refugees to see that the Conservative government chose to pander to the public's fears about terrorism and national security as part of its strategy to win re-election.

Certainly, the rise of these anti-democratic and racist forces made us very concerned about how we might counter the government's strategy. We were well aware that the government planned to use the new legislation to highlight the fact that it was the party that could best protect Canadians against an invoked growing terrorist threat. Coupled with its niqab ban and its cuts to refugee health care, these policies were designed to consolidate the party's support among their supporters who harboured anti-immigrant sentiments.

The reaction of the organizations advocating for human rights and immigrants was swift and uniform. We saw the use of this new, thinly disguised anti-immigrant rhetoric as a threat to the most fundamental values of our society. Worse still, by exploiting these anti-immigrant and anti-Islam sentiments in this manner, the government made it acceptable for persons to express these views. Suddenly we were told that certain conduct was "un-Canadian." We had no choice but to respond with an aggressive public-relations campaign. The new citizenship legislation was condemned because it denied citizens due process, because it made citizenship inaccessible to many immigrants and refugees, and because it attempted to manipulate the public's concerns over national security by introducing legislation that did nothing to protect our society but pandered to the fears of the public.

Despite the almost universal condemnation of the legislation from civil society, the Conservative government pushed the legislation through parliament. During the legislative process, human-rights groups launched a petition against the bill that garnered over 110,000 signatures and a media campaign to rally opposition to the legislation. Most of the groups who appeared before the parliamentary committee studying the legislation condemned it. Many argued that it did not comply with the Charter of Rights and Freedoms and denied citizens a fair hearing. Despite these criticisms, the citizenship reforms were rushed through, and the legislation was passed by parliament in June 2014.

Having failed to convince the government to modify the legislation, human-rights organizations and those dedicated to protecting the rights of refugees had to develop a strategy to challenge the legislation. The first prong of this strategy involved a legal challenge. Once the legislation came into force, two civil-society organizations decided to launch litigation. The Canadian Association of Refugee Lawyers (CARL), an organization of which

I am founder, and the BC Civil Liberties Association (BCCLA) announced their legal challenge in August 2015. They challenged the legislation under sections 7, 12, and 15 of the Charter of Rights arguing that it created two classes of citizens and that it did not provide a fair process when persons faced revocation.

At the same time, human-rights and immigrant groups launched a media campaign aimed at educating the public during the election. We argued that there should not be second-class citizens in Canada and that all citizens should be provided with due process. Election campaigns are difficult to predict. Although it was clear that the Conservative government wanted to appeal to anti-Islamic feelings in Canada and counted on this legislation to be its key plank, no one anticipated that these issues would come to dominate the campaign. But with the appearance of the tragic photo of Alan Kurdi, the young Syrian child whose body washed up on a beach in Turkey after his family's attempt to reach the Greek island of Kos, everything changed. Suddenly, immigration, and in particular our lack of compassion toward refugees, became an election issue. With the sudden emergence of immigration as an issue, and with attempts by the Harper government to use Islamophobia as a tool to mobilize its base, the campaign was turned into a campaign about values.

Both main opposition parties opposed the changes to the citizenship legislation. The Liberals campaigned against the changes to the citizenship law, maintaining that there are no second-class citizens and promising that they would revoke the Conservative government's changes to the law if they were elected – and made this promise one of the highlights of their campaign. Human-rights and immigrant groups used their resources to reach out to the immigrant communities, warning that the changes to the citizenship law represented a serious threat to the rights of all immigrants. The issue had a great deal of resonance in ethnic communities and likely had an impact on the vote in key ridings in Toronto, Montreal, and Vancouver.

With the victory of the Trudeau Liberals, we believed that all the concerns related to the changes to the Citizenship Act would be resolved and that the newly installed government would repeal the Conservative legislation. Indeed, the newly installed Liberal regime introduced as one of its first measures Bill C-6, an Act to Amend the Citizenship Act. But although the legislation reversed some of the contentious aspects of the changes introduced by the Conservatives' legislation, it did not fully repeal it. The bill eliminated the provisions that allowed for revocation of citizenship on grounds of terrorism. It eased the residency and language requirements and eliminated the requirement that citizens promise to reside in Canada after they obtain citizenship. However, it did not modify the revocation process; citizenship could still be revoked without a hearing based on written submissions received by an official.

In response to this, BCCLA and CARL mounted an intensive lobbying campaign. We met with dozens of members of parliament, highlighting how unfair it was to allow officials to revoke citizenship without a hearing. Many of the members of parliament we met expressed their agreement with our concerns and promised to support changes to the legislation that would require a hearing before a person's citizenship could be revoked. When C-6 was sent to committee after second reading, numerous witnesses highlighted the unfairness of a revocation process that did not require an oral hearing before the decision-maker. In response to this lobbying, the Minister of Immigration, Refugees and Citizenship appeared before the parliamentary committee studying the bill and, although he refused to amend it to allow for a hearing, he promised that he would introduce legislation that would provide for an oral hearing in the near future.

In the face of this intransigence by the government, lawyers continued their legal challenge to the revocation process. We argued that a process that allowed for revocation of citizenship was unfair and violated the guarantees in the Charter and Bill of Rights. In January of 2016, the Federal Court held that there were serious concerns with the fairness of the revocation process and granted an injunction, preventing the government from applying the procedures to the persons who had launched the legal challenge in the court.

While the litigation continued, the bill was sent to the Senate for consideration. Prime Minister Trudeau had recently appointed a large number of new, independent senators. Up and until the appointment of the independent senators, the Senate had not been considered a useful place to conduct lobbying. Of course, when the Senate considered legislation, non-governmental organizations were often invited to appear before its committees. But the senators generally voted along party lines, and when the governing party had a majority in the Senate, which was usually the case, given the prime minister's unfettered power to appoint senators, we did not expect the Senate to approve significant amendments to government legislation.

However, no one knew how the independent senators might affect the new Senate, and we saw their appointment as a new opportunity to lobby for change. With this in mind, we approached Senator Ratna Omidvar, the sponsor of the government's bill in the Senate and a strong champion of human rights, and asked her to lead the call for amendments to create a fair revocation process. She agreed, and an amendment was prepared that would ensure all persons subject to revocation were provided with an oral hearing. As the bill slowly made its way through the Senate, members of CARL and the BCCLA lobbied intensely, trying to convince the senators on all sides to support an amendment. Given the new composition of the Senate and expected opposition to the amendment from Conservative senators, it was essential to get the support of all of the independent senators and of the Liberal Senate caucus in order to ensure that the amendment passed the Senate.

But it was clear that, even if the Senate passed the amendment, it would not be passed into law if the Liberal government did not support it. Despite the earlier promises that the government would amend the revocation procedure, there was considerable debate inside the government as to whether it should accept the proposed changes to the revocation process. The officials in charge of the revocation process argued that the new procedure was fair enough, and that it was needed in order to allow the government to process the large backlog of cases that were being considered for revocation. They argued that the new system was a fair, cost-effective way to deal with the large-scale fraud that had allowed a large number of people to obtain citizenship that they did not deserve. As the Senate debate of the legislation continued, the minister appeared before the Senate committee and defended the revocation procedure, arguing that it was fair enough.

During this time, members of non-governmental organizations continued to meet with officials in the office of the Minister of Immigration, Refugees, and Citizenship in order to convince them to support the amendment. However, the government did not firmly commit to support the amendment that would allow for a fair hearing in revocation cases. Then, on 10 May 2017, the Federal Court released its decision in *Hassouna v Minister of Citizenship and Immigration*. The court held that the revocation procedure was unfair, as it violated the guarantees for a fair hearing provided for in the Bill of Rights. The court also held that a process that did not provide for an oral hearing or a fair process allowed the prosecutor to act as judge, and struck it down.

After the Federal Court decision, the die was cast. Faced with the ruling that the revocation procedure enacted by the Harper government violated the Bill of Rights, the Liberal government had little choice but to accept the Senate amendment. But the amendment still had to pass the Senate. The Conservatives opposed it, but with the support of the Liberal and independent senators, the amendment was passed in May 2017, days after the Federal Court decision.

The legislation was returned to the House of Commons in June 2017, and the minister announced his acceptance of the amendments. The bill was passed and proclaimed into law. The new fair revocation procedure did not come into effect until February 2018. Now all persons faced with the possibility of revocation of their citizenship have a right to make submissions on humanitarian grounds as to why their citizenship should not be revoked; and have the right to ask for an oral hearing in the Federal Court.

The efforts to challenge the Conservative government's citizenship legislation, which began in 2014, ended successfully in February 2018. Those involved employed all the tools available to them – planning media campaigns; giving testimony before the parliamentary committee; raising the issue during the election; lobbying in both the House of Commons and the Senate; and, finally, legal challenges. It was the combination of all these measures taken together that led to the success of this campaign. While the current government has abandoned the anti-immigrant rhetoric of the former government, there will be times in the future when political parties will attempt to exploit these sentiments. In such a circumstance, our experience has taught us the importance of uniting all the democratic forces and of developing a coherent and comprehensive strategy that involves all the tools at our disposal. We must not shy away from using legal challenges as a tool to challenge unjust laws, but we must understand that such challenges must be used in conjunction with all of the other tools available to us if we are to succeed in resisting the racist sentiments that are far too prevalent in our society.

PART FOUR

SOCIAL MOVEMENTS
FOR CHANGE

29

ALT-RIGHT, ALT-LEFT, AND ANTIFA

Richard J.F. Day

Many people are surprised and aghast at the recent rise of white nationalism – sometimes referred to as the "alt-right" – across Europe and North America. It's as though that sort of thing just shouldn't be happening in "advanced democracies." But the more historically aware among us are quick to point out that the nation-states of the Eurocolonial world have *always been* fascist to the core, that white supremacy is their point of origin, as well as the energy behind their perpetuation. Thus, it is not wise, it is not safe, to try to ignore or downplay the threat presented by this new generation of Angry White Men. Communities of all sorts, of all political persuasions, can and must take them seriously.

Given the focus of this book on Canada and the United States, there is perhaps no better place to look for intersections in anti-fascist organizing than in the mainstreaming of militant tactics that has occurred alongside the resurgence of the fascists themselves. As recently as 2016, the only people who used the word "antifa" were embedded in anarchist subcultures, or tasked with policing them. Now we can hear about militant anti-fascism on CNN, read about it in the *New York Times*, and listen to its blustery, angry opponents on conservative talk radio, who have deployed one of their favourite obfuscation tactics by naming militant anti-fascists the "alt-left." What has happened, in this short period of time, to bring both these identifications out of the shadows? And what are the perils and possibilities of militant anti-fascism for both the communities out of which antifa tactics emerge and the mainstream spaces where they combine with their anti-particles to release their elemental energy?

I should note that I've been only incidentally involved in anti-fascist direct action. I've never organized these kinds of events, but I have participated in them in various places, at various times. My energy for the past ten years or so has been focused on re-skilling for a life further outside of the current dominant order and building stronger, closer relations with the people whose land I've been on. It may sound like this is an escapist path, but I would argue that trying to ignore what the mainstream societies are doing, while creating alternatives to them, is bad strategy from almost every conceivable perspective. Everyone who is working, in whatever ways, to reform, destroy, or render redundant what has been called "the fascist creep" (Ross 2017), needs to work together in networks of mutual aid and support – because, as I mentioned, fascism is everywhere and always ready to emerge from within our own communities, our own bodies.

Three Kinds of Anti-Fascism

According to an excellent recent study, there are three main approaches to working against fascism: state-legislative, liberal, and militant (Testa 2015, 2–3). In order to better understand why people gravitate to militant tactics, I want to very briefly go through the possibilities and limits of the state-legislative and liberal approaches.

In the United States, it is often thought that there are no hate-crime laws on the books, because of the unshakable commitment of so much of the populace to "freedom of speech" – a different, and (for many), mutually exclusive principle. But after the Civil Rights Act of 1964 made racial segregation illegal, follow-up legislation has explicitly addressed crimes based on race, colour, religion, or national origin, exclusion from housing, as well as destruction of religious property. In 2009, these protections were extended to attacks based on gender and sexual orientation and disability (via the Shepard-Byrd Act). These laws seem progressive, but there are substantial hurdles in actually applying them. They effectively protect perpetrators of hate crimes (rather than their victims) in many parts of the country, so that, as of 2016, only seventy-two cases were tried, and forty-five convictions obtained (US Department of Justice 2017). On a rough calculation (Southern Poverty Law Center 2017), it takes approximately five thousand hate incidents to produce one conviction.

As a country known for its multicultural tolerance and harmony, we would expect Canada to be doing better on this front. Indeed, the protections offered by the Criminal Code of Canada are more expansive than those in the United States. But the number of hate crimes that it takes to generate a conviction is of the same order of magnitude: in Canada, about twelve thousand incidents are required before a perpetrator is fined or put in jail (Statistics Canada 2017). In both Canada and the United States, then, it seems that the state-legislative approach is suffering from serious limits to its efficacy, leading, as Barbara Perry notes in this volume, to an increasing ascendancy of right-wing extremism.

According to Testa (2015), liberal tactics involve trying to "help" fascists by "deradicalizing" them, trying to convert them with rational arguments, or, if all of that fails, shaming them out of polite company. Grouping all "radicals" into one category is both empirically misleading (since anti-fascists are fighting in the streets with fascists, so there must be quite a lot they don't have in common) and politically unsupportive (an issue I will address later in this essay, and which Lesley Wood's chapter discusses in the context of the policing of social movements). This aside, it is difficult to quantify the success of these efforts, but it does seem likely that shaming by liberals was what had driven the fascists in North America to cut themselves off from the public sphere for so many years. Recently, as already mentioned, that has changed drastically. White nationalists hold large rallies, speak at university campuses, and enjoy "cover" (i.e., support in their ability to pass as "normal") from major news outlets such as Fox News – and, of course, from the president of the United States, who has referred to them as "good people." Although they get less press than in the United States, either "positive" or "negative," White nationalists are also on the rise in Canada. Protests are now popping up against the paranoid supposition that "Sharia Law" is being imposed on the country, and in 2019, the Quebec government passed a clearly Islamophobic statute that forbids the wearing of any religious symbol by public servants, including the hijab. There are very few people on any side of the issue who don't know that An Act to Foster Adherence to State Religious Neutrality, is aimed precisely at Muslim women. And, since two-thirds of Canadians say they would like to see a similar law in their own province (Abedi 2017), it cannot be justified by the historical oppression of the Québécois people by an anglophone majority.

This inability to put fascists in jail, or at least to keep their anxieties from driving public policy, signals a clear limit of state-legislative/liberal approaches. In fact, rather than being co-opted into the liberal mainstream and thereby being tamed, the fascists have increasingly managed to seduce the liberal mainstream into legitimating *their* points of view. This undoubtedly has something to do with why so many people are now turning to more militant approaches to anti-fascism.

What Is "Antifa"?

The answer to this question, of course, depends upon whom you ask. As I've mentioned, until recently, antifa didn't appear at all in mainstream discourses in North America, and that has led to a lot of surprise and confusion. According to CNN, "the exact origins of the group are unknown," but one thing seems clear: antifa supporters are identified with "violence" and "property damage" (Suerth 2017). In an interview with Mark Bray, the author of a recent book on anti-fascist resistance (Bray 2017), a reporter for Vox asked the very leading question: "Why do [antifa activists] think physical violence, as opposed to nonviolent resistance, is both justifiable and effective?" (Illing 2017). Bray responded by noting that antifa is: (1) not new (there is a long history of this kind of organizing in North America, mostly under the banner of Anti-Racist Action [ARA], and in Europe it goes back to the rise of fascism itself); (2) not a group, but a tactic (anyone can gear up and take part in militant direct action); and (3) not only about fighting in the streets.

This last point is important enough that I want to dwell on it for a moment. According to a Toronto ARA bulletin from 1998, the ARA network was united by four principles: (1) "We go where they go – never let the Nazis have the streets" (this is the part that sometimes involves fighting); (2) "Don't rely on the cops or the courts to do our work" (a critique of state-legislative/liberal anti-fascism); (3) "Exercise non-sectarian defence of other anti-fascists" (they commit to protecting those who stand alongside them, even if they don't agree on all matters of politics, strategy, and tactics); and (4) "Do the hard work necessary to build a broad strong movement against racism" and all other forms of oppression (Toronto ARA 1998).

This is a necessarily condensed attempt to see beyond the headlines regarding the recent increase in visibility of the street-engagement component of militant anti-fascism. What I'm trying to do is highlight the fact that street engagement is only one component of a much-broader approach, which is itself tied to many decades of struggle on the part of anarchist and other autonomous communities.

What Are Some of the Challenges and Opportunities Facing Anti-Fascist Organizing in North America Today?

In what remains of this essay, I want to focus on the legacy of knowledge and debate that has emerged over the many years of militant anti-fascist activity, in the hope of helping to foster a broader mutual understanding among all of the opponents of fascism in North America, and to address the third question asked of contributors to this volume, "What needs to be done to surmount these challenges and to strengthen the common good in Canada?" In the interest of brevity, and to focus on questions and challenges rather than seeming to provide definitive answers to particular actors, this discussion will be highly condensed and driven by responses to some Frequently Voiced Objections.

"You're as bad as the fascists because you support violence."
The critique of direct physical engagement as a form of "violence" tends to come mainly from outside antifa circles. It is usually answered by noting the failures of liberal–state-legislative approaches, the need to protect communities that the police simply cannot, or will not, serve, and arguments about what does and does not constitute "violence." But there is also a version of this critique that comes from inside militant subcultures such as anarchism, which is strongly associated with antifa tactics, and is driven by the high value that anarchists place on means-ends identification. By attempting to solve problems with fists, sticks, knives, and guns, it seems that the means of militant anti-fascism are way out of alignment with the ends of a consensus-based, mutual-aid-driven society. But it should be noted that *all* ways of defending our communities against those who would destroy us are dissonant in this way. For example, liberal societies claim to value individual freedom, but are quite quick to deprive people of this good (for example, by putting them in jail) for what eventually may turn out to be not terribly harmful transgressions, such as smoking marijuana or having sex with the "wrong" kind of person. For another example, state socialist

societies of the twentieth century, such as the Soviet Union, killed and imprisoned people for voicing political positions that dissented massively from the "common sense" of their time. It's a problem inherent to human societies, so perhaps the deeper question is about how radical communities might be better able to support, accept, and limit the potential problems that arise when some people take on these necessary roles.

"This is just a bunch of White guys strutting their macho stuff."
This critique is related to the previous one, but comes primarily from within anarchist subcultures, which are famously committed to battling oppression on all axes, and which (in my experience) have yet to find consistent and productive ways to deal with the deadlocks that this commitment incessantly creates. In this case, the clear and present need to "fight fascists where they are" clashes with the clear and present need to fight patriarchy and male violence where *they* are, and to prioritize movement-building over fighting with cops and fascists. The great popularity of "riot porn" seems to attest to the fact that, for some people, "this shit is fun." But not all people who get some satisfaction out of street fighting are male-bodied, and not all of them are White-identified. Is it possible that the identification of street fighting with only one segment of our communities can itself function as a mode of oppression? Given the necessity of defending those communities against violence, without appealing to agents of the state, it is perhaps wise to differentiate between inward- and outward-directed moments of physical engagement, that is, to try to disentangle community defence from the perpetuation of patriarchy.

"You're alienating those who would otherwise support your cause and/or making the fascists stronger."
Both forms of this argument have always struck me as tautological – they presume what they should be trying to argue for. People who don't believe in direct action will never support it, no matter what form it takes; and fascists will never mistake their most fervent enemies (liberals and militant anti-fascists) for their friends. People on each side would have to become *someone other than they are* in order to even begin to have anything like a "reasoned discussion" in a "shared space of communication."

So, instead of arguing over the abstract validity of various approaches from entrenched ideological perspectives, it might be better to adopt a mutual respect for diversity of strategies and tactics. We could leave the fighting in the streets to those who are willing and able to do it, while validating their efforts and sacrifices. We could leave the fighting in the courts, the mass media, and elections, to those who see this as their calling. We could all take on the "Nazi sympathizer next door" (Fausset 2017) when he is living near *our* place, in whatever ways we deem to be fitting to the task.

Conclusion – On Living Differently, Together

As the author of *Militant Anti-Fascism* attests, "it's possible for many different kinds of anti-fascists to work together successfully" (Testa 2015, 6). This is not only possible, I have tried to suggest, but absolutely necessary, because fundamental social change is ultimately won and sustained only through our day-to-day interactions. Thus, our ultimate power against the current rise of fascism lies where our power always lies – in ourselves, as we organize to live the kinds of lives we want to lead.

REFERENCES

Abedi, Maham. 2017. "68% of Canadians Want Quebec's Face-Coverings Ban in Their Province." *Global News*, 17 October. https://globalnews.ca/news/3828752/quebec-face-covering-ban-support-canada-poll/.

Bray, Mark. 2017. *Antifa: The Anti-Fascist Handbook*. New York: Melville House.

Fausset, Richard. 2017. "A Voice of Hate in America's Heartland." *New York Times*, 25 November. https://www.nytimes.com/2017/11/25/us/ohio-hovater-white-nationalist.html.

Habermas, Jurgen. 1984. *The Theory of Communicative Action*. Boston: Beacon Press.

Illing, Sean. 2017. "'They Have No Allegiance to Liberal Democracy': An Expert on Antifa Explains the Group." *Vox*, 25 August. https://www.vox.com/2017/8/25/16189064/antifa-charlottesville-activism-mark-bray-interview.

Ross, Alexander Reid. 2017. *Against the Fascist Creep*. San Francisco: AK Press.

Southern Poverty Law Center. 2017. "FBI: Hate Crimes Reach 5-Year High in 2016, Jumped as Trump Rolled Toward Presidency." 13 November. https://www.spl center.org/hatewatch/2017/11/13/fbi-hate-crimes-reach-5-year-high-2016-jumped-trump-rolled-toward-presidency-0.

Statistics Canada. 2017. "Police-Reported Hate Crime, 2016." 28 November. https://www.statcan.gc.ca/daily-quotidien/171128/dq171128d-eng.htm.

Suerth, Jessica. 2017. "What Is Antifa?" CNN, 14 August. http://www.cnn.com/2017/08/14/us/what-is-antifa-trnd/index.html.

Testa, M. 2015. *Militant Anti-Fascism: A Hundred Years of Resistance*. San Francisco: AK Press.

Toronto ARA. 1998. *On the Prowl* [zine]. no. 11 (Spring): back cover.

US Department of Justice, Civil Rights Division. 2017. "Hate Crime Laws." 28 July. https://www.justice.gov/crt/hate-crime-laws.

30

THE PRINCIPLE OF SOLIDARITY

Stephen D'Arcy

The right-wing populist project of people like Trump is, on the one hand, the very opposite of everything the left stands for and defends. It is racist, sexist, anti-worker, and xenophobic. On the other hand, however, it takes pains to present itself as a kind of successor to the left: a new force to defend the downtrodden worker against the rich and powerful elites of Washington and Wall Street. In one of his early executive orders, for instance, Trump expressed a commitment "to create higher wages ... for workers in the United States, and to protect their economic interests." In a White House policy statement, couched in anti-Establishment rhetoric, Trump is depicted as the only force willing to stand up to economic and political elites: "For too long, Americans have been forced to accept trade deals that put the interests of insiders and the Washington elite over the hard-working men and women of this country."

It is easy to point out the hypocrisy and cynicism, to say nothing of the veiled racism, of these populist appeals to workers, and their superficial denunciations of nameless insiders and elites. What's harder to acknowledge is the left's own role in allowing this rhetoric to gain a foothold, by failing to offer to the wider multiracial working class a credible, potent form of authentically anti-Establishment, pro-worker politics, founded on solidarity and equality. But this lack – the absence of a potent left force to attack the Establishment and defend vulnerable workers' livelihoods from the relentless neo-liberal onslaught – is not rooted in indifference to the fate of workers or a disavowal of the responsibility to resist. Instead, it is rooted in real challenges to building solidarity, challenges posed in large part by antagonisms and inequities – the privilege of some, the marginalization of others – that pervade what would have to be the social base of any left-populist resurgence: the 99 per cent, in George Jackson's now-famous formulation (Jackson 1972, 9).

The divisions and antagonisms within the 99 per cent are nothing new, of course. Marx's call for workers of the world to unite was not a description of an already-reliable solidarity; it was an exhortation to embrace solidarity as a way forward for the left. Since the nineteenth century, the principle of solidarity – "an injury to one is an injury to all" – has been widely understood to express the basic norm of trade unionism. Yet many of us would go further, regarding the principle as crucial for all projects in which people try to liberate themselves from exploitation and oppression through struggle, including feminism, anti-racism, and anti-colonialism. The problem is, we're not always sure what "solidarity" means. I want to address this question by considering a parable that I think can clarify both the left's present predicament and how solidarity can help.

Imagine that a passenger jet is carrying two hundred passengers. Two of the passengers have used makeshift knives to commandeer the plane. Call them the 1 per cent. Their intention is to use their position of power over the other passengers, the 99 per cent, to extract money and compliance under the threat that non-compliant passengers will be penalized in various ways, such as by being denied adequate food or a decent place to sit. Conversely, they offer passengers who don't make trouble and help the hijackers out in various ways some special advantages, including extra comforts and more freedom to move around. We can call the penalized passengers "the worse off" and the rewarded passengers "the better off." It occurs to many of the passengers that even two armed hijackers could easily be overpowered by the combined force of 198 others, or even a substantial segment of them. And yet, the great majority of passengers make no attempt to challenge the hijackers. Why not?

Are they too comfortable? Do they have too much to lose? Maybe. But even if this explanation rings true for the better-off passengers, who get special advantages, we would still need to explain why the less-advantaged members of the 99 per cent are *also* reluctant to rebel.

It is no mystery, surely. This is a "collective action problem." This occurs whenever the action that would be most advantageous to a group of people, *were they to cooperate with one another*, is disadvantageous to each of them individually *in the absence of such cooperation*. It would be advantageous to attack the hijackers only if enough other passengers *also* did so, in a coordinated way. It would be self-defeating to do so in isolation, one or two passengers at a time. A few might still try, hoping to spark a wider revolt. But when the others see how easily the rebellion is crushed, the likely effect would be to reinforce the impression that the only sensible option is to make the best of a bad situation, doing what one can to please the hijackers in order to extract some relative advantages for oneself. Indeed, the situation may give many of the passengers – especially the ones who are treated relatively well – a strong motive to identify with the hijackers, to imagine that those who are treated harshly by them must have done something to provoke their mistreatment. After all, by doing as they are told and playing by the hijackers' rules, they find a way to access certain benefits and avoid the worst abuses.

This, in short, is the structure of the situation that exploited and oppressed people face today. It is important to emphasize that some workers – a small but precious minority – do try to put up a serious fight, sometimes winning important gains. But all too often those who rebel are defeated by the superior strength of the powerful. Were all or most of the exploited and oppressed to challenge the system at once, in a sustained and coordinated way, there is little doubt that the rebellion could prevail. But this kind of sustained, broad-based coordination does not exist, and everyone knows it, so revolt against the system just does not seem, to most people, to be a sensible course of action. Are we just stuck, then? Or is there a way out of this impasse?

It is here that the principle that "an injury to one is an injury to all" can help, but only if we avoid misreading it. The worst reading would be a *common-fate* interpretation, according to which it means that *whenever anyone is injured in some way, then everyone is injured in that way*. If that's what the principle means, it's simply false. The fact that one worker is fired unjustly, or sexually harassed, doesn't entail that the same thing happens to every worker. So, we can discard this reading immediately.

A better option is the *common-interest* interpretation: *Whenever one member of the relevant group is harmed in some way, it reveals a form of vulnerability to harm that is shared by all members of the group, so that all share an interest in minimizing their vulnerability*. This reading is not obviously false, but it too is defective. Even if we concede that injuries to some of us reveal vulnerabilities shared by all of us, this still ignores the fact that vulnerability may be distributed very unequally. For instance, although *all* workers might be vulnerable to police violence, Indigenous or Black workers are much *more* vulnerable to it. To claim that, because all are vulnerable in some way, all must share an interest in minimizing the vulnerability is a bit too optimistic. Those with a lesser degree of vulnerability would presumably have much less to gain by reining in the police. They might even think the benefit of reduced crime outweighs the risk *to them* of continued aggressive policing. When we notice the unequal distribution of vulnerability, we become far more circumspect about the idea that common vulnerability automatically generates a common interest in removing its source.

Where does this leave us? The point of solidarity is to identify something people have in common. The problem is that we can't base our strategy on ignoring or denying the real differences between people, and that's what both the common-fate and common-interest readings seem to do. Maybe an old distinction made by the philosopher Hegel can help. He distinguished between two ways people can have something in common. A *found commonality* is a similarity shared by members of some group that is *discovered* to be already there. An *achieved commonality* is not there in advance, but has to be *forged* by people who find a way to come together in some way (Hegel 1841, 54). In a found commonality, people act in common because they are in some crucial respect *similar* to one another. In an achieved commonality, people are similar only because they have undertaken a course of joint action. With this in mind, we can start to see that solidarity may be less a *description* of us, than an *offer* to us.

What the principle of solidarity offers is proposed terms for an alliance, in which we forge a common bond: *It would be advantageous for each member of the group to commit to defending all others in the group from any harms or injuries, as long as all the others can be counted on to defend each individual in turn.* According to this *common-front* interpretation, the point of solidarity is that it pays off for everyone who lives by it, as long as others reciprocate, but it doesn't rely on people being in "the same boat." If we think back to the hijacked plane, it is clear that the "more advantaged" members of the 99 per cent are actually getting a share of the benefits that are denied to the less advantaged. Therefore, they do not have especially "common interests." But a common front would give them access to the kind of coordination and reciprocal defence that would make ending the whole ordeal a realistic prospect.

This makes it clear why the principle of solidarity can help us map a trajectory out of the collective-action impasse laid out in the parable. What solidarity requires of us is not that we pretend we are all the same, but only that we jointly commit to having one another's back. Yet, this in turn requires that we forge bonds of reciprocal trust and mutual support, and even doing that much can seem like a tall order from our present weak position. How can we make a real start in this direction?

Traditionally, working-class social movements knew exactly how to do this. They systematically cultivated norms and practices that reinforced habits of reliable coordination: the movements took great pains to inculcate the "working-class values" of co-operation, mutual aid, and mutual defence. Unfortunately, changes in modern capitalism have tended to "decompose" these forms of mutual defence and co-operation. These changes include the bureaucratization of unions, the displacement of self-organized practices of mutual aid by professionalized state services, the legalistic routinization of "labour relations," and the reorganization of workplaces to disempower and de-skill workers. The effect has been to weaken the grip of expectations of solidaristic behaviour, to the point where now the "bourgeois" norms of competition, social climbing, and careerism have come to prevail, even within large parts of the working class, which for so many generations opposed these norms as anti-egalitarian.

But this can be reversed. A recomposition of the bonds of solidarity won't be easy, but it can be done, if we take up the challenge of constructing new forms of solidarity, co-operation, and mutual aid, while reinvigorating (where possible) the old forms. One part of this will be the emergence of new styles of struggle, more effective in today's context than the domesticated and defanged varieties of collective action that now predominate, too often integrated into the official political process or the state-supervised labour-relations regime. Just as crucial will be the revitalization of co-operative production and distribution systems that can draw us out of the seemingly totalitarian reach of market and commodity relations, on the one hand, and bureaucratic "command-and-control" systems, on the other hand. A resurgence of grassroots collectivism could offer a much-needed reminder of our capacity to support and sustain one another, outside and against capital and its state.

A firm embrace of the principle of solidarity, understood as setting out the terms of a mutually advantageous practice of reliable and reciprocal defence of one another, *as if* we were each defending ourselves, has to be returned to the centre of left politics. Only a concerted and persistent commitment to this process of regenerating the shared sense that "an injury to one is an injury to all" can begin to turn the tide against neo-liberalism and weaken the appeal of right-wing populism and its cynical deployment of "anti-Establishment" rhetoric.

REFERENCES

Hegel, G.W.F. 1841 [1807]. *Phänomenologie des Geistes.* Berlin: Duncker und Humblot.
Jackson, George L. 1972. *Blood in My Eye.* New York: Random House.

31

RESISTANCE LIES IN DEFENDING HUMAN RIGHTS

Alex Neve

At a time when we are indeed called to redouble our efforts to resist injustice, inequality, and violence – in our communities, across our country, and around our world – my rallying call remains the great promise of universal human-rights protection. For as a courageous and besieged woman defending human rights at the frontline of strife and repression in Zimbabwe once told me, "If I do not stand up for my own human rights, who will? If I do not stand up for the rights of other Zimbabweans, will they stand up for mine?"

It has been over seventy years since world governments gathered in December 1948 at the newly established United Nations, and committed themselves to the stirring vision that "recognition of the inherent dignity and of the equal and inalienable rights of all members of the human family is the foundation of freedom, justice and peace in the world" (United Nations 1948). In adopting the Universal Declaration of Human Rights they promised every woman, man, and child on every continent that "all human beings are born free and equal in dignity and rights" and "everyone is entitled to all the rights and freedoms set forth in this Declaration, without distinction of any kind" (United Nations 1948). These words from the Universal Declaration are a source of deep inspiration and hope; and at the same time of cruel and bitter betrayal. For the truth is that seven decades later these promises are not merely broken, but shattered, for hundreds of millions of people in every corner of the world every single day, including across Canada.

As we move past the seventieth anniversary of this precious human-rights instrument, we certainly face turbulence and division. These are not easy times for human rights. The turbulence is undeniable, as around the world situations of strife, conflict, and mass atrocities seem on the rise, and the list of countries and of peoples whose lives have been torn apart by ethnic cleansing, war crimes, and unrelenting human-rights abuse grows longer not shorter. We continue to witness conflicts: the Rohingya are facing a devastating crisis in Myanmar, in addition to ongoing and often-deepening human rights and humanitarian catastrophes in Syria, South Sudan, Yemen, Libya, Iraq, the Central African Republic, and far too many other countries.

Faced with situations of such dire need, more often than not the world responds with a mixture of geopolitical deadlock and self-interest on the one hand, and indifference and fatigue on the other. Divisiveness grows, within and between countries, as we face a rapid rise in the politics of hate, fear, and scapegoating in far too many corners of the world. Ugly bigotry and discrimination are nothing new; far from it. But after decades of anti-racism campaigns and education, we hoped that there would have been some progress in relegating it to the margins of most societies, the fodder of extremist politicians and tabloid headlines. But instead it has become disturbingly mainstream.

Hate won the most recent contest for the White House. Hate seems to be at the heart of elections and referenda every time Western Europe goes to the polls. The truth is that the world over, leaders with poisonous views that vilify and demonize some of the most marginalized groups within society – women and girls, refugees and migrants, people living in poverty, LGBTQ communities, and racial, ethnic, and religious minorities – are no longer at the outer edges of public discourse; they have come to power or forged governing alliances in the United States, Brazil, Russia, Hungary, the Philippines, Turkey, Austria, and a lengthy list of countries that risks expanding with each election.

And let us not lull ourselves as Canadians into believing that we are cocooned away from these disturbing global trends. First and foremost, of course, we still have a long way to go in addressing our disgraceful record – both historical and contemporary – of utter disregard for the rights of Indigenous peoples across the country. And while recognition that we all must rise to the responsibility of reconciliation grows, the realities of poverty, discrimination, and neglect faced by First Nations, Inuit, and Métis people in every province and territory simply do not change.

A recent national inquiry examined the scandalous levels of violence faced by Indigenous women and girls in Canada. But during the four years the inquiry was being established and then was underway, governments across Canada did not pursue the changes and reforms that we already know are desperately needed to keep Indigenous women and girls safe. More shelters for Indigenous women and girls escaping violence in remote communities would be a good starting point.

At long last the federal government has stopped fighting the determined First Nations Child and Family Caring Society and has accepted that First Nations children living on reserves across Canada experience serious discrimination when it comes to the provision of services meant to keep them safe and with their families. Easily said; yet at the same time the same government feels it is okay to fail to take the steps the Canadian Human Rights Tribunal has ordered, repeatedly, so as to end that discrimination.

And amidst stirring talk of new relationships and an enthusiastic embrace of the United Nations Declaration on the Rights of Indigenous Peoples, it sadly seems to be business as usual when it comes to sacrificing the land rights of Indigenous peoples when powerful economic interests are in play. The controversial Site C dam in northeastern British Columbia is a glaring case in point, a development fiercely resisted by the First Nations communities who look forward to the flooding and destruction of lands central to their traditions, culture, and way of life. Yet in July 2016, when Justin Trudeau's government had an opportunity to demonstrate that the promise of new respect for Indigenous peoples would be backed up by decisions that put their rights first for once, the promise was broken and permits from two ministries were issued, allowing dam construction to continue.

And, in December 2017, when John Horgan's new provincial government in British Columbia had the same opportunity, having sworn during the election campaign that reconciliation and regard for the UN Declaration on the Rights of Indigenous Peoples would be the hallmarks of his administration, those promises were again quickly put aside and the dam allowed to proceed. In defence, Premier Horgan offered the blithe explanation that he was not the first leader to "disappoint Indigenous peoples" (Kurjata 2017). It is a stunning indictment to hear that a politician believes that a valid justification for a decision that violates the rights of Indigenous peoples is to simply point to the fact that such violations are part of a long-established pattern.

Clearly Canadians cannot risk smugness in jumping to quick conclusions that rights and justice are safe and secure here. Beyond the rights of Indigenous peoples, we are reminded of that on many other fronts as well.

While these days the federal government promotes an important message of #RefugeesWelcomeHere, not long ago we were faced with immigration ministers who spoke unceasingly instead of bogus refugees abusing our system, and pursued policies overwhelmingly designed to punish and restrict refugee claimants. Even now, with a positive new tone, the refusal to lift the Safe Third Country Agreement belies that commitment. The agreement makes it difficult for refugees, who are fearful of the implications of Donald Trump's punitive measures against migrants, refugees, and Muslims, to look north to Canada for protection instead.

We cannot forget how relatively quick and easy it was for Stephen Harper's government to take steps on many fronts in an effort to punish, sideline, and silence voices of dissent in the country. While this was obviously not comparable to the situation in countries where critics disappear at the hands of death squads, it was a wakeup call to see how readily the space for advocacy and dissent came under siege in Canada. Individual activists were singled out for sharp criticism and even surveillance. Groups that opposed the government's agenda when it came to the environment, pipelines, women's equality, and the rights of Palestinians were vilified as foreign agents and subject to threatening audits by Revenue Canada. The accusation? That advocating for and defending human rights constituted impermissible political activity, justifying that they be stripped of charitable status.

Intolerance, hate, and violence continue to rear their heads in Canada, sometimes with deadly consequences. One need only recall the barbaric-cultural-practices hotline proposed by the Conservative Party in the 2015 federal election, marginalization of women who wear the hijab in Quebec by Bill 21 (An Act Respecting the Laicity of the State), and the cold-blooded killing of six men following evening prayers in a Quebec City mosque in January 2017.

In times of turmoil and divisiveness, it is most certainly time to link up and stand in solidarity, with each other and with the communities – close to home and halfway around the world – that experience the repercussions most directly. It is certainly a time to stand strong in resistance, refusing to accept the normalization of a world of bigotry and atrocities. It is time for an agenda of resistance with universal human rights as its rallying cry. It is an agenda with five key considerations at its core.

First, we must, at every opportunity, *turn the channel on hate*. That means going beyond the obvious moments. We must do this not only when a politician needs to be called out on bigotry, or a newspaper's hate-filled editorial demands a letter in response. We must do it when we encounter the hate – in both glaring and subtle ways – every day in our own lives. Far too often we ignore the intolerance and hate we witness around us, be it in our workplace, a public bus, or a street corner. We don't have enough time. It does not feel worth the bother. It's not my business. What difference would it make anyway? But every time we walk away, hate gains a foothold. That is what we must resist.

Second, we absolutely must actively *reject indifference*. We cannot continue to accept that we live in a world that shrugs its shoulders in the face of mass atrocities, entrenched discrimination, and extreme poverty. It is not okay to regretfully say that's simply the way it is when the United Nations is paralyzed in the face of a staggering crisis like Syria. It is not okay to say, just another tragedy in Africa, when conflict and famine erupts in South Sudan. And it is certainly not okay to justify ongoing violations of the rights of Indigenous peoples by pointing to a long history of disappointment. Resisting indifference means being a voice that consistently says it does matter and must change.

Third, now is the time to *embrace equality*. There has been a conversation about women's rights and equality unlike anything we have seen in many years. Sparked by the Harvey Weinstein case and the #MeToo movement, there is at long last a growing chorus that rejects silence and resists the stereotypes and norms that lie at the heart of gender-based violence and sexual harassment. But we have been here before. This time it must take hold and lead to real, lasting societal change.

Fourth, it is time to *insist on justice*, no matter what. That is the necessary flip side to resisting injustice. Canadian companies responsible for human-rights abuses in other countries? There must be justice and accountability. Architects of genocide and crimes against humanity face no consequences, retain power, and amass great wealth? There must be justice and accountability. Indigenous peoples, African-Canadians, and other racialized minorities are disproportionately targeted for arrest and imprisonment? There must be justice and accountability.

and political changes that often include violence and warfare. The United Nations High Commissioner for Refugees (2017) reported, "We are now witnessing the highest levels of displacement on record. An unprecedented 65.6 million people around the world have been forced from home."

Settler-colonial regimes like the Canadian state are seeking to undermine Indigenous sovereignty and destroy Indigenous existence, even as they nod to reconciliation. Indigenous communities lack access to clean water, decent housing, and education for their children. Governments and corporations have renewed attacks on Indigenous sovereignty, because it impedes the extraction of profits from natural resources, for example through pipeline construction. Indigenous existence also points to other ways of living that are rooted in collective sovereignty rather than individualism and market exchange.

Finally, the ecological disaster of our times is a huge source of insecurity. The devastating impact of two hurricanes on Puerto Rico in 2017 shows what happens when increasingly severe weather events driven by climate change meet social infrastructure (like the electricity grid) that has been undermined by underfunding due to neo-liberal economic restructuring and colonial debt. Scientists and activists make it absolutely clear that policy changes are lagging far behind the ecological damage.

This insecurity is so pervasive that it can feel like a force of nature, as inevitable as the weather. The neo-liberal era has hollowed out politics, as the main political parties across the spectrum, ranging from Conservative to Social Democratic (like the NDP in Canada) have all embraced its pro-market agenda. The major organizations for the exercise of power from below, ranging from unions to community organizations, have been weakened by the restructuring of work and changes in the rhythms of everyday life that have undermined a sense of collectivity. This has produced the "impoverished condition of contemporary public discourse" in which there is little space for serious debate about the political decisions that shape our collective futures (Harvey 2005, 183).

Insecurity and the Rise of the Right

Employers and state policy-makers have deployed neo-liberal strategies to create widespread insecurity and undermine confidence in our collective powers to change the world from below. This has opened a space for the growth of the far right, which offers false solutions to insecurity based on the misdirection of fear. At the level of the state, terrorism is cast as the greatest threat to security. Politicians and government officials offer up ethnically targeted surveillance, immigration controls, and overall militarization, claiming these measures will reduce the threat level for the population as a whole.

The right thrives on the misdirection of insecurities. Richard Saull (2017, 40) argues that the far right has a long history of misdirecting the anxieties generated by economic vulnerability toward forms of racial and cultural exclusion: "Indeed, there is continuity here – at least in form – with the earlier manifestations of the far right, in that questions of socio-economic insecurity and crisis have always been presented in cultural/racial terms."

Dörre, Kraemer, and Speidel (2006, 123–4) conclude from their analysis of right populism in Europe: "there is an interconnection between the increase in precariousness of work, the recurrence of social insecurity and the occurrence of right wing populist orientations." People facing greater insecurity without a sense of collective efficacy tend to be open to the identification of racialized or marginalized workers as competition undermining their social position. The fear of decline in income and working conditions or of unemployment is real, but the cause is economic restructuring and cuts to social services, not migration. The far right has drawn some of its fuel from the decline in the living and working conditions of particular sections of the working class, misdirecting their anger at deteriorating life circumstances away from the corporate elite and their allies in government and toward vulnerable groups like migrants, people who are Indigenous or racialized, and trans people.

Security and insecurity have never been evenly distributed across the working class. Certain sections of the working class, disproportionately White and male, won a degree of security over the period from the Second World War to the 1970s through unionization and the spread of social programs associated with the welfare state. In this sense, security could be considered part of the wages of whiteness described by W.E.B. Du Bois. Even when their incomes were low, White workers "were compensated by a sort of public and psychological wage … [t]hey were given public deference and titles of courtesy because they were white" (Du Bois 1935, 700–1).

John Narayan (2017, 2491) argues that the right is rising today by promising "to re-supply the wages of whiteness in the absence of wages." He characterizes this as a "racially regressive reaction to the effects of neo-liberal
globalisation's decimation of (white) working class and middle class economic and political power" (Narayan 2017, 2491). The right has drawn
specifically on ideologies of masculinity and whiteness to encourage White
men to see their perceived loss of social position as the result of the rise of
feminism and lesbian/gay/bisexual/transgender rights, rather than the restructuring of work, attacks on union rights, and cuts to social services.

Other Possible Worlds

Effective resistance against the far right must include the development of
movements from below that address the real sources of insecurity. It is
crucial to mobilize against fascism, a movement built on intimidation and
fear. This needs to be combined with struggles in workplaces, schools, and
communities to win improvements in living and working conditions. Such
mobilization is a particular challenge now, because the left has been weakened by over thirty years of neo-liberal restructuring. The workplaces that
were the powerhouses of the union movement, such as mines and factories,
have been shut down or dramatically downsized. Communities that had
long radical histories have been undermined by the relocation of work, gentrification, and attrition of political spaces.

Effective resistance from below does not simply come from insecurity
and anger. People need to deliberately develop capacities to mobilize against
the institutional advantages of the ruling elite, who control the corporations, much of the media, and the state. Activists in the past have successfully created spaces to nurture resistance capacities. This has included
everything from union education to socialist and anarchist organizations,
from participatory cultural activities to alternative media. Collectivity needs
to be learned in a society that teaches us from the youngest age that we are
pitted against each other in a competitive struggle to survive.

Students at an individual level might feel intimidated by their teachers.
However, when they begin to coordinate, they feel their power. This can
happen informally, for example near the end of a dull university lecture,
when students start to pack up and put on their jackets, indicating that the
class is over even if the professor is still talking. At a more formal level, Que-

bec students have a long history of striking against tuition-fee increases, most recently in 2012, shutting down many post-secondary institutions in an unlimited strike that mobilized hundreds of thousands and stopped a 76-per-cent tuition increase.

Collective organization of workers, students, and community members is essential to building the confidence and power from below to defeat the politics of insecurity. Callum Cant both participated in and wrote about the mobilization by Deliveroo workers in Britain. Management regards these bicycle and moped couriers as self-employed contractors, organized through an app along the lines of Uber drivers. Pay for workers began to fall in 2017, as more riders joined the company, so the growth of the workforce was outstripping the increase in orders. The couriers began to organize collectively, launching meetings and demonstrations, producing a monthly bulletin called the *Rebel Roo*, and calling strikes. These workers used their collective power to win demands around pay and conditions by bringing work to a grinding halt through wildcat strikes, even without formal union organization, in part drawing on the opportunities to communicate with each other that were built into the organization of work (Cant 2017).

The Deliveroo mobilization is just one example of people forging new forms of collectivity to fight the insecurity of life under neo-liberal capitalism. Black Lives Matter has mobilized to take direct action against the brutal racist policing and mass-incarceration policies that have increasingly blighted the lives of Black, Indigenous, and other racialized people during the neo-liberal era. The Fight for $15 and Fairness campaign organized to successfully win an increase in the Ontario minimum wage and important changes in employment law. This campaign started by mobilizing precarious workers, many of whom were migrants, and gradually winning union endorsement. Indigenous resurgence has seen powerful demands for the transformation of educational institutions and the use of sovereignty to protect the land and water by resisting the incursions of resource-extraction industries. Younger people mobilized in large numbers in 2017 to work for the election of Jeremy Corbyn's anti–neo-liberal Labour Party in Britain, building energetic rallies and active campaigns to persuade others to vote, boosting the turnout of students and young people.

People fighting back against insecurity are challenging the core logic of neo-liberalism and providing a glimpse of other possible worlds. These struggles against insecurity must feature genuine solidarity built around redress, reparation, and reconciliation that addresses the damage done by generations of domination and oppression. This will require a process of mobilization, experimentation, and deliberate learning, in which the left works toward an integrative anti-racist, anti-colonial, ecological, feminist, and queer class politics. We will be sustained in this process by a serious commitment to change the world, and also from a joyous understanding of liberation as an unleashing of human potential in every area of life.

REFERENCES

Cant, Callum. 2017. "The Warehouse Without Walls: A Workers Inquiry at Deliveroo." Submitted to *Ephemera*, November. Cited by permission.
Dorre, Klaus, Klaus Kraemer, and Frederic Speidel. 2006. "The Increasing Precariousness of the Employment Society: Driving Force for a New Right Wing Populism." *International Journal of Action Research* 2 (1): 98–128.
Du Bois, W.E.B. 1992. *Black Reconstruction in America, 1860–1880*. New York: The Free Press.
Hales, Jessica. 2017. "City Is Ignoring Toronto's Shelter Crisis" *Toronto Star*, 9 October. https://www.thestar.com/opinion/commentary/2017/10/09/city-is-ignoring-torontos-shelter-crisis.html.
Harvey, David. 2005. *A Brief History of Neoliberalism*. Oxford: Oxford University Press.
Narayan, John. 2017. "The Wage of Whiteness in the Absence of Wages: Racial Capitalism, Reactionary Intercommunalism and the Rise of Trumpism." *Third World Quarterly* 38 (11): 2482–500.
Saull, Richard. 2015. "Capitalism, Crisis, and the Far-Right in the Neoliberal Era." *Journal of International Relations and Development* 18: 25–51.
United Nations High Commissioner for Refugees. 2017. Figures at a Glance. http://www.unhcr.org/figures-at-a-glance.html.

33

GRASSROOTS AND INTERFAITH

A Foundation for Activism?

Lisa Kowalchuk and Cynthia Levine-Rasky

Like the moment one heard of the death of a revered public figure like John Lennon or John F. Kennedy, the night of Tuesday, 8 November 2016 is seared into our memories. Almost immediately, a widely shared recognition set in that the election of the 45th President of the United States would bode ill for society, and not just for American society, but for *all* of society. The vulnerability of communities marked by religion, refugee status, racialization, low income, sexual difference, and disability increased dramatically overnight. But fears spread beyond these positions. We intuitively understood that environmental gains, Indigenous claims, and LGBTQ rights would come under attack, and that the erosion of the welfare state, especially the gap between rich and poor and the attrition of political accountability, would intensify. We took a big collective breath and prepared to hold it for what we expected would be a long time, and we cast our eyes about for potential allies. We are still holding our breath, but the irony of the bleak shift in the political climate is that many of us have found allies. Some of them were found in places that had been completely unexplored, opening up possibilities for grassroots community building and renewal of all kinds. The question is, to what end?

This essay describes an action that Cynthia took shortly after the US election, and together we consider its potential to contribute to social change. The election impelled her to seek ideas for what she could do, to whom she could reach out, and where she could deal with her anguish. In scanning her Facebook feed just after the election, she saw a post for an interfaith organization for Muslim and Jewish women. The Sisterhood of Salaam Shalom (soss) immediately caught her attention. Identifying as a secular, but a positively identified Jewish woman most comfortable in the Reform movement, Cynthia's membership with a congregation has waxed and waned throughout her adult life. Since her childhood involved very little Jewish education, she dedicated herself to learning the Sabbath liturgy and

Passover Seder later in life. As a result, she enjoys prayer, perhaps a bit unusual for a thoroughly secular Jew. Her idiosyncratic identity and practice led her to appreciate religious identities and practices of others, regardless of their degree of observance or personal expression. In the sisterhood, she saw a place to turn for allies in a campaign for social justice. That it furnished a way to build community with ostensible religious adversaries made it acutely and urgently right.

In December, she contacted the director of the organization in the United States. This was followed by a phone conversation early in January 2017 and an agreement that Cynthia would co-lead the first Canadian chapter in Toronto. She was not alone taking this initiative; after November, the number of soss chapters surged from 50 to over 150 across North America, with the Toronto group the first in Canada. With Muslim co-leader Sabreena Ghaffar-Siddiqui, and with patient outreach, social media, word-of-mouth, and some media coverage, membership had grown to over one hundred by the end of 2017. Members are more or less evenly divided between Muslims and Jews, and are diverse in age, ethnicity, and religious observance. Due to its burgeoning size and the geographic dispersal of members around the Greater Toronto Area, the group divided into five smaller "circles" in 2018. Face-to-face dialogue in the group concerns personal identity, experiences, community-building, religious practices, and social values, but the circles also coordinate responses to local anti-Muslim and anti-Jewish acts, and for Christmas 2017, organized a Sadaqa-Tzedakah Day around the donation of gifts to a community drop-in centre. More ideas for sessions are in the works and are now accomplished by each autonomous circle.

The sisterhood's primary goal is to "build trust, respect, and sustainable relationships between Muslim and Jewish women," and to "take action to diminish any acts of anti-Muslim and anti-Jewish sentiment." The relationship between these two goals is not obvious, since some members, like any collection of individuals, may be more or less inclined to activism. Members' personal interest in activism range from avoidance to avid engagement, and as with personal preferences in religious expression and politics, is accepted without judgment.

Journalists and others have asked Cynthia, as the group's spokesperson, why the sisterhood appeals to Canadian Muslim and Jewish women when it arose in the United States in response to what they may see as an American problem. She explains that hatred knows no geographic borders, and that the impact of the US political leadership is felt everywhere. This is certainly suggested by increased news reports during 2017 of violent acts perpetrated on Canadian streets (see Perry and Scrivens 2016; and Perry in this volume) by groups whose names should not be further publicized. For 2015, Statistics Canada (2017) showed that police-reported hate crime motivated by religion comprised 35 per cent of the total number of 1,362 incidents reported that year. Jews continued to be the most common targets of such crimes, with 178 incidents, but crimes against Muslims increased by 61 per cent to a total of 159. For 2017, these figures increased. Forty-one per cent of all hate crimes were motivated by religion; Jews were targeted in 360 incidents, and Muslims were targeted in 349 incidents (Statistics Canada 2019). These numbers do not reveal the conflation of crimes against racialized groups and against those assumed to be Muslim. There is also no estimate of actual hate crimes committed as a ratio of those reported.

As the essays by Jamil, Elghawaby, and Farber and Rudner attest, organized and random acts of anti-Muslim and anti-Jewish violence are ongoing. The day Cynthia wrote this, a Muslim sister sent her an image of someone's graffiti scrawled in huge orange lettering on a major highway barrier in Vaughan, a region directly north of Toronto. It reads, "Hitler was right!" Four weeks prior to that, arsonists destroyed a car belonging to Mohamed Labidi, the president of the Quebec Islamic Cultural Centre, just thirty-six hours after Quebec City mayor Régis Labeaume announced the purchase of city-owned land for a Muslim cemetery. The Islamic Centre was the site of the mass murder of six Muslim men who were shot while praying at that mosque on 29 January 2017.

The Sisterhood of Salaam Shalom through the Prism of Social Movements

The sisterhood is a grassroots, community, interfaith organization of women in solidarity with each other against racism. While the simple act of standing alongside each other is in itself a powerful political act of resistance, can it be effective in countering the almost daily incidents of racism in our communities? Does dialogue fall too far short of activism, or does it create bonds of authentic reciprocity that are necessary to sustain engagement with activism? Can it do both? In the end, the question is, can soss participate in a social movement? And, given its gender and faith-based composition, can soss stand as an example of how to build an intersectional coalition to combat the nativist bigotry of the far right and contribute to an inclusive common good?

Answering these questions hinges partly on how we define social movements. The Trump election and its emboldening effect on the far right in the United States, Canada, and many other countries "has inspired activism on multiple fronts … [and] given rise to a plurality of political acts against a common target" (Rose-Redwood and Rose-Redwood 2017, 646). We view the sisterhood as one instance of such activism. That said, it is not a conventional social-movement organization that forms mainly to press authorities or elites for policy changes, often through campaigns that encompass public protests. Nor does it exist primarily to campaign for changes in the realm of attitudes and values, directing its messaging outward to society or to particular publics. Neither of those modes of activism is the appropriate prism through which to consider soss's potential as a change-maker. Rather, we think soss should be seen as part of a broad anti-racist and anti-patriarchal "social movement community," a term coined by Buechler (1990) to refer to a set of actors of many different types – organizations, individuals, informal networks – that are "loosely connected" and that share values, beliefs, and aspirations for social change (Buechler 1990; Staggenborg and Taylor 2005).

The recognition of social-movement communities reflects a gradual evolution in scholars' thinking about movements. The still highly influential "contentious politics" paradigm in social-movement studies regards clashing interests, public claim-making by formally structured organizations, and the use of extra-institutional channels to express those claims as definitional elements in social movements (McAdam, Tarrow, and Tilly 2001). But movement scholars such as Diani (2000), Haug (2013), Rupp and Taylor (1987), Melucci (1996), and Staggenborg and Taylor (2005) have increasingly come to regard movements "as networks of informal relationships between a multiplicity of individuals and organizations, who share a distinctive collective identity, and mobilize resources on conflictual issues" (Diani 2000, 387). Arguably many kinds of movements that are "based on fundamental social cleavages" (Staggenborg and Taylor 2005, 48) are associated with a movement community. The concept stems originally from studies of feminist organizing, reflecting in part the fact that "women activists frequently avoid conventional politics and even disavow being 'political' and turn, in-stead, to everyday forms of activism deriving from their community roles and identities as women" (Staggenborg and Taylor 2005). While we will address gender more fully below, this certainly corresponds with the diverse range of views and experiences that come together in soss.

The very diversity in the types of actors that make up a social-movement community means that they can "combine mass demonstrations, direct ac-tion, and conventional political actions with consciousness-raising, self-help, performative, cultural, and discursive forms of resistance oriented to cultural and social change" (Staggenborg and Taylor 2005, 46). So, while some actors direct demands toward elites or toward counter-movement groups, others, like the sisterhood, engage in a variety of activities that en-ergize and nurture movements between periods of intense, publicly visible, campaigns. As Rose-Redwood and Rose-Redwood observe of international post-Trump women's mobilizing, "backstage work is just as important to social movements as mass public spectacles" (2017, 650).

The sisterhood's main mode of interaction has the potential to con-tribute crucially to anti-racist resistance. In particular, the regularity of face-to-face encounters among the members constitutes the space for the "backstage" work of generating and sustaining a movement (Haug 2013; Poletta 1999). In observing the importance of face-to-face interactions in movement networks, some scholars emphasize the bolstering of strategic and instrumental capacities. When people meet regularly to share their life experiences, develop and solidify friendships, and develop their analysis of their situation, they can establish an "infrastructure of dissent" (Lafrance and Sears 2016). They also acquire experience in collective decision-making, whereby they can respond effectively and quickly to a changing environ-ment for protest, especially compared to digitally convened groups that scale up quickly but are not built on prior face-to-face networks (Tufekci 2017). Face-to-face interactions also have impacts that are more indirect, affective, and expressive; in this regard Jasper (1997) talks about the joys of collective action as crucial to people's commitment. The "emotion cultures" created by movement-identified groups and networks like soss can serve as a resource for more overtly contentious actions (Staggenborg and Taylor 2005, 44). Based on her case study of the women's movement in Indiana, Staggenborg notes that "activists who interact in the community infect one another with their enthusiasm for related causes" and that this is "critical to the emergence and survival of social movements" (1998, 199). This is reminiscent of the approach favoured by famed civil-rights figure Ella Baker: "For Baker, elections, court decision, and even legislative victories were the events that punctuated the real ongoing political process, which consisted of a discursive exchange, the building of a set of trusting relationships, individual and organizational, the transmission of skills and confidence, and the forging of a shared democratic vision for the future" (Ransby 2003, 271).

To fully address our questions about the sisterhood's relationship to a broad movement of resistance, we must also consider the relevance of its gender composition. It is useful to reflect on why it is women have come together in this enactment of solidarity, caring, and love between two groups that are major targets of recently resurgent nativist bigotry, and what difference this makes. In this regard, Cynthia observes from experience that there are things that sisterhood members can take for granted in the group that would not be the case otherwise, such as the demands of parenting and their roles in the nuclear family, the experience of the female body as objectified, and women as traditionally subordinate in religion and culture. All these factors combine to serve as a foundation that would be absent in a mixed group.

Furthermore, we cannot ignore the patriarchal character of the threat we as a society are currently confronting in the far-right resurgence. As Gokariksel and Smith (2017, 631) observe in relation to how the landscape has changed in the United States, the "political strategy" at the highest echelon of this threat ironically "centers white masculinity both as victor (the President) and as victim (the voters in the deindustrializing Midwest and South)." This is a government that "invests in strengthening masculinist state institutions like law enforcement and the military, while divesting from feminized state institutions that are associated with the care, well-being, and education of the population and the soft power of diplomacy" (Gokariksel and Smith 2017, 630).

Several essays in this volume – such as Irving, Jiwani, Shaker, Watts, and Tufts, Thomas, and MacDonald – underscore the relationship between nativist, patriarchal white supremacy and a deepening of a right-wing neoliberal agenda that, especially in the United States, is enjoying a freer rein than ever before. In light of these twinned threats, there has perhaps never been a more urgent time than the present to confront interlocking oppressions. The fact is that countless women's organizations have emerged around the world in recent decades to do just that, and have often done so across lines of race, religion, immigration status, sexual orientation, and nation-state borders (Carastathis 2013). These coalitions reflect, and are a response to, the compounding of sexism and gender-based violence with the suffering and injustice inflicted by neo-liberalism, neo-imperialism, militarism, and environmental degradation.

It goes without saying there are innumerable challenges in forging an intersectional solidarity. Gokariksel and Smith observe that women in resistance to the far right and neo-liberalism need "a politics that begins from and builds on … differences, rather than claiming an easy sisterhood that obscures divisions" (2017, 632). The obvious fact of plurality in the sisterhood's membership, and the fact that neither "woman," nor "Muslim," nor "Jewish" is a stand-alone category, means that there may well be internal disagreements. But it need not be a barrier to unified action. On the contrary, because we are not dealing with "single-factor stratification systems," but rather "multiple systems of domination" (Taylor and Whittier 1992, 111), we think that the distinctive backgrounds and experiences that the sisterhood brings together are a kind of resource or "fund" (Carastathis 2013) for activism. As Carastathis (2013) has noted of other multi-ethnic feminist coalitions, participants are "members of multiply oppressed groups" (Carastathis 2013, 960) that are each outraged by, and are pushing back in various ways against, these systems of oppression. The sisterhood regards this as a strength, not a weakness.

Returning to the question posed in our title, the sisterhood is clearly a potential foundation for anti–far-right activism. Undoubtedly, many of its members already take part in additional, more-contentious activity in and outside the institutional political arena to delegitimize and defeat far-right, neo-liberal forces. Others, animated by their more avidly activist sisters, may eventually do so. But by forging friendship and community between two groups sometimes considered to be intractably at odds, the sisterhood is already building the alternative society its members want, one in which marginalized groups stand up for each other's dignity and inclusion, surely an enactment of the common good.

REFERENCES

Buechler, Steven M. 1990. *Women's Movements in the United States.* New Brunswick, NJ: Rutgers University Press.

Carastathis, Anna. 2013. "Identity Categories as Potential Coalitions." *Signs* 38 (4): 941–65.

Cole, Elizabeth R. 2008. "Coalitions as a Model for Intersectionality: From Practise to Theory." *Sex Roles* 59 (5/6): 443–53.

Diani, Mario. 2000. "Social Movement Networks Virtual and Real." *Information, Communication, and Society* 3 (3): 386–401.

Gokariksel, Banu, and Sara Smith. 2017. "Intersectional Feminism Beyond US Flag Hijab and Pussy Hats in Trump's America." *Gender, Place, and Culture* 24 (5): 628–44.

Haug, Cristoph. 2013. "Organizing Spaces: Meeting Arenas as a Social Movement Infrastructure Between Organization, Network, and Institution." *Organization Studies* 34 (5/6): 705–32.

Jasper, James. 1997. *The Art of Moral Protest: Culture, Biography, and Creativity in Social Movements.* Chicago: University of Chicago Press.

Lafrance, Xavier, and Alan Sears. 2016. "Infrastructure of Dissent: The Case of the Québec Student Movement." In *A World to Win: Contemporary Social Movements and Counter-Hegemony,* edited by William Carroll and Kanchan Sarker, 159–75. Winnipeg: ARP Books.

McAdam, Doug, Sidney Tarrow, and Charles Tilly. 2001. *Dynamics of Contention.* New York: Cambridge University Press.

Melucci, Alberto. 1996. *Challenging Codes: Collective Action in the Information Age.* Cambridge: Cambridge University Press.

Perry, Barbara, and Ryan Scrivens. 2016. "Uneasy Alliances: A Look at the Right-Wing Extremist Movement in Canada." *Studies in Conflict and Terrorism* 39 (9): 819–41.

Poletta, Francesca. 1999. "Free Spaces in Collective Action." *Theory and Society* 28 (1): 1–38.

Ransby, Barbara. 2003. *Ella Baker and the Black Freedom Movement: A Radical Democratic Vision,* vol. 2. Chapel Hill: University of North Carolina Press.

Rose-Redwood, CindyAnn, and Reuben Rose-Redwood. 2017. "'It Definitely Felt Very White': Race, Gender, and the Performative Politics of Assembly at the Women's March in Victoria, British Columbia." *Gender, Place, and Culture* 24 (5): 645–54.

Rupp, Leila J., and Verta Taylor. 1987. *Survival in the Doldrums: The American Women's Rights Movement, 1945 to the 1960s.* New York: Oxford University Press.

Staggenborg, Suzanne. 1998. "Social Movement Communities and Cycles of Protest: The Emergence and Maintenance of a Local Women's Movement." *Social Problems* 45 (2): 180–204.

Staggenborg, Suzanne, and Verta Taylor. 2005. "Whatever Happened to the Women's Movement?" *Mobilization* 10 (1): 37–52.

Statistics Canada. 2017. "Police-reported Hate Crime in Canada, 2015." http://www.statcan.gc.ca/pub/85-002-x/2017001/article/14832-eng.htm.

Tufekci, Zeynep. 2017. *Twitter and Tear Gas: The Power and Fragility of Networked Protest.* New Haven: Yale University Press.

34

RESISTING THE RESURGENCE OF
WHITE SUPREMACY

Pamela Palmater

Of the many crisis-level issues facing world leaders today, none seems to have received the amount of attention as the purported problem of "others." French President Emmanuel Macron delivered a speech to the G-20 summit several months after his election in May 2017 that highlighted his specific concerns about Africa: "The challenge of Africa, it is totally different, it is much deeper, it is civilizational today" (Wildman 2017). Macron went on to explain that "when countries still have seven to eight children per woman – you can decide to spend billions of euros, you will not stabilize anything" (Wildman 2017). President Donald Trump, elected only a few months before Macron, also shared his concerns about Africa, specifically immigration from Haitian and African countries: "Why are we having all these people from shithole countries come here?" (Dawsey 2018). Trump, instead, prefers immigration from countries like Norway (Dawsey 2018). Trump's solution for preventing the immigration of Mexicans, who he claimed were "bringing drugs. They're bringing crime. They're rapists" (Kopan 2016) is to build a giant wall on their shared border.

However, it would be too easy to point to US President Donald Trump and make him the villain or the "cause" of this phenomenon. He has been described as racist, sexist, and classist – his views representing every hateful "ism" that exists. Yet, he was, in fact, elected by millions of Americans. We are no better in Canada. It's just that Canadian politicians tend to be a little more nuanced about it. It is important to note that Canada recently came out of a decade of right-wing Conservative rule under former Prime Minister Stephen Harper. His government was critical of the United Nations and engaged less with international human-rights treaty bodies. Harper himself often skipped meetings of the United Nations and, in general, promoted human rights less than former governments (Canadian Press 2013; Gallow 2015). It should be no surprise then that their core policy issues included "immigration" control and anti-terrorism measures – which some called draconian and others called outright racist (Fitzpatrick 2011; Mair 2015).

In addition to Trump's giant walls to stem the flow of non-White migrants, the United Kingdom's "Brexit" debate took on an Islamophobic tone, with supporters playing on fears of isis attacks and migrants taking up all the state-supported social programs (Robertson 2016). Brexit racism seemed to inspire a "frenzy of hatred" in Britain – a very public "celebratory racism" (Khaleeli 2016). Italy may well be headed down the same path. Matteo Salvini, one of the candidates who ran in Italy's presidential election, also recently expressed concerns about the "invasion" of non-White immigrants into Italy – namely Muslims (D'Emilio 2018). He publicly defended the candidate for the governorship of Lombardy Atillio Fontana, who said that immigrants pose a real threat to the "white race." He explained: "We must decide if our ethnicity, if our white race, if our society must continue to exist or if it must be cancelled out" (D'Emilio 2018). As shocking as these statements are, this is not a new phenomenon. Another former world leader held similar views against "immigration" and made it the mission of his country to "assemble and preserve the most valuable racial elements … and raise them to the dominant position" (Editors 2017). That leader was Adolf Hitler.

What's clear about these messages is that they are less about immigration and more about the open and often public resurgence of racism, white supremacy, and anti-human-rights rhetoric. Though much of the focus has been on Trump and his overtly racist comments, world leaders, especially those in the G-20, have been equally racist in their policies, albeit under the guise of immigration or anti-terrorism. While some may call this a rise in racism and anti-human rights, these sentiments have always been there. They are not shared by everyone, but there are large segments of society in many of these countries – including Canada and the United States – that have always felt this way. The core difference between the 1980s and today is the very public nature in which racism and white nationalism have resurfaced. Incredibly, even some in the mainstream media seem to believe that the very merits of racism are back up for debate and have provided a platform to air these views. Take, for example, the most recent study on reporting in Australia, where content in mainstream media was found to be so racist that it would likely contravene their code of conduct on racism (Ho 2017). In Canada, all "White" panels of political commentators are the ones who get to decide whether US President Trump's derogatory comments about African countries were in fact racist (Khan 2018). A recent report on the controversy over removing statues of those who committed human-rights atrocities saw CBC give a platform to a White supremacist to justify the genocide against Indigenous peoples without anyone to counter his hateful views (Huffpost 2017), leading to all kinds of social-media debate on the so-called merits of racism. It is as if we have turned back the clock on humanity itself by allowing racism, white supremacy, and anti-human-rights discourse to be legitimized in the media (Balgord 2017) and justified in government policies.

This is certainly not where we thought human rights were headed. Since the Universal Declaration of Human Rights was proclaimed in 1948, it was hoped that, over time, this would become the minimum standard in countries worldwide (UN General Assembly 1948a). The Convention on the Prevention and Punishment of the Crime of Genocide was passed in the same year after the horrific atrocities committed by Hitler's Nazis (UN General Assembly 1948b). Various other international treaties, declarations, and conventions addressing anti-racism, anti-sexism, and non-discrimination were also touted as the new standards by which democratic countries and UN member states agreed to abide. Many of these countries adopted their own domestic laws and policies protecting human rights. Canada is often celebrated for its federal and provincial human-rights acts, its Charter of Rights and Freedoms and commitment to international human rights (Government of Canada 1982). Ironically, countries like Canada, the United States, and the United Kingdom have long used those international human-rights standards by which to judge the actions of other countries like China, Iran, and North Korea.

This rise in white supremacy in society seems to be fuelled by the publicly racist, hateful, and nationalist views of White men in positions of power, like Donald Trump. However, White supremacists have always been here – timing their overt presence with various political issues (climate change, economics, labour, war/conflict), riding the wave of public fear, and strategically laying blame on the "other." Their hope is to cover their hatred under the guise of unity, nationalism, and public security, i.e. protection from the others who they claim pose these threats. The rise in racism, white supremacy, and anti-human-rights discourse would, at first glance, seem to unravel the decades of hard work, advocacy, and, indeed, loss of life by human-rights defenders.

The current anti-human-rights backlash also has a unique and disproportionate impact on Indigenous peoples worldwide. Indigenous peoples have already suffered through the brutal colonization of their nations and territories by foreign powers; the devastating impacts of state laws, policies, and actions intended to eradicate their cultures and identities; and the ongoing poverty and ill health that has resulted from the theft of their lands and resources. The genocidal acts[1] committed upon Indigenous peoples, such as scalping bounties, forced sterilizations, violent rapes, starvation policies, murders, theft of children forced into White families to be assimilated, and the torture, rape, and experimentation on Indigenous children in residential schools (boarding schools) were all based in racist ideologies about white supremacy and entitlement to the lands, resources, and lives of non-White peoples. Indigenous resistance to racism and white supremacy has been a long road that never ends but merely changes forms.

Sustained resistance against racism and oppression by Indigenous peoples went hand in hand with their advocacy for human rights, and led not only to the creation of the United Nations Permanent Forum on Indigenous Issues, but also resulted in the negotiation, drafting, and passing of the United Nation Declaration on the Rights of Indigenous Peoples (UNDRIP) (UN General Assembly 2007). This declaration protects their land rights, treaties, their right to self-determination, and freedom from assimilation, relocation, and discrimination. Many of the rights contained within UNDRIP are already contained in other UN human-rights declarations. However, it was necessary for Indigenous peoples to have this declaration, because many states did not see or treat Indigenous peoples as human beings – and thus they did not enjoy even basic human rights within their own territories now controlled by states. Their ability to establish an international standard is quite an achievement; yet, despite this success, Indigenous peoples are experiencing a second wave of violent colonization by states and corporations, which are intent on developing Indigenous lands and resources.

At the start of 2017, the UN Special Rapporteur on the Rights of Indigenous Peoples, Victoria Tauli-Corpuz, expressed deep concern that there were "serious retreats" in Indigenous rights, specifically noting the threat of the extractive industry to Indigenous lands (Yakupitiyage 2017). She also noted that international trade agreements, like the Trans-Pacific Partnership (TPP), poses a significant threat to Indigenous land rights, since the TPP "grants more rights to transnational firms, often at the expense of Indigenous rights" (Telesur 2016). A collective of special rapporteurs issued a joint statement raising concerns about the "retrogressive" effects these trade agreements may have on human rights and pointed out that they may in fact make Indigenous peoples even more vulnerable (United Nations 2015). Concerns about the growing tensions in the relationship between states and Indigenous peoples has been developing for some time. James Anaya, former Special Rapporteur on the Rights of Indigenous Peoples, noted that, in the decade under Harper, Canada's relationship with Indigenous peoples had declined and become even more strained (Anaya 2014). Indigenous peoples have long had to resist the ever-present threat of racism, white supremacy, and anti-human-rights efforts – the issue we now face is that this racism has become very public or mainstream. This is so much the case that in Canada some media outlets have had to discontinue public comments on their online stories related to Indigenous peoples because of the racism and hatred posted after each story (Office of the General Manager 2015).

While abuses of Indigenous rights have generally happened in plain sight for decades, more recent events surrounding the Dakota Access Pipeline (DAPL) land and water defence by the Standing Rock Sioux Tribe, highlight the rise of overtly racist sentiments in some segments of state and society. As a result of hundreds of Indigenous tribes and First Nations gathering to protect the lands and waters of Standing Rock Sioux Tribe against the construction of the DAPL (which could poison their water systems), North Dakota proposed legislation to legalize the "accidental killing" of native protestors. The Special Rapporteur emphasized that: "This law ... is really not consistent at all with international human rights law ... how can you justify running over or violently treating a protestor when every person has the right to protest? (Yakupitiyage 2017). This is especially the case, she explained, when Indigenous peoples are merely trying to protect their lands (and waters) (Mclaughlin 2017). As if a harbinger of things that might come unless we stem the tide of hatred, a man drove his vehicle into peaceful anti-white-supremacy protestors in Charlottesville, Virginia, killing one and injuring many (Wilson 2017). Imagine the ramifications if this kind overt and violent act of racism became legal?

While measures in the United States may seem extreme, Canada's tactics are equally insidious. Former Conservative Minister of Indian Affairs Bernard Valcourt told parliament that Indigenous peoples – namely treaty Chiefs – were "threats to national security" (Barrera 2014). In other words, Canada considers First Nation Chiefs who publicly and peacefully defend their treaties, lands, and Indigenous rights, to be domestic terrorists. To this end, Canada now has anti-terrorism legislation (Bill C-51, Anti-Terrorism Act), national-security protocols, and law-enforcement policies that specifically target the activities of Indigenous peoples and their advocacy activities. Despite the election promises of the Liberal Party, at the time of writing, Prime Minister Justin Trudeau's Liberal government had not amended Bill C-51 to address these blatant human-rights violations. Under Canada's anti-terrorism policies, national security, economic well-being, international relations, territorial integrity, sovereignty, and elections all become justifiable excuses to violate the human rights of Indigenous peoples. National security and anti-terrorism discourse is being used as a vehicle to trample human rights and justify (with renewed vigour) racist practices like racial profiling, overpolicing of racialized minorities, and the suspension of basic civil rights and liberties all over the world.

All these developments in racism, white supremacy, and anti-human-rights efforts paint a very bleak picture of countries that were thought to have grown past the struggle for basic human rights into an era of concrete implementation and protection. But we will be okay. It wasn't governments that gave us our human rights; it was the people that fought for them and won. Our hope is in the people. We have come too far and made too many sacrifices to allow the value of human life to be traded for either state power or corporate wealth. Keep in mind, Indigenous peoples survived one of the most lethal genocides in history – deliberate spreading of disease via small-pox-infected blankets, scalpings, forced sterilizations, rapes, torture and murders in residential schools, medical experimentation, deaths in police custody, forced starvation, and the disappearances of Indigenous women and girls. Yet, Indigenous peoples are still here, we are still holding on to our identity and culture, and we are the first ones on front lines to protect the lands, waters, and core human rights and freedoms for all peoples.

Resistance is about resilience and a never-ending faith in the power of the real governments – the people – to rise against any backward slide into the hatred of racism, white supremacy, and anti-human-rights discourse. This very book is a testament to the many ways, means, and perspectives of human-rights defenders from all different backgrounds and philosophies to come together to ensure that white supremacy or nationalism do not take hold of our families, communities, or Nations. Going forward, we need to inspire others with our historical successes, celebrate the many achievements in human rights, and challenge the backward slide. Society went from belittling environmental-rights activists as hippies, anti-poverty rights as a "charity" issue, women's rights as a feminist issue, and Indigenous rights as ancient grievances to seeing the complex, inter-relationship of human rights among all peoples as the foundation of all our relationships. Everything we do must be measured by the impact it has on human life and the ecosystems upon which we depend and share with other living creatures. Whether in law, politics, governance, trade, or the economy, the protection of human rights and freedom from racism must be at the fore.

We have new tools at our disposal to equip our resistance movement with powers we didn't have in the past. Global information and communications had long been held and controlled by the richest and most powerful in society, and now, through the Internet and social media, we have levelled the playing field in many ways. We also have a new generation of children and youth who grew up in this age of information, insight, and communication and are eager for change and passionate about taking action to bring about that change. However, we must also constantly adapt to the means and methods by which those enveloped in racial hatred and white supremacy seek to counter our resistance movements. We must get out in front, arm each other with the facts, insights, and analyses that will help us publicly counter the age of fake news, government propaganda, and corporate misinformation. We live in an age where social revolutions have been fuelled and supported by social media and – with an increasingly informed society – people will want better for themselves and their children. The move from historical entitlements based on class, race, or gender are already making way for people who believe we are privileged for the ecosystem in which we live and that with human rights comes a responsibility to live, assert, and defend those rights for all. It's on us all to prevent the slide backwards to racism and hatred. Resistance is renewal, revitalization, and resurgence of our human rights and dignity, and our participation in this resistance will be the hope that our next generation needs to carry our humanity forward.

NOTE

1 National Inquiry into Murdered and Missing Indigenous Women and Girls, "Reclaiming Power and Place: The Final Report of the national Inquiry into Murdered and Missing Indigenous Women and Girls" (Ottawa: National Inquiry into Murdered and Missing Indigenous Women and Girls, 2019), https://www.mmiwg-ffada.ca/final-report/. The National Inquiry found, as a matter of fact and law, that Canada is guilty of both historic and ongoing geno- cide against Indigenous women and girls through its racist and sexist laws, poli- cies, practices, actions, and omissions that lead to violence against Indigenous women and girls. See also: National Inquiry into Murdered and Missing Indige- nous Women and Girls, "Supplementary Report: A Legal Analysis of Genocide" (Ottawa: National Inquiry into Murdered and Missing Indigenous Women and Girls, 2019), https://www.mmiwg-ffada.ca/wp-content/uploads/2019/06/ Supplementary-Report_Genocide.pdf.

REFERENCES

Anaya, James. 2014. "Report of the Special Rapporteur on the Rights of Indigenous Peoples." A/HRC/27/52/Add.2, at 6, para.14.
Balgord, E. 2017. "CBC Admits Botching Gavin McInnes Interview on Power and Politics." *CanadaLand*, 6 July. http://www.canadalandshow.com/cbc-gavin- mcinnes-interview/.
Barrera, J. 2014. "Valcourt Attacks Confederacy of Nations, Calls Chiefs 'Rogue' and Threats to National Security." *APTN News*, 16 May. http://aptnnews.ca/2014/05/ 16/valcourt-attacks-confederacy-nations-calls-chiefs-rogue-threats-national- securit/.
Canadian Press. 2013. "Re-Engage with the United Nations, Harper Urged." *CBC News*, 23 September. http://www.cbc.ca/news/politics/re-engage-with-the- united-nations-harper-urged-1.1864618.

Dawsey, J. 2018. "Trump Derides Protections for Immigrants from 'Shithole' Countries." *Washington Post*, 12 January. https://www.washingtonpost.com/politics/
trump-attacks-protections-for-immigrants-from-shithole-countries-in-oval-
office-meeting/2018/01/11/bfc0725c-f711-11e7-91af-31ac729add94_story.html?utm_
term=.5cd8e235c317.

D'Emilio, F. 2018. "Italian Candidate for Premier Defends 'White Race' Remark."
ABC *News*, 15 January. http://abcnews.go.com/International/wireStory/italy-
candidate-immigration-endangers-white-race-52358033.

Editors. 2017. "Encyclopaedia Britannica, Mein Kampf: Works by Hitler." London:
Encyclopaedia Britannica, 28 December. https://www.britannica.com/topic/
Mein-Kampf.

Fitzpatrick, M. 2011. "'Draconian' Anti-Terrorism Laws Not Needed, Opposition
Says." CBC *News*, 7 September. http://www.cbc.ca/news/politics/draconian-anti-
terrorism-laws-not-needed-opposition-says-1.1118337.

Galloway, G. 2015. "Canada's Global Promotion of Human Rights Has Declined:
Internal Memo." *Globe and Mail*, 29 September. https://www.theglobeandmail.
com/news/politics/leaked-government-document-claims-canadas-international-
clout-under-threat/article26583397/.

Government of Canada. 1982. Canadian Charter of Rights and Freedoms. Part I of
the Constitution Act, 1982, being Schedule B to the Canada Act 1982 (UK), 1982, c.11.

Ho, Christina. 2017. "Racist Reporting Still Rife in Australian Media." *The Conversation*, 14 December. https://theconversation.com/racist-reporting-still-rife-in-
australian-media-88957.

Khaleeli, H. 2016. "'A Frenzy of Hatred': How to Understand Brexit Racism."
Guardian, 29 June. https://www.theguardian.com/politics/2016/jun/29/frenzy-
hatred-brexit-racism-abuse-referendum-celebratory-lasting-damage.

Khan, J. 2018. "An All-White Panel Debating Trump's Racism Isn't Just Wrong, It's
Irresponsible." *Flare*, 19 January. http://www.flare.com/news/janaya-khan-on-
canadian-media/.

Kopan, T. 2016. "What Donald Trump Has Said about Mexico and Vice Versa."
CNN, 31 August. https://www.cnn.com/2016/08/31/politics/donald-trump-
mexico-statements/index.html.

Mair, R. "Exploiting Fear Is Wrong and Racist." *The Tyee*, 23 February. https://the
tyee.ca/Opinion/2015/02/23/Exploiting-Fear/.

Mclaughlin, T. 2017. "North Dakota Lawmakers Vote 'No' on Protecting Drivers

Who Hit Protestors." Reuters, 14 February. https://www.reuters.com/article/
us-north-dakota-bill/north-dakota-lawmakers-vote-no-on-protecting-drivers-
who-hit-protesters-idUSKBN15T2D5.

Office of the GM and Editor in Chief. 2015. "Uncivil Dialogue: Commenting and
Stories about Indigenous People." CBC News, 30 November. http://www.cbc.ca/
newsblogs/community/editorsblog/2015/11/uncivil-dialogue-commenting-and-
stories-about-indigenous-people.html.

Paling, E. 2017. "CBC Interview with 'Proud Boys' Founder Gavin McInnes Goes Off
the Rails." Huffington Post, 6 July. http://www.huffingtonpost.ca/2017/07/05/cbc-
interview-with-proud-boys-founder-gavin-mcinnes-goes-off-t_a_23018129/.

Robertson, N. 2016. "A Look at Brexit: Why Are the Brits Thumbing Their Noses
at Europe." CNN, 24 June. https://www.cnn.com/2016/06/24/europe/brexit-after
math-robertson/index.html.

Telesur. 2016. "TPP Threatens Indigenous Land Rights Says the UN." TeleSUR
English, 18 February. https://www.telesurtv.net/english/news/TPP-Threatens-
Indigenous-Land-Rights-Says-the-UN-20160218-0042.html.

UN General Assembly. 1948a. Universal Declaration of Human Rights, 10 December
1948, 217 A (III).

– 1948b. Convention on the Prevention and Punishment of the Crime of Genocide,
9 December 1948, 260 A (III).

– 2007. United Nations Declaration on the Rights of Indigenous Peoples, 2 October
2007, A/RES/61/295.

United Nations. 2015. "UN Experts Voice Concern Over Adverse Impact of Free
Trade and Investment Agreements on Human Rights." 2 June. http://www.ohchr.
org/FR/NewsEvents/Pages/DisplayNews.aspx?NewsID=16031&LangID=E.

Yakupitiyage, T. 2017. "'Serious Retreats' in Indigenous Rights Protection, Says UN
Rapporteur." Inter-Press Service, 26 January. http://www.ipsnews.net/2017/01/
serious-retreats-in-indigenous-rights-protection-says-un-rapporteur/.

Wildman, S. 2017. "French President Emmanuel Macron Is in the Middle of a
Social Media Firestorm." Vox, 10 July. https://www.vox.com/world/2017/7/
10/15949392/macron-women-children-7-or-8-g20-stumble-twitter-storm.

Wilson, J., E. Helmore, and J. Swaine. 2017. "Man Charged with Murder after
Driving into Anti-Far-Right Protestors in Charlottesville." Guardian, 13 August.
https://www.theguardian.com/us-news/2017/aug/12/virginia-unite-the-right-
rally-protest-violence.

35

BUILDING DISABILITY ACTIVISM IN THE TRUDEAU AND TRUMP ERA

Melissa Graham

I have been a disability activist since before I realized what it meant. Like many disabled people, I started out not knowing that such an identity existed. I was born with a disability, and grew up in a small town without much accessible infrastructure. To have access meant writing letters and doing what I could to make myself heard. It was just about me back then; I hadn't yet connected to the bigger picture. Activism wasn't something I "did" at that point. It was about survival.

My transition into broader activism came slowly, with a little help from people who were more seasoned activists than myself. I was privileged enough as a student to work under someone who had chained himself to a bus back in the 1980s in a struggle for accessible transit. He lived in what we often think of as the glory days of disability activism. His experiences seemed to have come from a bygone era, but the knowledge he shared stayed with me. Without knowing it, I think he planted a seed.

Being a disability activist in the twenty-first century has its challenges. It's rare to find someone who would be willing to chain themselves to buses these days. Disability activists of the 1980s and 1990s were successful, so successful that they managed to compel the Canadian government to include disabled people as a protected group under the human-rights code, and Ontario started accessibility legislation in 2001. In my beginnings as an activist, I would enter conversations about other forms of oppression, and try to connect those conversations with other movements in which I was involved.

During the Occupy Movement in 2011, I founded the Toronto Disability Pride March (TDPM). This has grown into an annual event, with at least one hundred participants each year. Our organizing team is made up of grassroots disability activists, each with their own lived experience of disability. The march is focused on bringing forward the voices within the disability community that seldom receive the opportunity to speak, naming oppression and ableism for what it is, and taking the time to celebrate the disability and mad community. It started with wanting to include the disability movement and ableism in activist conversations, but it also became an opportunity to give those struggles a visible presence.

The TDPM has an organizing team of four people. We push above our weight in our work, but we also know that our very method of organizing challenges the status quo. With my fellow organizers, I've presented talks on the march and how we organize, in the hopes of spreading ideas across the country. As our ideas are heard and often challenged, it has helped develop the work we do, and enriched my own work and writings as an activist.

One of the things that has led to the continued success of the march is the fact that we're not just taking to the streets. We've grown, thanks to the collaboration and solidarity of other local activists in the International Socialists, the Ethno-Racial Coalition of People with Disabilities Ontario, People First, the Ryerson Student Union, and the Ryerson School of Disability Studies, among other organizations. These connections have given us opportunities to build and has broadened the conversation of disability rights brought to other communities.

We've also built our conversation on disability activism through social media. Through tools like Facebook, Twitter, and our own web page, we've been able to continue the discussions on various intersections of disability activism such as race and disability, gender-based difference, and impacts of poverty and disability. We've drawn attention to the housing crisis in Toronto and the health-care crisis in the United States, and encouraged solidarity with other movements such as Idle No More and the Vigil for Indigenous Youth Suicides at the Indigenous and Northern Affairs Canada offices in Toronto. Doing this kind of disability activism on the margins and intersections of disability often means challenging commonly held assumptions of mainstream disability movement. From the outside, the movement appears to be dominated by White men who usually have enough privilege to see only the environmental barriers. They are content with seeking reforms rather than challenging the system and its inherent ableism. Like other movements, the disability movement is increasingly represented by activists at the intersections, but those in power have not yet caught up with this shift.

Creating Meaningful Movement in the Aftermath of "Real Change"

Over the past decade, there continues to be growing acceptance of the disability movement, and ableism is slowly being acknowledged as a real and
present form of oppression. There is also a growing understanding that legislation and government will not save us from oppression, and certainly not
from the politics of austerity. Of course, activists are not the only people
who have noticed this shift. During the 2015 election of Prime Minister
Justin Trudeau, a collective of disability advocates known as Barrier Free
Canada began the call for a Canadians with Disabilities Act, a call that TDPM
and I supported. David Lepofsky, one of the main organizers for Barrier
Free Canada, was one of the key speakers at TDPM that year. We encouraged
our supporters to back that movement, and we pushed it even further by
including demands of immigrants and Indigenous people. The demand for
a Canadians with Disabilities Act became so widespread that Trudeau eventually added it to his collection of election promises.

The acknowledgment of the need for change from the Liberals did inspire many disabled people, but, like many groups, we're still waiting for
meaningful action beyond talking points and town-hall meetings. While it
is promising to see action on these standards, the direction in which the
federal government has taken the proposed legislation is less encouraging.
On behalf of the TDPM, I attended one of the town-hall meetings about
the proposed act. During the town hall, it became increasingly obvious
that the feedback obtained from these conversations would be limited to
the consumerism and employment opportunities for disabled people in
Canada. The Accessible Canada Act was introduced in June 2018, with specific standards yet to be released at the time of writing.

The provincial legislations in Ontario, Manitoba, and other provinces that
preceded the federal discussions is equally unapologetic in its neo-liberal
perspective. It's not about creating rights or reducing oppression, but instead tries to facilitate accessibility only in capitalist economic terms. Its
focus on employment, customer service, the built environment, and transportation is not in itself a bad thing, but focusing on those sectors alone
presents a problem. Through this lens, disabled people are seen as consumers
or potential employees, rather than as people with full lives. It is difficult to
expect a capitalist structure to make changes, since disabled people are not

seen as people of equal value. Consider that there is nothing in these standards about accessible housing, education, or even health care, and the gaps begin to surface. What the provincial standards have done is looked at the barriers of those of us who have the most privilege and opportunity, and attended almost exclusively to the barriers they face. The idea is that if disabled people have jobs and can be dependable consumers, then the government will have done its job with regard to accessibility needs for the disability community. Compliance and reporting in these areas has yet to meet expectations, at least in the province of Ontario.

The federal government could be doing much more to encourage equity for disabled people. During the nationwide town halls, the government hired disabled people to act as consultants for these meetings, and much of the work those consultants did was underpaid or unpaid work. Cuts to health and social transfers continue to impact the lives of disabled people across the country. In many provinces, disabled people are being placed in long-term care or hospitals, because services are not available to allow the person to live at home. This is something that disabled people have long fought against. The cuts also affect people needing assistance in their homes; the province of Ontario has subtly cut back services for Personal Support Workers, who enable persons with disabilities to do things like take a shower or get dressed, so they can get on with their day. These are the kinds of decisions that are made when the rights of disabled people are viewed primarily in economic terms. As Haiven affirms in this volume, "Resistance … is fundamentally about reclaiming and reinventing how we cooperate and relate to one another"; institutions that are tied to the terms of capitalism cannot create the change that is needed for all people to thrive.

The problem becomes more obvious when disability and citizenship intersect. One issue that continues since Trudeau's election is for the removal of the excessive-demand clause of the Immigration Act. This clause allows the federal government to deny citizenship to any person who could be deemed to pose an excessive demand on health and social services. Since disabled people often do have an increased need for health and social services, this clause amounts to a discriminatory practice of preventing disabled immigrants from becoming Canadian citizens. Recently the federal government has started to consider removing the excessive-demand clause, but, at the time of writing, it was unclear whether this change will happen.

Keep Moving Forward

For disabled people living in the United States, the stakes are much higher. Under Trump, disabled people are facing a lack of access to health care, cuts to services, a possible dismantling of the Americans with Disabilities Act, and a president who openly mocks disabled people. Their obstacles are much greater. Yet, in the United States, the rate of disability activism and protest is much higher than here in Canada. In this country, governments do a great job of making promises to disabled people, but they do not remain accountable for those promises. More importantly, these promises do a very effective job of silencing activists by telling disabled people to be happy and grateful for those promises and not to ask for more. In many ways, disability activists of my generation have reawakened the movement across the globe. Sometimes it looks like a protest or a rally, sometimes it is one-on-one conversations with people in the community to explain what ableism is or trying to convince someone that, yes, disabled people really are oppressed.

The outcomes of activist work are often difficult to measure, but sometimes I am reminded of the impact of the work I am doing, and that keeps me going. The 2017 Toronto Disability Pride March was a strong reminder of the impact of that resistance. One of our speakers was assaulted by police the day before the march, but the event was so important to her that she came anyway. That says more about the person she is than about the march, but her presence opened up a conversation around disability and police violence. On the same day, we celebrated the life of one of our key organizers, Beverly Smith, who had passed away the year before. Her energy kept us going while she was with us, and as we celebrated her life that day, it was obvious that she was still pushing us forward.

These are the things that remind me how far we have come. I have to believe that, if we continue to support each other and build, change will come. We cannot rely on those in power to make meaningful change for us, but we can continue to question power, to call it out. And that is what we must do. I've been doing this work for some time, but I'm still learning, and I think that's a responsibility of all activists. Movements grow stronger if we build beyond our own experiences, and find where our causes intersect with others. It's also important to give the people in your movement something to believe in. It's not enough to tell people the system is against them; most people already know that. Successful movements help people find their individual and collective power to make change.

Often I find myself wondering if the work I am doing has any real impact. It could be argued that the years I have put into organizing, marching, writing, and resisting have not changed anything, but that is not true. I see the power in the faces of people who march with me every year. It reminds people that they have power, that they have a voice, that they can make a difference. I hope that, year by year, that sea of faces will build a tidal wave of change.

RESISTING THROUGH
INTERSECTIONAL SOLIDARITIES

Yasmin Jiwani

Current Socio-Political Climate

The current socio-political climate reflects a zeitgeist of reactionary politics, a politics that clings to entrenched notions of the rights of the privileged, whether these be business/capital, whiteness, muscular masculinity, Christianity, ableism, or heteropatriarchy, the very characteristics that underpinned colonial and now neo-colonial power. Within this context, the far right represents a current that has always run deep within society. It is a current that mediates what is normative, acceptable, and tolerable. However, it has now solidified into a new and right-centred middle, occupying the zone of normativity by making acceptable right-wing attitudes, moves, and strategies, a point also articulated by Palmater in this volume.

Hence, the far right has long existed, but social shifts in attitudes, particularly after the counter-culture of the 1960s, tamed this politic into a median position, not always progressive but still more progressive than the state of affairs that existed before. Within that context, that which was other and strange had more acceptance, albeit often as exotic novelty, than was the case before. As much research has noted, the Bohemian turn of the sixties was directly related to the exoticization of the Other. Soft power, through popular media, diplomacy, and the like, concealed the hard power of brutal and explicit violence. Extreme right-wing attitudes, behaviours, and norms became more privatized, and, in public, simmered under the surface of a polite veneer.

The decolonizing movements in the global south impacted this as well, bringing to the fore an increased awareness of colonization and its ideological apparatus, evident in the academic and activist work that was produced in the immediate aftermath of the sixties and into the nineties, as for example in the works of Aimé Césaire, the Combahee River Collective, Angela

Davis, Frantz Fanon, Edward Said, Ella Shohat, Achilles Mbembe, and Himani Bannerjee, among others. Yet again, an outcome was a burying of the reactionary elements, not so that they disappeared but rather percolated away, spewing forth poisonous fumes whose stink could be smelled but whose materiality seemed transient except in extremist far-right organizations. That such organizations existed (and continue to exist) is undebatable. Rather, it is the way in which they were treated – as extremist marginalized groups – whose existence, let alone demands, could not be *seen to be* entertained in any serious fashion.

This shift towards normalizing and centring the politics of the far right can then be seen as a reactionary response to the increased globalization of the networked economy, the psychological sense of losing privilege as a result of advocacy efforts on the part of marginalized groups, and the general sense of defeat and impotency as evident in the failure of contemporary wars and other perceived losses in the arena of white, patriarchal supremacy. However, it is now undergirded by a sense of legitimacy; it is now articulated as a legitimate grievance. It is this legitimacy, the credibility that it is clothed in, that makes the far right now such a significant force impeding the fight for equity and equality. The mass media has endowed the far right with its legitimacy, amplified those sentiments and demands beyond the borders of the local community, and broadcast them into an international arena. In that context, the rising crescendo of "paranoid nationalisms," a phrase I borrow from Ghassan Hage, have fuelled the far-right claim to recuperate a "golden past" of the way things were, or a future devoid of colour, diversity, and variety.

The Nature of the Threat

Since the demise of the Russian bogeyman and the end of the Super Power conflict, Islam has emerged as the dominant threat to the West. Though made ostensibly more real with the continuous replay of the destruction of the Twin Towers, the construction of Islam as the quintessential enemy has a long and now-revivified history. From the usage of historic labels such as the "Crusades," down to the naming of various military operations, as for example, "Operation Freedom," Islam has become an iconic threat. As Elghawaby affirms in this volume, neither blowback nor imperial quests and invasions are the preferred explanatory paradigms; rather Islam as a pestilence that has to be eradicated is the prevailing paradigm. Islam has to be decimated – if not through the hard power of military might, then through the soft power of sanctions, coercive trade agreements, Hollywood films, and the mind share colonized by major corporations.

This reconstruction of Islam works as an intricate but highly dependable and threatening mirage, deflecting attention to other lands while the state wreaks havoc at home through privatization of public goods and the ascendency and entrenchment of a neo-liberal paradigm that justifies the erosion of services, making individuals responsible for their lacks and failures. The technocratic empire of the military-industrial complex ensures the surveillance of all, while investing in an increasing number of detention centres, prisons, and the production and export of arms. The carceral net, as Foucault described it, is everywhere, promulgated by technological capillaries of power and networks of transportation.

In the meantime, airport alerts, telephone hotlines, and the ever-pervasive cell-phone technology that captures normative violations, become the conduits for the surveillance that everyone carries out on everyone else. Sous-surveillance, as it is called, works extremely well. From hotlines that can be used to report on "honour killings" (as if domestic violence didn't exist before Muslims came), to frenzied cries about shariah law (as if religious mediators didn't exist before Muslims came), to cries about bogus refugees and bomb threats (as if these didn't exist before Muslims came), all work to erase the continuity of these practices and the constructed nature of these threats. Of course, bombs are real and bomb scares are scary, but they existed long before Muslims came to these shores.

"Islam is the new Black" paints the controversial artist Sarah Maple. While she satirizes this, the material reality of the phrase is rendered even more poignant by the physical criminalization, incarceration, and deportation of all those who inhabit a space of intersectionality – Black and Muslim. Disavowed bodies, they become the fodder of the military industrial complex that is driven by the unfettered need to capitalize on bodies, whether in prison chain gangs or in privately sanctioned spaces of terror, governed by private contractors doing the dirty work of the state (see Perry in this volume). But, the phrase "Islam is the new Black" also lateralizes the hierarchies of power and worthiness that traverse the social terrain. The phrase also decontextualizes and dehistoricizes relations of power. That "Islam is the new Black" is a misnomer when we think about Black Muslims who have left a powerful legacy in the United States; the phrase decontextualizes the relationship between Islam and Europe as an aggressive oppositional dynamic, ignited by the Crusades and Christendom's seizure of lands and dislocation of peoples, similar to the relationship of the United States to countries ruled by Muslim leaders, where oil has been the impetus for many of the conflicts, not to mention contested lands.

Current interactions are shaped from the colonial legacies of previous encounters, predicated on the theft of land, labour, and bodies. Take the role of the Muslim woman, who colonizers sought to unveil, just as they fought to conquer the lands in which women lived. So it is today that we see the passage of numerous bills in Quebec and elsewhere which seek to forcibly unveil women. The passive Muslim woman is, as scholar Jasmine Zine notes, an ambivalent character: imperilled as Sherene Razack describes her, and waiting to be rescued by the White knights of imperial civilizations, she is nonetheless a threat, dangerous in her abilities to engulf the dominant culture through kith and kin. As for the dangerous Brown man, as Gargi Bhattarcharrya has so eloquently noted, his implied tenacity for the destruction of society is as merciless as the barbarian that Foucault caricatured in his work *Society Must Be Defended*. Thus it is that the barbarian must be banned, exiled, or destroyed, and the women tamed, if they are to be made more like "us." This is the nature of the constructed threat that faces us today.

Tactics of Resistance

To succumb to the myth of powerlessness is futile for obvious reasons: it doesn't get us anywhere. In his oft-cited quote, Antonio Gramsci speaks about the optimism of the will and the pessimism of the intellect. Power, amassed power, congealed power, in the form of state institutions and its various apparatuses, lattice the social order, but the crevices in between are the spaces of tactics, as Michel de Certeau has insightfully noted. Tactics are mobile, transient, and temporary. But tactics, amassed as a volley of targeted nodes, can puncture the seemingly resistant hide of dominant ideologies, even if only temporarily.

These tactics are continually being enacted from the margins, through talk, text, performances, and the like. Slowly but surely, through infiltration, they insert other ways of seeing the world. How else can one explain the changes that have accrued, and the backlash that such changes have spawned, as for example in the endless battle against gendered-based violence? But tactics cannot work in isolation. This is where solidarity across tactical interventions needs to occur. We cannot take on Islamophobia alone; we need to engage on multiple fronts, forging bonds of solidarity across different terrains. We need to, as bell hooks argues, "talk back." And in that oppositional stance, we need to adopt an intersectional point of view that defines the points where numerous oppressions are enacted and condensed. It is at those nodal points that power is most felt, and it is where power is most visible that tactics can be most demonstrably effective. Contemporary social movements are examples of such effective tactics, though they have not always been inclusive, marred by a single-issue focus that drowns out the intertwined complexities of multiple and intersecting oppressions. An example of such transversal solidarity is apparent in the Occupy movement, which though critiqued by women of colour, undertook steps to foreground the voices and perspectives of the most marginalized. The work of the women of colour and Indigenous women's group called Incite! offers us a compelling example of such solidarity at work, a solidarity that stretches across race, gender, sexuality, religion, and class. Similarly, the Black Lives Matter movement and its cross-border solidarity and exchange of information with Palestinian youth in the Occupied territories is yet another cogent example of transversal politics that transcend nation states.

Analytical precision is crucial in this regard. What does Islamophobia represent in the layered accretions of historically sedimented hatreds? Where does it draw its power, its potential as a rationalized exclusion? What other hatreds feed into it? These are the questions we need to ask if we are to make naked the power of domination that is common as a substrate through all these multiple forms of oppression. This is not simply to make the personal political but also the political personal.

That 'We Resist' is apparent in our being here, rooted in this land, albeit as a result of a settler-colonial society, its history and continued legacies of colonization. But being here also means ensuring that the beneficiaries of power do not remain comfortable in their zones of privilege, but rather are irritated enough to make changes that, while they may appear to be cosmetic, allow us the spaces to continually demand equity. Such spaces can be forged only when we work together on issues that appear as disparate as violence against women, Islamophobia, anti-Black racism, precarious labour practices, ecological violence, and the ongoing violence of colonization, which are all intricately linked to what I call the valences of power. Such valences, which act as the scaffold upholding the infrastructures of power, are buried and become more apparent when we analyze the relations of power that define values of worthy/unworthiness, deserving/undeserving, and disposable/indispensable bodies – an analytic that is forcefully revealed in the struggles of Indigenous women.

37

YET WE RISE
Cultivating a Resilient Transgender Community that Overcomes Systemic Barriers

Morgane Oger

I am a trans-rights activist and progressive Canadian politician working to increase equality and justice for all Canadians. I advocate mostly in the contexts of LGBTQ2+ rights, education policy, health policy, and housing security, with a focus on bringing down systemic barriers and addressing discrimination on the basis of gender identity or expression in Canada. This is the basis of the mission statement of the Morgane Oger Foundation.

My trans activism normalizes the experiences of transgendered and non-binary people in an effort to advocate for the frameworks and policies that protect us from discrimination so trans people can live their lives to their fullest, free from discrimination. Another aspect of the activism relies on sharing Canada's example with other countries, addressing bias in policy implementation. That trans folks thrive in Canada without any change in crime statistics or proof of harm demonstrates that proposed legislative changes in other countries that follow Canada's example will contribute to a better situation.

One embodiment of my activism and that of the foundation is the act of resisting trans erasure and pathologization through the normalization of the perception of our lives. We demonstrate that trans people are everywhere, and that being transgender is not, in of itself, a meaningful impediment to living one's life authentically in our society: we exist, we are here, and we have no patience left.

The Lay of the Land

At the time of writing, xenophobic incidents have been growing steadily in the Americas for a number of years. Hate violence has been on the rise in Canada since 2013, and in British Columbia we observed a 30-per-cent increase of hate violence in 2016 and 47 per cent in 2017. A corresponding increase in severity of incidents has accompanied this increase of hate-induced violence. Canada's worst hate-based incident since the 1989 gender-motivated mass murder at École Polytechnique de Montréal during which fourteen women were targeted and murdered was the 29 January 2017 Quebec City mosque mass shooting at the Islamic Cultural Centre of Quebec City. Six worshippers were killed and nineteen others injured by a gunman during evening prayers.

Religious extremists and white supremacist groups are organizing in British Columbia, and there have been a growing number of hate-based anti-trans flyers distributed there. The Soldiers of Odin, a white-supremacist organization with violent tendencies, currently patrols a number of British Columbia neighbourhoods. An anti-LGBT conservative group known as Culture Guard, led by Kari Simpson, has been combining homophobic and transphobic hate at rallies which are now a regular occurrence in British Columbia. Culture Guard, the KKK, and the Soldiers of Odin are organizing and fundraising openly.

As we know, vulnerability to oppression stems in part from having insufficient power in a society and from an inability to find protection in the systems it puts at our disposal. When we are not protected by laws, policies, and attitudes, we are vulnerable, as reflected by hate-crime data. This disconcerting rise of intolerance in Canada is the root cause that motivated the creation of the Morgane Oger Foundation: to help combat supremacist bias through policy change that narrows the gap between our laws and their application on the ground.

Visibly Take Up Space

Those who enter spaces that have not yet been opened up to transgender persons and demonstrate that "transness" is irrelevant help shift the bias that comes from a lack of familiarity. This is one way that activists have been steadily eroding the existing systems of oppression against our communities, because it is much harder to hate a friend you respect simply because they are trans. In order to increase awareness that our society's rules also need to allow for the increasingly normalized realities of trans folks, trans activists work to show we exist with the knowledge that we need to be seen to be included. The change-makers who are first in these closed spaces show by example that whatever stigma must be eroded is caused by bias and unfamiliarity, rather than by underlying truths or pathology. They also often demonstrate by example that there will be consequences for those who ignore the intention and letter of the law as it pertains to letting us live our lives fully and equally. Awareness of diversity and inclusion is the first step to respecting the rules that protect diverse communities.

Participate Fully

The trans community needs to continue fighting to ensure our voices are present at decision-making time in all contexts that matter. As the expression "nothing about us without us" goes in documenting our lives, so does it apply to the workplace, policy-making, and governance. Trans folks need to see members of our community working in role-model careers. Young transgender and non-binary persons need to see that we are not only being given space in cisgender society, but that our voices shape society: we are equal participants, and we are seeing signs of progress.

In Canada, as of winter 2019, there is finally one out, elected transgender person, Julie Lemieux, mayor in Très-Saint-Rédempteur, Quebec. Canada came close to having an out transgender lawmaker elected (me, in 2017), but that goal remains frustratingly elusive. So far in Canada, all laws that affect trans or non-binary people have been enacted by legislative bodies that excluded us and failed to sufficiently consult with us.

There is one transgender judge in Manitoba and a handful of lawyers sprinkled throughout the nation. We are even seeing handfuls of doctors and nurses. At the University of Victoria, there is one transgender person who is the only chair of transgender studies in Canada. There are a few transgender or gender-diverse professors in Canadian universities studying trans experiences. We see more and more transgender people holding onto jobs and careers through their transition. We are even seeing trans students graduate and find employment – often in their field of study. Of course, trans professionals describe a significant disadvantage with employment due to bias or its consequences. We are still some way off from a time when being trans is without consequence in somebody's career; it is still tantalizingly over the horizon.

These working folks are doing something for us all by existing as role models and living out their daily lives. Their reality calls into question the all-too-prevalent narrative that transgender folks are inherently broken persons requiring either sympathy or charity. Their increasing ordinariness replaces the discourse of a presumed dysfunction – amplified by deeply held biases – with the truth that trans and non-binary people thrive when provided the oxygen we need to breathe freely.

Working on one's career is still an act of defiance for too many trans or non-binary folks. After all, far too many companies still resist putting a transgender or non-binary person in front of their client. The trans folks among us who are breaking through stigma and the barriers it puts in our way are making inroads in our cis-normative culture to take hold of positions of power and privilege. We still have to be louder and pushier than cisgender people, and are usually still the only one of our kind we know of at any job. Yet we can now show a growing roster of role models and enjoy our newly minted explicit protection from discrimination in Canada. Sadly, that success in establishing our rights in recent years is causing growing pushback from those who oppose our equality and still see us as abominations or damaged goods. The laws may protect us on paper, but attitudes on the ground have some distance to catch up before we can truthfully claim to have reached equality in Canada.

Brace Yourself for the Pushback

When looming legislation was promising to finally ensure equality for trans persons in Canada in 2015, socially conservative organizers began to realize that the age-old bathroom-predator trope had been exhausted after years of fruitful seeding of moral panic. As a result, opponents focused on new targets: A handful of academics, led by University of Toronto professor Jordan Peterson, fomented opposition to trans rights on the basis of the still-new-to-many *singular they* pronouns that many non-binary persons prefer. Opponents brought out ill-conceived-yet-compelling free-speech arguments in their pushback on Bill C-16, a bill that amended the Canadian Human Rights Act to add gender identity and gender expression to the list of prohibited grounds of discrimination.

Reinvigorated since the 2016 US presidential election, "alt-right" and supremacist movements joined in arguing that transgender equality law tramples on free speech and criminalizes freedom of expression. This refrain continues today, with an intensity that seems to be amplified by the fact it applies to the needs of transgender people. Meanwhile, the religious right is reeling at the policy and procedural consequences of equal protection of trans people in society, including in schools and social spaces. Conservative Christianity, in particular, is fomenting a growing pushback, claiming that helping trans kids is "child abuse," famously stated in a public Facebook post by Chilliwack School District trustee Barry Neufeld in 2017 (Durang and Benning 2017).

Take Control of the Narrative and Overcome the Pushback

When we are working to convince people to change policy, there is a need to engage in debate over the validity of our claims. In order for this to work, it is necessary for our narrative to be told and heard as effectively and as widely as the opposing side's ideas, or preferably more so. In a situation like trans-rights advocacy, we are working asymmetrically to change the status quo. The new idea that we are promoting is at a significant disadvantage; to succeed in winning hearts and minds, trans-rights activists need to displace the existing narrative and replace it with our own. To get laws or major policies changed, we need to be supported by more than just the community seeking the change. In British Columbia, in order for the trans community to win equal protection from discrimination in 2016 from a government that was disinclined to provide it, activists had to demonstrate wide geographical and demographic support throughout the province. A similar tactic was used federally, leading to the 2017 passing of bill C-16. We did this in part with a petition campaign which allowed us to geocode thousands of supporters from across British Columbia. Going further, we also reached out into religious congregations, civic organizations, labour, and private businesses and convinced them to write the government in support of our campaign. Using these tools, we successfully showed that support was widespread and came from many communities. It helped a lot that we convinced evangelical Christian congregations to support us, breaking down the then–BC Liberal government's perception, seeded by Culture Guard and their ilk, that the faith communities were against transgender protections.

Once we have a majority of voices in support of an idea, we have to overcome those who are fanatically opposed to our view. They are few in number, but their reach and determination are disproportionate. In the case of transgender rights, the fanatic opposition is made up of two highly distinct communities. Trans-Exclusive Radical Feminists (TERFs) adhere to an essentialist perspective that centres the patriarchal oppression against women entirely on female bodies. The TERFs frame their ideas using essentialist terminology like reproductive rights and issues related to patriarchal control of female bodies and questions about body autonomy. The second is the socially conservative right, most notably North American evangelical Christians and conservative Catholics, who view transgender bodies as either an abomination against their belief system or as a sign of debauchery. These two unlikely allies strongly oppose any increase in transgender inclusion and tend to be well funded and organized. Because they are well established, they easily access media and public opinion through their networks. When working to reset the narrative to one that benefits our goals, the challenge lies in accessing the traditional and social media at a scale that benefits us to change their perception. Despite Trump's campaign to portray mainstream media as tainted and biased, when we are working asymmetrically for equality, accessing the traditional press continues to be important. There are still many, many people who get all their news from the TV, the radio, or the websites of established outlets.

When working to control the narrative, we need to be seen by the audience as being more reasonable, more evidence-based, and more sympathetic than those who oppose us. Yet even though we are trying to convince the public of our story, it is rarely the point of our campaigns. Our actual goal is to get our audience to act for us. We have to tell them what to do. We are educating, but we also are aiming to have the largest-possible effect through our audience. For example, we may want our audience to contact the decision-makers or persuade their friends to do so. We may want money. We may want them to take some other specific action.

To control the narrative, trans activists have to ensure we do it in a like-able and approachable way. In political training, they tell us that you will win someone's heart (and vote or contribution) if they have a good experience with you. This is especially true if they see themselves as being very different from you. In the thick of resisting an oppression invisible to most cis people, this is particularly important. We always have to manage the dosage of information for our audience and stay within their own perception of what is plausible or reasonable. If we start with transphobic homi-. cide statistics and follow it with the success rates in court for transgender people fighting for their lives, we seriously risk losing them. There are places for these conversations, like awareness-raising events in universities or at the second or third meeting with allies, but initial contact or advocacy with the public need nuanced statements that the audience can digest. Managing these experiences must not be confused, however, with pandering to people who hate us. Nor should it mean sweeping major problems under the rug. Whereas much of the advocacy we are doing has forced the trans community to deal with people who openly hate us or consider us abominations, we are required to remain polite and engaging while staying firm and continuing to move toward our goal. We still need to tread lightly, because the only way to people's hearts is by not calling them bigots too often, even if it feels deeply satisfying to mention the elephant in the room. That said, I personally give only so many chances, and some individuals have earned my utter contempt as human beings.

In Other Words

The fight for equal rights never ends. First the rights must be won, and then they must be forever defended. To keep safe the very rights that protect us, we must maintain our lore and cultivate our voice. We must lift our role models and use them as examples to us all. We must encourage our future leaders to prepare for the coming work that we opened up for them, so they will protect us when we are too old to fight.

A community is protected by its institutions and by public policy. We must build these up to ensure our needs are met and to help us see any coming storms before the trouble takes hold. We must know what to do if conflict looms, because the best way to withstand any future transphobic storm is to never allow it to build up. For our community to stay safe, we must be vigilant and ensure that efforts to erode our rights and protections fail.

REFERENCES

Duran, Estefania, and Kyle Benning. 2017. "Trans Rights Activist Reaches Out
     to Chilliwack School Trustee Who Compared Gender Transitioning to 'Child
     Abuse.'" *Global News*, 26 November. https://globalnews.ca/news/3882044/trans-
     activist-on-barry-neufeld-chilliwack-school-trustee/.

38

BEYOND CAPITALIST AUTHORITARIANISM
The Radical Imagination

Max Haiven

The Power of the Imagination: Financialized or Radicalized?

My activism, my academic research, and my writing have been dedicated for some years to the problem of the politics of the imagination. Generally, this has led me in two directions: the study of the imagination that reproduces power, and the imagination that reproduces resistance and reinvention.

In the first case, a lot of my writing, teaching, and public speaking over the last few years has been dedicated to trying to understand the imagination behind finance capital, by which I mean that aspect of the capitalist economy that is known as the FIRE sector (Financial, Insurance, and Real Estate) (Haiven 2014b). Ultimately, the matters this field deals in are basically imaginary: there is no such physical thing as a credit default swap or collateralized debt obligation. A deed to a house or a piece of land is ultimately a piece of paper with some words on it. I'm interested in two things: first, how is it that, as a society, we are in the thrall of this imaginary stuff; second, how does the power of finance transform our imaginations more broadly. Somehow, today everything has become an "investment" or an "asset," from education to relationships (see Martin 2002, 2007).

But such questions lead one to a broader realization that most of our social institutions, norms, and power structures are always at least somewhat imaginary (see Castoriadis 1997). Money today is really just tokens (or, increasingly numbers in a database) given functional value by our shared belief. Police are just an armed gang, except to the extent we imagine them to be legitimate public servants. Racism is, ultimately, based on imagined hierarchies. All these forms of power are deeply and tragically material, political, and institutional, but are also solidifications of the imagination.

Thus, the second dimension of my work focuses on the radical imagination. Radical here implies both a legacy of political radicalism, but also reflects the word's Latin etymology, referring to roots. The radical imagination is a force that questions and resists social institutions and power from the roots. Along with my colleague Alex Khasnabish, I founded the Radical Imagination Project in Halifax, an activist-research initiative (see Haiven and Khasnabish 2014). We theorized the radical imagination not just as something an individual *has*, but something we, as a society and as collectivities, *do* together. The radical imagination sparks and burns bright through activism, debate, conflict, struggle, and transformation.

For this reason, we as researcher-activists couldn't be content to just observe the radical imagination; we felt a responsibility to trigger or catalyze it. Thus, our research took the form of working *with* a diversity of social movements in the city to organize debates, talks, events, training sessions, workshops, film screenings, and free schools to create an ecosystem for the radical imagination. We wanted to see if activists-scholars could work outside but alongside social movements for social justice in ways that were additive and collaborative, rather than extractive.

Capitalist Authoritarianism and Its Monsters

As much as I am dismayed and heartbroken at the resurgence of authoritarianism in recent years, I am hesitant to characterize it as a threat to democracy for two connected reasons. First, I have never believed we have lived in a democracy. While our governmental system provides a veneer of democratic participation, the reality is that decisions continue to be made by a small political elite, and political participation is laughably minimal. Further, while we might aspire to greater democratic modes of government, the capitalist economy is ultimately authoritarian, with a tiny elite claiming almost all the power and benefits. Indeed, I am of the belief that the authoritarian nature of capitalism has always fatally undermined substantial democracy wherever they have sought to coexist. It is certainly true that some democratic institutions have been stronger in the past than we find them today. I prefer to see these institutions as part of a yet-unsuccessful democratic project, or the results of a compromise between that radical democratic project and capitalist authoritarianism. Their decline is the result of the weakness of a radical democratic project, and that weakness has a lot to do with our failure to adequately challenge the economic authoritarianism of capitalism. This weakness has allowed for the recent rise of political authoritarianism as well.

Second, I think there is a danger in suggesting that the recent rise of explicit political authoritarianism is not "democratic." Sadly, most of the "new" ugly authoritarians around the world today enjoy widespread "democratic" support, as for instance in the case of the United States, Turkey, the Philippines, or India. The problem for me is not so much that authoritarianism has hijacked democracy, but that our already mortally flawed oxymoronic system of "capitalist democracy" has unleashed its own inevitable demons. In moments of crisis, when capitalism is imperilled, we should not expect anything less. So long as we accept, as we generally have, that capitalist economic order that is fundamentally authoritarian can coexist with formal political democracy, the former will consume the latter as capitalism undergoes its inevitable periodic crises, which is what is happening now to a large extent.

The crisis of capitalism which opened the gates to authoritarianism is a series or cascade of intertwined crises. On the economic level, the 2008 financial crisis is, in reality, the tip of an iceberg of unprecedented inequality unleashed by neo-liberal policies since the mid-1970s, which has gradually made a huge number of people dependent on debt, as real wages fell relative to inflation (Brown 2015). Relatedly, it is a crisis of masculinity, as the patriarchal ideals of the postwar economy have fallen apart, thanks both to changing economic realities and the vitality of feminist and queer rebellions (Fraser 2013). It is a crisis of race and racism as, on the one hand, precariousness and exploitation continue to disproportionately negatively affect non-White people and, on the other, resilient narratives of white supremacy offer convincing answers for many dispossessed people with access to whiteness (Taylor 2016). It is a crisis of settler colonialism, as the unfolding financial crisis drives an ever-more-frantic race to extract and monetize the world's "resources," necessitating the removal of Indigenous people from their land (Coulthard 2014). It is an ecological crisis, for obvious enough reasons (Klein 2015; Moore 2015).

Overall, it is a crisis (or many crises) of the imagination as well (Haiven 2014a). Neo-liberal ideology and culture, which insists that there is "no alternative" to capitalism, has led to what the late Mark Fisher (2009) called capitalist realism, which has robbed us of our utopian visions of liberation and convinced us resistance is futile. Meanwhile, the existential pressures of living amid so many interlocking crises grow, and we seek a release for the anxieties and rage of constantly failing to thrive in the midst of such incredible wealth. For some, mostly those who had imagined themselves entitled to some share of capitalism's booty (largely White, straight, "able-bodied" men), authoritarian politics provides the answer based on a misrecognition of the problem (Kimmel 2015; Hochschild 2016). Cultural and economic efforts to make capitalism slightly less unequal, exploitative, and oppressive are reframed in the authoritarian imagination as the cause of both declining economic vitality and increasing alienation.

Like all phobic reactions, today's authoritarianisms are ultimately murderous to the imagination: they must vanquish the possibility of other alternatives for social organization, relationships, and ways of being. Such authoritarianisms necessarily always narrate themselves as the right and inevitable course of action, based on a fabricated notion of history, spirituality, economics, or human nature. Religious fundamentalist authoritarians of all types retroactively justify their politics with recourse to their interpretation of tradition or scripture, insisting it provides iron-clad rules for how gender and society should be governed. Neo-liberal economic authoritarians make recourse to the myths of the market and of inherently competitive human nature to justify the inevitability of free markets and the pathology of any alternatives. Ultra-nationalists hallucinate a (categorically racialized) history of the nation-state to legitimate a "return" to what is imagined to be normal. In all cases, the imagination is put to work precisely to kill the imagination, to stifle curiosity and empathy, and to dehumanize human beings. All authoritarianisms violently insist that their formations of the imagination are not only correct, but that to question or challenge them is heresy, morally or materially dangerous to the social fabric (Giroux 2015).

Yet we should not lose sight of the fact that all these forms of "new" authoritarianism have emerged under the economic authoritarianism of financialized neo-liberal capitalism. While many obtain power by mobilizing antipathy toward economic "elites," the reality is that these new authoritarianisms often work hand in glove with – or at least do nothing to challenge – the overarching economic authoritarian regime of global capital. It should also be noted that, in spite of some charismatic female or gay leaders, all these new authoritarianisms depend on reactionary gender politics, usually tying their project to a "return" to some mythic bygone patriarchal fantasy.

Meanwhile, all these "new" authoritarianisms also mobilize race and racism, often by mobilizing a myth of the betrayed generosity of those now cast as the "silent majority," who, we are told, was *too* accepting, patient, and welcoming to late-coming "others" (see Mackey 2016; Razack 2004).

Towards the Commons: Actuality, Ethos, and Horizon

If the radical and anti-authoritarian imagination is to awaken, it will need to emerge not from platitudes or isolated intellectual activities but, as mentioned earlier, from actual on-the-ground activism, solidarity-building, and struggle. The way out of the present suicidal deadlock of authoritarianisms will emerge from a direct struggle for collective liberation, from building a difficult alliance among freedom-seeking people. Such a struggle would be dedicated to more than "resisting" avowed authoritarianism in order to return the deposed "liberal" capitalism to its tyrannical throne. It would, to my mind, need to begin with the recognition that the present moment is not the exception to, but the culmination of, the contradictions of a system of racial capitalism that has always been authoritarian at its core. It would need to link the authoritarianism of settler-colonialism to the authoritarianism of heteropatriarchy to the authoritarianism of racial capitalism (Taylor 2017; Walia 2013).

Rather, what I am dreaming of is already being built in the proverbial streets, although these streets are also day-care centres, bingo halls, and prisons. It stems from one of the strange gifts this moment has given us, which is the recognition that there is no turning back, that things will not get better, that we can only rely on ourselves. While no doubt there is an important role to be played by the state in whatever comes next, and while struggles over policy and programs are important, the struggles that will change the world will be those that are based not only on ideology and protest, but also on practising life and care differently (Gibson-Graham, Cameron, and Healy 2013).

Ultimately, capitalism is a poisonous and exploitative methodology for orchestrating human "co-operation," for organizing our energies as a co-operative species. Here I mean both "productive" labour (the production and exchange of things) and "reproductive" labour (the recreation of life biologically and socially), though really the distinction is artificial (Federici 2012; Bhattacharya 2017). But co-operation and work are not only physical;

they are also imaginative activities. Capitalism, like any system of domination, has always conscripted our imagination, not only for its legitimation, but also to shape how we co-operate. Resistance, then, to capitalism and other systems, is fundamentally about reclaiming and reinventing how we co-operate and relate to one another. For this reason, and also because life is likely to get a lot harder for all of us in the context of the assassination of what remains of the welfare state and imminent ecological breakdown, the task before us is to reimagine and rebuild living infrastructures of care and relationality on the level of neighbourhoods, communities, and ecological zones (see Wright 2010). There are a vibrant plurality of courageous experiments around the world, ranging from small neighbourhood agricultural projects to worker co-operatives (Ness and Azzelini 2011) to whole regions, such as the grassroots and participatory democratic revolution in Rojava (Bookchin 2018). They have in common a recognition that, although "top down" legislative change can be important (especially in abolishing huge systems and institutions like prisons, capitalism, and white supremacy), such changes will never occur until and unless there are massive, vibrant grassroots movements transforming the fabric of daily life and the network of human and non-human relationships, and thereby making the current order functionally impossible.

For these reasons, I have kept faith with the radical notion of the commons, as developed by theorists, including Silvia Federici (2012) and Massimo De Angelis (2017) and others, and as implemented by, among others, the inspiring Jackson Rising movement (Nangwaya and Akuno 2017). The commons takes its inspiration from the shared lands seized from English peasants during the transition to capitalism, and today can be used to name the way certain lands, or what we call "resources," can be held and cared for in common, not under the regime of private property. For instance, there are powerful movements around the world demanding that water be treated as a commons, or the Internet, or urban space itself: these are things we must share and also care for collectively, not commodify (see Bollier and Helfrich 2015).

There are several challenges for the notion of the commons. First, it has been adopted by and incorporated into neo-liberal thought as a means to address "market failures" (see Haiven 2016). Second, here in Canada and in other settler colonies we need to work very diligently to square the notion of the commons with the reality of the ongoing genocidal theft of Indigenous lands and "resources" (Fortier 2017; Pictou 2017). These challenges often stem in part from a kind of confusion of many different notions of the commons. For this reason, I have sought elsewhere (Haiven 2016) to distinguish three conjugations of the commons: first, the *actuality* of the commons, by which I mean the existing resilient examples and experiments in holding and caring for the "natural" and the "built" environment in common; second, the *ethos* of the commons, by which I mean the dispositions, beliefs, practices, and skills for "commoning" that cut through all those different examples and experiments, and are also a sort of underground reservoir acting within, against, and beyond the capitalist society in which we are forced to live; and finally, the *horizon* of the commons, which means for me the concrete utopianism and pragmatic strategizing for wholesale transformation that emerges from the active experience of *commoning* – in other words the radical imagination. All three of these must be present in movements for the commons if we are to succeed.

REFERENCES

Bhattacharya, Tithi, ed. 2017. *Social Reproduction Theory: Remapping Class, Recentering Oppression*. London: Pluto Press.

Bollier, David, and Silke Helfrich, eds. 2015. *Patterns of Commoning*. Commons Strategies Group. http://patternsofcommoning.org/.

Bookchin, Debbie. 2018. "How My Father's Ideas Helped the Kurds Create a New Democracy." *New York Review of Books* (blog), 15 June. https://www.nybooks.com/daily/2018/06/15/how-my-fathers-ideas-helped-the-kurds-create-a-new-democracy/.

Brown, Wendy. 2015. *Undoing the Demos: Neoliberalism's Stealth Revolution*. New York: Zone.

Castoriadis, Cornelius. 1997. "Radical Imagination and the Social Instituting Imaginary." In *The Castoriadis Reader*, edited by David Ames Curtis, 319–37. Cambridge and New York: Blackwell.

Coulthard, Glen. 2014. *Red Skin, White Masks: Rejecting the Colonial Politics of Recognition*. Minneapolis and London: University of Minnesota Press.

De Angelis, Massimo. 2017. *Omnia Sunt Communia: On the Commons and the Transformation to Postcapitalism*. London: Zed.

Federici, Silvia. 2012. *Revolution at Point Zero: Housework, Reproduction, and Feminist Struggle*. Brooklyn, NY, and Oakland, CA: Common Notions (PM Press).

Fisher, Mark. 2009. *Capitalist Realism: Is There No Alternative?* London: Zero Books.

Fortier, Craig. 2017. *Unsettling the Commons: Social Movements Within, Against, and Beyond Settler Colonialism*. Winnipeg: ARP.

Fraser, Nancy. 2013. *Fortunes of Feminism: From State-Managed Capitalism to Neoliberal Crisis*. London and New York: Verso.

Gibson-Graham, J.K., Jenny Cameron, and Stephen Healy. 2013. *Take Back the Economy: An Ethical Guide for Transforming Our Communities*. Minneapolis and London: University of Minnesota Press.

Giroux, Henry A. 2015. *Dangerous Thinking in the Age of the New Authoritarianism*. London and New York: Routledge.

Haiven, Max. 2014a. *Crises of Imagination, Crises of Power: Capitalism, Creativity and the Commons*. London and New York: Zed Books.

– 2014b. *Cultures of Financialization: Fictitious Capital in Popular Culture and Everyday Life*. London and New York: Palgrave Macmillan.

– 2016. "The Commons Against Neoliberalism, the Commons of Neoliberalism, the Commons Beyond Neoliberalism." In *The Handbook of Neoliberalism*, edited by Simon Springer, Kean Birch, and Julie MacLeavy, 271–83. London and New York: Routledge.

Haiven, Max, and Alex Khasnabish. 2014. *The Radical Imagination: Social Movement Research in the Age of Austerity*. London and New York: Zed Books.

Hochschild, Arlie Russell. 2016. *Strangers in Their Own Land: Anger and Mourning on the American Right*. New York: New Press.

Kimmel, Michael S. 2015. *Angry White Men: American Masculinity at the End of an Era*. New York: Nation Books.

Klein, Naomi. 2015. *This Changes Everything: Capitalism vs. the Climate*. New York: Knopf.

Mackey, Eva. 2016. *Unsettled Expectations: Uncertainty, Land, and Settler Decolonization*. Halifax and Winnipeg: Fernwood.

Martin, Randy. 2002. *Financialization of Daily Life*. Philadelphia, PA: Temple University Press.

– 2007. *An Empire of Indifference: American War and the Financial Logic of Risk Management*. Durham, NC, and London: Duke University Press.

Moore, Jason W. 2015. *Capitalism in the Web of Life: Ecology and the Accumulation of Capital*. 1st ed. New York: Verso.

Nangwaya, Ajamu, and Kali Akuno, eds. 2017. *Jackson Rising: The Struggle for*

Economic Democracy and Black Self-Determination in Jackson, Mississippi.
Montreal: Dajara Press.

Ness, Immanuel, and Dario Azzellini, eds. 2011. *Ours to Master and to Own: Workers' Control from the Commune to the Present.* Chicago: Haymarket Books.

Pictou, Sherry. 2017. "Be Prepared to Win: Indigenous Struggles and the Radical Imagination." In *What Moves Us: The Lives and Times of the Radical Imagination,* edited by A. Khasnabish and M. Haiven, 153–61. Halifax and Winnipeg: Fernwood Publishing.

Razack, Sherene. 2004. *Dark Threats, White Knights: The Somalia Affair, Peacekeeping, and the New Imperialism.* Toronto: University of Toronto Press.

Taylor, Keeanga-Yamahtta. 2016. *From #BlackLivesMatter to Black Liberation.* Chicago, Illinois: Haymarket Books.

– ed. 2017. *How We Get Free: Black Feminism and the Combahee River Collective.* Chicago: Haymarket Books.

Walia, Harsha. 2013. *Undoing Border Imperialism.* Oakland, CA, and Edinburgh: AK Press and the Institute for Anarchist Studies.

Wright, Eric Olin. 2010. *Envisioning Real Utopias.* London and New York: Verso.

CONTRIBUTORS

PAT ARMSTRONG's research on women's work, women's health, health care, and social policy is primarily interdisciplinary and collaborative, and is focused on making change. Working with colleagues, students, community organizations, government agencies, and unions, her research is concerned with policy and turning evidence into practices, is written in a manner accessible to broad audiences, and is focused primarily on Canada in a comparative perspective.

MATTHEW BEHRENS is a writer who coordinates the Homes not Bombs non-violent direct-action network, providing civil disobedience/creative protest workshops. He's been privileged to work with everyone from Indigenous land defenders and refugees fighting deportation to high-school students interested in "deschooling" and women behind bars for defending themselves against male violence.

AZIZ CHOUDRY is associate professor and Canada Research Chair in Social Movement Learning and Knowledge Production, Department of Integrated Studies in Education, McGill University, and visiting professor at the Centre for Education Rights and Transformation, University of Johannesburg. He is a board member of the Immigrant Workers Centre, Montreal.

JOHN CLARKE became involved in anti-poverty struggles in London, Ontario, in the early 1980s, when he helped to form the London Union of Unemployed Workers (LUUW). In 1990, he moved to Toronto to become an organizer with the newly formed Ontario Coalition Against Poverty (OCAP) and has worked in that role ever since.

EDWARD C. CORRIGAN was called to the bar of the Law Society of Upper Canada in 1992. Certified as a specialist by the Law Society of Upper Canada in citizenship, immigration, and immigration and refugee law, Ed's academic area of expertise is the Middle East. His articles appear in *Middle East Policy, Middle East International, Outlook,* rabble.ca, and *Z Magazine.* His law office is located in London, Ontario.

STEPHEN D'ARCY is associate professor in the Department of Philosophy at Huron University College and a climate-justice activist. He is the author of *Languages of the Unheard: Why Militant Protest Is Good for Democracy.*

RICHARD J.F. DAY is an autonomy-oriented practitioner and theorist who lives on a regenerating former gravel pit on Denman Island. He has been involved with a number of radical projects over the years, from community education to food and housing co-ops, Indigenous solidarity, urban social centres, and rural intentional communities. He is the author of *Gramsci Is Dead* (2005) and (with Greig dePeuter and Mark Coté) *Utopian Pedagogies* (2007).

CAROLYN EGAN is president of United Steelworkers Local 8300 and a long-time activist in the women's movement. She is on the organizing committee for International Women's Day in Toronto and has been involved in anti-racist organizing for many years.

AMIRA ELGHAWABY is a journalist and human-rights advocate. She served as human-rights officer and later as director of communications at the National Council of Canadian Muslims between 2012 and 2017. Amira lives in Ottawa with her husband and three children.

BERNIE M. FARBER is one of Canada's most recognized authorities on antisemitism and hate groups. A past CEO of the Canadian Jewish Congress, the Paloma Foundation, and the Mosaic Institute, today Bernie is retired, though continues his social-justice work as a consultant to government agencies, school boards, law enforcement, and community groups. He is also a writer and columnist for various newspapers and magazines.

MELISSA GRAHAM is the founder and one of the key organizers for the Toronto Disability Pride March, which began in October 2011. She is an activist involved in disability issues throughout Ontario and has written for publications such as *Abilities* magazine and *The Monitor*. She holds a Master of Social Work, with a concentration in social justice. She can often be seen at rallies or enjoying the occasional wheelchair bungee jump.

MAX HAIVEN is Canada Research Chair in Culture, Media, and Social Justice at Lakehead University in northwest Ontario and director of the ReImagining Value Action Lab (RiVAL). He is the author of books including *Crises of Imagination, Crises of Power: Capitalism, Creativity, and the Commons* (2014) and *Art after Money, Money after Art: Creative Strategies Against Financialization* (2018).

MOSTAFA HENAWAY has been an organizer with the Immigrant Workers Centre in Montreal since 2007. He holds a master's degree from the Global Labour University.

ALIA HOGBEN is a social worker who has worked in services for child protection, for women who have been abused, and for individuals with disabilities. She has taught at a community college and currently writes a regular column in the *Kingston Whig-Standard*. Alia is the executive director of the Canadian Council of Muslim Women. Among her many awards, she is very proud of her Order of Canada for activism on behalf of women and girls.

PHILIP S.S. HOWARD is assistant professor in the Department of Integrated Studies in Education at McGill University. He works in the areas of critical race studies, anti-colonial studies, and Black Canadian Studies in education. His interests are in the pedagogical processes and epistemological frames that mediate how we come to know ourselves, create community, and exercise agency and resistance with/in/against racialized social relations.

DAN IRVING is associate professor in the Human Rights and Social Justice and Sexuality Studies Minor program at Carleton University. He is the co-editor of *Trans Activism in Canada: A Reader*. His work has been published in *Radical History Review*, *Sexualities*, and *Australian Feminist Studies*.

UZMA JAMIL is a researcher and visiting scholar at McGill University. Her expertise and publications are on the securitization and racialization of Muslims in the context of the war on terror, Islamophobia, and racism. She is on the editorial board of *ReOrient: The Journal of Critical Muslim Studies*.

YASMIN JIWANI is professor in the Department of Communication Studies and Concordia University Research Chair in Intersectionality, Violence, and Resistance.

CAITLYN E. KASPER is an Anishinaabek woman from the Chippewas of Georgina Island First Nation. She holds an Honours specialist degree in political science from the University of Toronto and a Juris Doctor from Osgoode Hall. She practised in Northern Ontario for David M. Gibson and Associates before opening her own law office. In 2014, she joined Aboriginal Legal Services as legal counsel and has since represented clients at every level of court, including the Supreme Court of Canada.

EL-FAROUK KHAKI runs a refugee lawyer practice focusing on sexual orientation, gender, gender identity/expression, and HIV. A public speaker, writer, author, and media commentator, El-Farouk is also the co-founder and imam of el-Tawhid Juma Circle (2009), also known as The Unity Mosque, a recipient of The Harmony Award in 2017. El-Farouk is currently working on his first book, exploring intersectional identities, global issues, sexuality, social justice, and spirituality.

LISA KOWALCHUK is associate professor of sociology at the University of Guelph. Her research looks at the labour conditions of nurses in El Salvador and Nicaragua, and how these have been affected by post–neo-liberalism. She has published her work in several peer-reviewed journals, including *Critical Sociology, Social Movement Studies, Latin American Politics and Society*, and *Sociological Quarterly*.

CYNTHIA LEVINE-RASKY is associate professor in the Department of Sociology at Queen's University. Her books are *Whiteness Fractured* (Routledge [Ashgate], 2013) and *Writing the Roma* (Fernwood, 2016). Her writing also appears in *Canadian Dimension, Canada's History, Ricochet, The Conversa-*

tion, and *National Observer*. Cynthia's current research interests concern narrative writing, intersectionality, and whiteness.

IAN MACDONALD is assistant professor at the École de relations indus-trielles, Université de Montréal. His research interests include union re-newal, labour politics, radical political economy, and labour geography, with current projects on the organizing of precarious workers and labour strat-egy in Quebec.

TIM MCCASKELL is a Toronto writer, LGBT activist, and educator. He is au-thor of *Race to Equity: Disrupting Educational Inequality*, on the struggle for equity in Toronto public schools, and *Queer Progress: From Homophobia to Homonationalism*, a history of the impact of neo-liberalism on LGBT or-ganizing in Toronto.

NEIL MCLAUGHIN teaches sociological theory at McMaster University and writes about public intellectuals and the sociology of disciplines, ideas, and knowledge. His most recent publications include (with James Lannigan) "Professors and Politics: Noam Chomsky's Contested Reputation in the United States and Canada," *Theory and Society* 46 (2017): 177, and a forth-coming essay with Iga Merger, "Who Gets to Be a Public Intellectual in Canada," dealing with the missing or erased women intellectuals in our public sphere.

DAVID MURAKAMI WOOD is associate professor and a former Canada Re-search Chair (Tier II) in Surveillance Studies at Queen's University. He is a widely published specialist in the sociology and geography of global sur-veillance and comparative urban security, and a founder of the open-access journal *Surveillance & Society*. He is also a long-time activist for ecological and social justice and for human rights.

ALEX NEVE has been Secretary General of Amnesty International Canada since 2000. Alex has an LLB from Dalhousie University, an LLM in Interna-tional Human Rights Law from the University of Essex, and three honourary doctorates. He has served on the Immigration and Refugee Board, taught at Osgoode Hall Law School and the University of Ottawa, been affiliated with

York University's Centre for Refugee Studies, and worked as a refugee lawyer. Alex is an Officer of the Order of Canada.

JANICE A. NEWSON is professor emerita in the Department of Sociology, York University. She has been an active critic of the corporatization of the university. Her latest publication is with Claire Polster, *A Penny for Your Thoughts: How Corporatization Devalues Research, Teaching, and Public Service in Canada's Universities* (Ottawa: The Centre for Policy Alternatives, 2015).

MORGANE OGER, through the work of the Morgane Oger Foundation and her political activity, works to narrow the gap between Canada's laws and lived experiences of marginalized Canadians. She is recognized as a leading Canadian change-maker, working for transparency and justice. Morgane has helped shape human-rights law, improve public policy, and win progressive change.

PAMELA PALMATER is a Mi'kmaw citizen and member of Eel River Bar First Nation. She has been a practising lawyer for twenty years, specializing in Indigenous law, politics, and governance. She was one of the spokespersons and educators for the Idle No More social-justice movement. She currently holds the position of associate professor and chair in Indigenous Governance at Ryerson University in Toronto.

BARBARA PERRY is professor in the Faculty of Social Science and Humanities at the University of Ontario Institute of Technology. She has written extensively on social justice generally, and hate crime specifically. Barbara has made significant contributions to the limited scholarship on hate crime in Canada, including work on anti-Muslim violence, hate crime against LGBTQ communities, the community impacts of hate crime, and right-wing extremism in Canada.

MARGARET REID is a journalist and PhD in Communication and Culture. She is the Jackman Humanities Institute's Journalism Fellow for 2018–19. She created a podcast called "lower case truth" and also works as a radio documentary producer for CBC's *Ideas*. She has been an active participant in communications policy through both advocacy work and regulatory interventions to the CRTC. Her dissertation research looked at personal branding in journalism and how this impacts the governing values of the profession in a context where the business model for news has collapsed. She has published academic works as well as pieces for j-source, IP Osgoode, and CWA Canada.

KIKÉLOLA ROACH is Unifor Sam Gindin Chair in Social Justice and Democracy at Ryerson University. She studied law at Queen's University in Kingston, Ontario, and at Université Jean Moulin in Lyons, France. She has been an advocate for accountability and reform in policing and detention centres for many years. Kiké is co-author of the book *Politically Speaking*, on feminism and Canadian politics.

MICHELLE ROBIDOUX is an activist and socialist, and a founding member of the War Resisters Support Campaign. She is co-chair of the Toronto and York Region Labour Council Rapid Response team, established to counter hate activity by the far right.

LEN RUDNER, formerly with the Centre for Israel and Jewish Affairs and Canadian Jewish Congress, has spoken at international conferences on the topics of antisemitism, Holocaust denial, and hate speech, and been qualified as an expert witness in proceedings dealing with hate and bias crimes. He now engages in human-rights advocacy as an independent consultant.

KIM SAUDER is a PhD student in critical disability studies. She has a BA (Hons) in women and gender studies, where her research focused on disability and motherhood. Her master's degree, also in critical disability studies, focused on media representation of disability in film adaptations of gothic fiction. She is also a blogger and disability-rights activist. When she isn't working on her PhD, she can be found engaging with other disability-rights activists on social media.

ALAN SEARS teaches sociology at Ryerson University. He is an activist with Faculty for Palestine and the New Socialist Group. He has written about movement activism in *The Next New Left: A History of the Future* (Fernwood,

2014), *The Democratic Imagination: Envisioning Popular Power in the Twenty-first Century* (with James Cairns) (University of Toronto Press, 2012), and other publications.

STEPHEN SHEPS's research straddles two distinct subfields: the sociology of sport and sociology of education. He is currently focused on a project on the rise of advanced analytics in the NHL. Stephen has taught at Queen's University, Trent University, and the University of Tennessee at Chattanooga before coming to Ryerson University as a limited-term faculty member.

KEITH STEWART is a senior energy strategist with Greenpeace Canada. He has a PhD from York University, and is a part-time faculty member at the University of Toronto, where he teaches energy and environmental politics.

MARK P. THOMAS is associate professor in the Department of Sociology at York University in Toronto. His current areas of research include the enforcement of employment-standards legislation in Canada and labour, austerity, and populism in urban North America.

STEVEN TUFTS is associate professor in the Department of Geography at York University in Toronto. His current areas of research include union strategy, labour-market adjustment, unions and urban austerity, and populism and labour in North America.

LORNE WALDMAN has been practising immigration and refugee law since 1979. He was appointed to the Order of Canada in June 2017 "for his commitment to upholding justice through his work as an immigration and refugee lawyer." In 2007, he was awarded the Louis St Laurent Award by the Canadian Bar Association for his contribution to the legal profession. On three occasions, he was chosen as one of the twenty-five most-influential lawyers in Canada by *Canadian Lawyer* magazine.

VANESSA WATTS is Mohawk and Anishinaabe Bear Clan from Six Nations of the Grand River. She is currently academic director of Indigenous studies and assistant professor in the Department of Sociology at McMaster University. Her research examines epistemological and ontological interventions on place-based, material-knowledge production. Vanessa is particularly interested in Indigenous feminisms and other-than-human relations as forms of Indigenous ways of knowing.

LESLEY J. WOOD is interested in how ideas travel, how power operates, how institutions change, how conversations influence practices, how people resist, and how conflict starts, transforms, and ends. She published *Crisis and Control: The Militarization of Protest Policing* (Pluto/Between the Lines, 2012) and *Direct Action, Deliberation, and Diffusion* (Cambridge University Press, 2012). She is associate professor of sociology and department chair at York University and also a member of the Ontario Coalition Against Poverty.

270, 289; and homelessness, 194–5, 263; and police, 153–6; and Pride, 78, 101, 103, 288, 292
Toronto Disability Pride March, 288–9, 292
transgender, 66, 70–72, 238; and activism, 300, 304–6; and Islam, 170; status of 302–3; treatment of, 303–4; violence toward, 66–71, 300–1
Trans Mountain pipeline 10, 35
Trudeau, Justin, 9–10, 196, 283; and citizenship legislation, 237–8; and climate policy, 10, 34; and Indigenous peoples, 32, 35; and Indigenous policy, 34, 90; and Pride, 79; and surveillance, 190
Trump, Donald, 3, 6–10, 39, 77, 126, 129–30, 143, 178, 193, 195, 228, 251, 260, 278–80, 282; and activism, 152, 155, 272; and Canada, 131–2, 179; and climate change denial, 220–1, 224–5; consequences of, 3, 115, 164, 177, 179, 199; and disability, 84–5; election, 7, 81, 155, 162–3, 228–31, 272; and media, 117, 181, 229, 305; and the "Muslim ban," 49, 81, 85, 115, 163; and racism, 231; and Serge Kovaleski, 81–2
Turkey, 229
Two-Row Wampum, 27–8, 90

United Nations, 83, 257, 259, 262, 264, 278, 280; Special Rapporteur, 90, 281–2
United States, 13–15, 79; and the Campus Reform movement, 130; and economic conditions, 75, 79; elections, 6–7, 14, 115, 129, 162, 181, 228–30, 269, 272
universities, 129, and corporatization, 123–5; faculty associations, 123; and funding, 123, 125; privatization, 123; and the public good, 126; and reforms, 124
The University Means Business, 124
University of Alberta, 92
University of New Brunswick, 92

Vancouver, 48, 165, 178, 181, 237. *See also* British Columbia

Wadud, Amina, 170, 172–3
war on terror, 49
White Canada, 48

white nationalism, 115, 118, 132, 218, 243, 245
whiteness, 62, 310; and Canadian identity, 118; in crisis, 50, 69; and heteronormativity, 67; and Islamophobia, 50–1; and nationalism, 67; and privilege, 68; in sports, 140; and violence, 68–70; and working-class insecurity, 265–6; and working-class masculinity, 67–70
White Ribbon campaign, 71
white supremacist groups, 60, 62, 92, 159, 177–8, 280, 301; and media, 117. *See also* Canadian Nationalist Party; far right; hate crime; Heritage Front; La Meute; Proud Boys
working class, 16, 115, 117, 163, 194, 196–7, 201, 204, 207, 209–10, 212, 232, 251, 265–6; men, 67–71